Leisure Services UK

Leisure Services UK

An Introduction to Leisure, Entertainment
and Tourism Services

Edited by Norman Borrett

MACMILLAN

First published in 1991 by
THE MACMILLAN PRESS LTD
Houndmills, Basingstoke, Hampshire RG21 2XS
and London
Companies and representatives
throughout the world

ISBN 0–333–52554–X

A catalogue record for this book is available
from the British Library.

Printed in Malaysia

10   9   8   7   6   5   4   3   2
00 99 98 97 96 95

Contents

Acknowledgements

The editor and publishers wish to thank the following for permission to use copyright material in the text of this book. The Policy Studies Institute, for data in Tables 1.1, 1.3, 1.4, 1.6 and 3.1, from *Cultural Trends 1989* (1989) and for Table 3.3 from *Cultural Trends into the Eighties* (1990); Library and Information Statistics Unit, Loughborough University, for CIPFA data in Tables 2.1 and 2.2, and Figure 2.1, from M. Donoghue and P. H. Mann, *Public Library Statistics 1987–88: A Trend Analysis* (1988); NALGO, for data in Table 5.1, from *Governing Bodies of Sport* (1985); Institute of Public Finance Ltd, for CIPFA data in Tables 5.2 and 7.4, from *Leisure and Recreation Statistics Estimates*, 1985 and 1988–9; Forestry Commission, for data in Table 5.3, from 'Recreation in Forests' in *The Forestry Commission and Recreation Commission Policy Paper No. 2* (1988); Play Board, for data in Table 6.1, from *Survey of play staff working in 11 local authority areas* (1986), and in Table 6.2 and Figure 6.1, from *Playwork Training, Qualifications, Conditions of Service: a survey of playstaff employees and local authorities*, D. Clarke, J. Coffin and C. Parkinson, Play Board/LGTB, August 1985; Sports Council, for data in Tables 7.1 and 7.2, from *Sport in the Community: Into the 90s* (1988), and in Table 7.3 from the *Annual Reports* of the Sports Council, the Sports Council for Wales, the Scotish Sports Council and the Sports Council for Northern Ireland; RSL Sportscan, for data in Table 7.5, from *Marketing/Sportscan Quarterly Survey* (May 1989); The Henley Centre, for data in Tables 7.6 and 7.7, from *Leisure Futures* (1986); BTA for data in Table 8.1, from *National Facts of Tourism* (1989), in Table 8.2, from *Britian's Tourism* (September 1989), and in Figure 8.1, from *British Travel Brief* (1987); Countryside Commission, for Figure 4.1, from *Survey of Countryside Recreation* (1986), and Figure 4.2, from *Recreation 2000 – Enjoying the Countryside . . .* (May 1987); Unwin Hyman Ltd, for Figure 4.3 from *Countryside Conservation* (1981); Central Council of Physical Recreation for data from *Down with Rates* (1990).

Every effort has been made to trace all the copyright-holders, but if any have been inadvertently overlooked the publishers will make the necessary arrangement at the earliest opportunity.

The editor would like to acknowledge the skill and dedication of Sue Davies who typed numerous drafts of the manuscript. Thanks Sue for your good humour and tolerance.

Notes on the Contributors

Oliver Bennett is Head of Arts Administration at Leicester Polytechnic, and Chief Executive of the Phoenix Arts Centre. He has worked in Arts administration for over 15 years and has served as a member of the Arts Council of Great Britain's Regional Committee and Combined Arts Sub-Committee. As well as teaching a range of undergraduate studies in Arts Administration, he is also developing an MA in European Arts and Cultural Policy, with the support of UNESCO and the European Commission. He sets and marks examination papers for the Institute of Leisure and Amenity Management (ILAM). He regularly directs student performance work, and plays tenor saxophone in a small jazz ensemble.

Norman Borrett is Senior Lecturer in Leisure and Recreation Studies at Bradford and Ilkley Community College. Prior to moving to Yorkshire he worked in both the Teaching Studies Department and the Business School at the Polytechnic of North London, where he was course tutor for the BTEC Higher National Diploma in Leisure and Tourism, and the MA in Leisure and Recreation Studies. He has served as a member of the Executive Committee of the Leisure Studies Association, and currently is a BTEC Moderator for courses in leisure and tourism. He has had experience preparing students for ILAM examinations and currently teaches leisure policy and leisure management.

Anthony Gentil is Deputy Head of Horticulture at Cheshire College of Agriculture. He has published material for Capel Manor Open Learning Unit, NALGO correspondence course leading to the ILAM Certificate, Ashford Press and Manchester Open Learning Unit, and various trade publications. He has experience as an examiner for ILAM and for the Master in Arboriculture of the Royal Forestry Society, and is a BTEC Moderator in Leisure Studies. He is a member of the British Institute of Management, and a Fellow of the Arboriculture Association and the Linnean Society.

Dr Graham Nicholson is Director of Leisure Services for Bury Metropolitan Borough Council. After completing his Doctorate in Tudor English History at Cambridge, he held a number of museum appointments, and was for several years Curator of the Castle Museum in York. He was until recently responsible for cultural services in Stockport, which included everything from public libraries and country houses to 'rock and roll' concerts. He has particular interests in marketing local history collections and archives, publishing in the library service, and the training of library staff.

Anne Partington-Omar is Assistant Chief Leisure Services Officer (Heritage and Culture) for Bury St Edmunds. Prior to starting her career in museum services, she trained as a microbiologist, and initially worked as a technical aquarist with Bolton Borough Council. She worked in Museum Education for Hull City and Doncaster M.B.C. before taking up a position as Curator for Epping Forest District Council. She has served as an Associate Member and Councillor of the Museums Association, Chairman of the MA's Education Board, and is currently a member of the Standing Registration Committee of the Museums and Galleries Commission. Her current responsibilities cover Museums, Arts, Tourism, Entertainments and Festivals.

Stephen Rennie is Director of The Play Co-operative Ltd (Playtech), a company concerned with training, research and the sale of goods and services in the field of play throughout the UK. Prior to joining Playtech, he was Regional Play Officer for Play Board. He has had an extensive career in children's play and has worked as a Youth Leader, Play Leader, and Play Officer for a number of Local Authorities. He has published widely, lecturers in Playwork at Leeds Polytechnic, and is External Assessor for the National Institute of Playwork.

Dr Terry Stevens is Head of the Department of Tourism, Leisure and Health Care at West Glamorgan Institute of Higher Education, and Business Adviser to the Wales Tourist Board. He is a member of a number of important committees including the Countryside Commission's Committee for Wales, the Wales Tourist Board Attractions Advisory Committee, and the Council of Europe Working Party on Cultural Tourism. He has extensive consultancy experience in the UK and overseas and has published over fifty articles in journals and books. As well as being a member and Examiner for ILAM, he is an External Examiner for the MSc and PhD programmes at the University of Reading, and a Fellow of the Tourism Society.

John Walsh-Heron was Head of Trade and Consumer Affairs for the Wales Tourist Board. He works on a number of committees including City and Guilds, the Council for National Academic Awards, and the British Tourist Authority. Following his training in Hotel Management, he worked for the Wales Tourist Board since 1970 and was responsible for Board policy relating to quality assurance, training, education, advisory services, and legislation. He established the first National

Tourist Board Inspection System in mainland UK and developed, in conjunction with the caravan industry, the basis for the first Grading System of Caravan Parks in the world. John Walsh-Heron has recently been appointed Managing Director of Tourism Quality Services Ltd, a company set up by the Wales Tourist Board to operate its inspection and advisory services.

Introduction

The Development of Leisure Services

Leisure services comprise public, commercial and voluntary organisations that influence every aspect of our lives: from the beginning of early play, to the cemeteries and crematoria that mark our final resting place; from the private spheres of home and family, to the public domain of stadia and theatre; from quiet reflections in a library or museum, to noisy and energetic pursuits on our playing fields or in discotheques. Whoever we are, whatever we do, and no matter how varied or limited our tastes, leisure services are there to supply our wants and nurture our needs.

Yet, the traditional leisure services that provide for us today have not always existed in their current forms, and the relationship between the various sectors of leisure provision has undergone substantial change. Two centuries ago public funding of leisure services hardly existed. The upper class fenced areas of land for their private use, developed various facilities for their own cultural advancement such as botanical gardens, libraries, museums, and art galleries, and sought to segregate themselves from the amusements of the masses. The poor took their leisure in the beer houses, in the streets, and at fairs and festivals. Public houses often formed the main centres for leisure activities including many kinds of collectors' clubs and societies, as well as events such as bowling, wrestling, boxing, horse-racing, card playing, and dancing.

The streets of the developing towns and cities became centres of attraction for entertainment of many kinds: buskers, preachers, Punch and Judy shows, music, bull baiting, and even public hangings. The streets were also the playgrounds for many children. At this time there was little public provision for leisure. However, by the middle of the nineteenth century, middle-class reformers including the Church and the police were aware that there was a great deal of drunkenness and coarseness within working-class recreation. Individuals and groups from the middle class decided to try and improve the leisure pastimes of the poor and make them more wholesome. Gradually, museums, public parks, libraries, and musical facilities were opened up to all sections of society. The government began to contribute money to secure open spaces for public use and to develop provision for the poor, and with the support of wealthy benefactors, a multitude of new facilities and events were established.

Supported by major technological advancements in printing, lighting, heating and transportation, the recreational opportunities for the masses underwent substantial change in a short period of time. In this book, this period forms a backcloth against which leisure services will be explored.

The 1990s will prove a challenging and exciting period for leisure services. Within the last few years changes in the economic and political environment have forced the public, commercial and voluntary providers to critically assess aspects of policy, planning and delivery. Public facilities have become privatised and are now open to private management through competitive tendering, commercial companies have developed interests in a wide variety of leisure concerns and sought partnership agreements with the public sector, and many voluntary and public bodies now make use of commercial sponsorship. The public sector has been forced to become more accountable in terms of economic efficiency and value for money, voluntary clubs and societies are encouraged to develop more efficient management methods, and the commercial sector has grasped opportunities to utilise new technology to improve profitability and develop exciting new leisure experiences.

It was in the mid 1960s that Michael Dower depicted four great waves engulfing society. The first three waves had already broken across the face of Britain. These were, the rapid development of towns during the period of the Industrial Revolution, the development of the railways, and the growth of car-based suburbs. The fourth wave was on the horizon, and was to be the world of leisure. It has been suggested that we are now caught in the tidal force of such a wave and that the society of leisure is upon us. There is a great deal of evidence to support such a claim – higher incomes, better communications, more leisure time, longer holidays, earlier retirement, and better facilities and services for leisure. However, there is a growing awareness among researchers that this picture is not as simple as it first appears.

There are, for example, major differences in opportunity in society today. There are those in secure, well-paid jobs, and those suffering many deprivations including poor housing and unemployment. There are sections of society suffering discrimination in various forms which makes access to leisure services difficult. There are also fundamental differences between leisure opportunities in the countryside compared with inner city environments. Increasing numbers of workers take second jobs, in many cases due to poor pay, and there are growing numbers of double-income households. Life can be viewed as a constant struggle for a limited number of resources and goods. Some are fortunate and have high disposable incomes, plenty of free time, and high levels of personal freedom. Others do not.

Within this book, the struggle for resources and the identification of priorities within an era of change will be discussed. Should more money be given to the development of popular arts, or should limited resources be concentrated on protecting a heritage based on 'high culture'? Should the countryside be utilised to build new towns and villages and better leisure and entertainment complexes, or should the countryside be protected from developers and tourists? What are the implications for a commercially-driven, deregulated broadcasting system? What would be the consequences of privatising our museums, libraries, parks and waterways? These and other issues will be addressed in the pages that follow.

Structure and Format

This text will explore the nature of leisure services, and introduce the reader to major aspects of policy, administration and finance associated with provision. The book will be an important text for those on leisure, recreation and tourism courses validated by the Business and Technician Education Council (BTEC) at National, Continuing Education, and Higher National levels, and those who are studying for the Institute of Leisure and Amenity Management (ILAM) examinations. Within a single cover, the book will also provide the new student of leisure and tourism at degree level with a broad understanding of leisure services within the UK.

This book can be used in a variety of ways. It can be read straight through to give the reader a sound overview of leisure services and many of the issues and problems faced by providers and consumers. Alternatively, the reader may wish to refer to a specific chapter that is appropriate to current studies. Those readers who are thirsty for further information and a deeper understanding can attempt some of the exercises and read from the list of recommended texts.

The first chapter, Entertainment and the Arts, has been given additional space as it includes such a diverse range of services. The first part of the chapter contains an exploration of provision and facilities under two broad headings: 'Staying In' – which includes a discussion of television, video, radio, hi-fi, and books; and 'Going Out' – which considers film and cinema, theatre, drama, concerts, opera, dance, cabaret, new variety, and other entertainments. Oliver Bennett goes on to examine consumer expenditure and the funding of Entertainment and the Arts. Finally, the author explores three significant policy issues that demand attention: the relationship between the free market and the cultural industries; the 'new-age' for broadcasting; and the role of public subsidy in support of the Arts.

Chapters 2 and 3 are shorter, as they deal with more specific areas of leisure servicing. Chapter 2 is on libraries, and Dr Graham Nicholson begins by examining the nature and extent of library provision. In the next section, the management and staffing of libraries, and the main sources of finance are analysed, followed by an examination of service planning and delivery, and an exploration of the crucial role of Information Technology within modern library services. Finally, the author considers 'libraries under threat' and highlights the future prospects for libraries during the 1990s.

Chapter 3 is on museums, and Anne Partington-Omar begins her analysis by considering three broad categories of museum service: national, local authority, and non-public/private museums. The author goes on to ask the question, 'What is a museum?' and contrasts traditional museums with the quickly expanding heritage industry. Following on from an analysis of museum funding, policy and planning, Anne Partington-Omar utilises a case study approach to critically evaluate the contentious issue of admission charges.

Chapters 4 and 5 share a common theme of 'the great outdoors'. In Chapter 4, Dr Terry Stevens begins by exploring the major features of provision in countryside recreation, concentrating on the structure, development and problems associated with our National Parks. In the next two sections the range of activities that take place in the countryside are depicted, as well as the management problems associated with expanding recreational use. Finally, the future prospects for the countryside are considered and the author argues for a sensitive approach to planning and management so that conservation and recreational use can exist in harmony.

Chapter 5, on parks and amenities, complements both Chapter 4 and Chapter 7. The author begins by highlighting the wide range of provisions and facilities that make up parks and amenities. These include urban and regional parks, gardens, sports grounds, allotments, trimtrails, cycleways, zoos, bird gardens, festivals and exhibitions, cemeteries and crematoria. Tony Gentil then reviews two principal organisations concerned with the administration and finance of parks and amenities: the Forestry Commission and the National Trust.

Chapter 6 is concerned with play and playwork. Stephen Rennie initially explores the range of provision in children's play from the public, commercial and voluntary sectors. The author then discusses the support services for supervised play provision, including play resource centres and the variety of national bodies associated with play and playwork. The third part contains a wealth of essential information on legislation, and provides the reader with a clear overview of Acts of Parliament as well as guidance and direction on standards of provision. The final sections are devoted to policy and planning issues in local authorities and future areas of concern for the provision of play.

Chapter 7 covers sport and physical recreation, and for completeness should be read in conjunction with Chapters 4 and 5. The first part consists of a summary of opportunities and facilities provided by the various sectors, and the importance of partnership agreements between them. Key funding bodies in the public and voluntary sectors are then contrasted with the financial and administrative remits of the commercial providers. In the final section, the future prospects for sport and physical recreation are explored.

The final chapter is on tourism, although it should be noted that many aspects of tourism are considered within other parts of the book. Indeed, the student of tourism would be well advised to note the wide ranging contributions supporting tourism made by areas discussed in previous chapters. John Walsh-Heron begins by exploring the range of accommodation that services tourism such as hotels, motels, caravans, camp sites, and self-catering establishments. The author then highlights the visitor attractions that play such an essential part in tourism, and the role of organisations such as the Tourist Boards and Local Authorities in the administration and finance of the industry. John Walsh-Heron concludes the chapter by considering three essential factors that will shape the future of tourism: population change, the European Community, and the Channel tunnel.

Within each chapter there are a variety of exercises to extend the reader and provide some practical underpinning to the issues raised. In carrying out these exercises the reader will develop a range of skills including information gathering and analysis; quantitative and numerate skills; design and visual discrimination; information processing; problem-solving; and communicating. For those who wish to expand their knowledge, each chapter contains a section on further study in which additional reading is suggested and questions are posed. By attempting the questions the reader will be able to assess his/her understanding of issues raised in the text.

Finally, at the end of the book, there is a selection of addresses of organisations that should provide an additional resource for information on each of the leisure services referred to. These organisations and institutes can provide a wealth of data to support project work and assignments.

Royal Ballet: *Romeo and Juliet* **(Sylvie Guillam and Jonathan Cope)**
(*photograph by Geoff Howard*)

1 · Entertainment and the Arts

Oliver Bennett

At the heart of the Entertainment and Arts industry is the product itself, which is enormously diverse. In the late twentieth century the industry not only reflects a wide range of tastes and cultures but also links with a complex international network of film companies, publishing houses, broadcasting agencies, and record companies. It can therefore be seen to encompass a vast range of activity, from Grand Opera to Pop Video, from New Variety to Soap, from Carnival to Repertory Theatre. The degree to which provision for this activity should be left to market forces, and the nature of any State intervention, remain the central question, in an analysis of British cultural policies.

'God help the Government that meddles with art', declared Lord Melbourne, the Whig Prime Minister of the 1830s. Although State support for some museums and galleries was introduced in the nineteenth century, the Melbourne view prevailed throughout the nineteenth century and through the first decades of the twentieth century. It was not until World War II that the Government significantly increased its support for Entertainment and the Arts. The Arts Council of Great Britain was established in 1946, and charged with the twin responsibilities of increasing accessibility to the Arts, and improving standards. These objectives, shared also by some local authorities which were permitted in 1948 to spend money on Entertainment and the Arts, and by the Regional Arts Associations which were formed in the 1950s and 1960s, have remained largely the same, but there have been significant changes in emphasis.

The certainties of the early years of public financial support of Entertainment and the Arts were gradually eroded during the 1960s and early 1970s, and the question of which Arts should be supported became highly contentious. No longer could the Arts Council declare, as it did in 1956, that the first claim upon its attention was the maintaining in London and the larger cities effective power-houses of opera, music, and drama.

During the 1970s, the most common criticism of Arts funding policies related to four areas. Firstly, the decisions on which kinds of artistic practice were to be supported from public funds were seen as arbitrary.

Why, for example, should the objective of improving standards apply only to professional work? Why should nineteenth-century Western European classical music be so much more worthy of support than jazz?

Secondly, the concentration of resources on maintaining the so called 'cultural heritage' was seen to be at the expense of supporting work by living artists and new forms of art. This related, thirdly, to the fact that the major centres for the Arts, and consequently a disproportionately high level of resources, were located in London at the expense of other regions in the country.

Fourthly, the cultural concerns of most of the Entertainment and Arts funding agencies were perceived to take account of the leisure pursuits of only a small minority of the white middle class. Cultural policies appeared largely to ignore both working-class culture and the multi-cultural nature of British society.

These divisions intensified in the 1980s with increasing pressures to reduce public expenditure. Although the commitment to public subsidy of Entertainment and the Arts was maintained, it was clear that major increases from public funds could not be expected, and that further developments would have to be funded through increased sales and private sponsorship. Managers of cultural organisations argued that they could no longer afford to take risks, and that they must 'play safe'.

The 1980s also saw a change in the language in which the Arts were discussed. The early emphasis on the social importance of the Arts gave way to an emphasis on the Arts as an economic commodity. The case for State support of the Arts was often made on the basis of the contribution the Arts made to the economy (for example, through tourism).

Up until the mid-1980s, British cultural policies on Entertainment and the Arts were largely discussed in terms of the subsidised sector – the world of theatres, arts centres, concert halls, and galleries. However, there has been a growing recognition that this is no longer adequate. 'Who is doing most to shape British Culture in the late 1980s?' ask Geoff Mulgan and Ken Worpole in their stimulating book *Saturday Night or Sunday Morning*, 'Next Shops, Virgin, WH Smith, News International, Benetton, Channel 4, Saatchi and Saatchi, the Notting Hill Carnival, and Virago, or the Wigmore Hall, Arts Council, National Theatre, Tate Gallery, and Royal Opera House?'

An adequate analysis of Entertainment and Arts provision needs to take account of not only the traditional concerns of the Arts Council, Regional Arts Associations, and local authorities but also the unregulated private sector, which is in cultural and economic terms the dominant force. With the special exception of broadcasting, this sector has received little attention from British cultural policymakers. 'It is as if', Mulgan and Worpole go on to argue, 'every energy has been directed to placing a preservation order on a Tudor cottage, while all around the developers were building new motorways, skyscrapers, and airports'.

The first section of this chapter sets the agenda for discussion by examining the full range of entertainments and arts that are promoted in the UK. Particular attention is given to the notion of the home leisure centre, equipped with TV, radio, video, and hi-fi, and supplied with an increasing number of products from the cultural industries – programmes, videotapes, recordings (on CD, cassette and vinyl), and books.

Provision and Facilities

Entertainers and artists work within a massive industry. A report published by the Policy Studies Institute in *Cultural Trends, 1989*, estimated that the industry had a turnover of £10 billion, and that this amounted to 2.5 per cent of all spending on goods and services by UK residents and foreign buyers. The scale of the industry, which was reckoned to employ around 496,000 people, was comparable to that of vehicles and energy.

The industry operates at many different levels, which often reflect conflicting values. It involves the private, the public, and the voluntary sector, and sometimes a combination of all three. There are the so-called cultural industries of broadcasting, film, video, music and publishing, sections of which are controlled by vast transnational corporations, such as CBS and News International, with cross-media interests in many countries.

There are the venues for live performances and for the visual arts – the theatres, the galleries, the concert halls, the clubs, the pubs, the civic halls and the arts centres. There are the festivals – the small local ones as well as the high profile ones such as Edinburgh and Glyndebourne. There are the schools and community projects, where artists in different disciplines can be found running workshops and classes. The list is not exclusive, but already it can be seen that the business is diverse, and that the different sectors may have sharply divergent objectives. However, there are two factors that these different sectors have in common. Firstly, they all have to compete for the consumers' attention, time, and money. Despite the increase in leisure time this remains a limited resource. Secondly, although the degree of independence enjoyed by the artist, and the motives for producing the work, vary from sector to sector, the artist's work is the foundation on which the industry has been built.

An appreciation of the range of provision and facilities can best be acquired by a brief examination of the characteristics of each of the main sectors. A number of questions need to be considered. What work is being produced, and by whom? How does the work reach its audience? Who is the audience? To what extent does one sector of the industry interconnect with others?

It is useful to think of the entertainment industry in terms of those activities which are home-based, and those which take place in public venues. The home as a leisure centre has gained strength as an idea, and it is important to remember that live entertainment now has to compete with a growing number of television channels and radio stations, video and hi-fi, and shelves stacked with records, tapes, videos, and books. The account that follows is not exhaustive, but the main sectors, many of which overlap, are considered.

Exercise
Choose five people, if possible of different ages and occupations, and ask them to keep a note of how much time they gave during one week to different Arts and Entertainment pursuits. Ask them to be as specific as possible, and keep a similar record for yourself. Analyse the results.

Staying In

Television

Since the launch of BBC TV's monochrome service in 1936, the growth and development of television has been spectacular, both in technological and cultural terms. Independent Television was launched in 1954, BBC2 in 1964, and colour introduced to BBC2 in 1967 and to BBC1 and ITV in 1969. Channel 4 went on the air in 1982, and Breakfast Television was introduced by the BBC in January 1983, followed a few weeks later by ITV's TV AM. Between 1982 and 1987, eighteen cable channels (of which 'Sky Channel' and 'Super Channel' are the most well-known) came into existence, delivering material via satellite, videotape, or interactive systems. The medium-powered satellite 'Astra' went into orbit late in 1988, and began transmitting direct to UK homes early in 1989 on a total of eight channels.

British Satellite Broadcasting (BSB) is another development, broadcasting on five channels through a high-powered satellite system (DBS) which requires smaller and less expensive reception antennae. However, owing to financial difficulties BSB has merged with Sky Television which uses one 'Astra' satellite; the future of the BSB technology is thus uncertain. Two new medium-powered satellites with multiple channel capacity, 'Eutelstat 2' and a second 'Astra' satellite, are also due to be launched soon. A fifth terrestrial channel, covering 65–70 per cent of the population, is planned for 1993, and beyond 1993 there is the possibility of a sixth terrestrial channel. There are also likely to be developments in the Multipoint Video Distribution System (MVDS), a technology which uses microwave frequencies to transmit television and sound channels from terrestrial transmitters across relatively short distances.

At the receiving end of all this distribution technology, the television set is at the centre of home-based entertainment. No other form of entertainment reaches so many people across such a wide spread of age, class, and race. According to *Cultural Trends*, edited by A. Feist and R. Hutchison, 97 per cent of all households now own a television set and the number of TV sets per household is on the increase. Only one third of households had more than one set in 1981, but in 1987 the number had risen to 57 per cent, with 17 per cent having three sets. The average person on an average day spends about three and a half hours watching broadcast television. Whether people are willing to spend even more time watching television, or whether the peak has been reached, remains to be seen. The average weekly viewing per person declined by just over 5 per cent between 1985 and 1988.

In its drive to increase competition and efficiency, the Government has given encouragement to the independent production sector, and the BBC and ITV companies have been set a target of commissioning 25 per cent of original material from independent producers. Both the BBC and the ITV companies are committed to achieving this target by 1992. Almost all of Channel 4's programmes are already commissioned from external sources.

As well as producing forms of entertainment that are unique to itself, such as the quiz show and soap opera, television is an integral part of many other sectors of the entertainment and arts industry. There are few forms of live entertainment that have not at some time been shown on it, or been adapted for it. The history of the film industry, in particular, is closely associated with that of television, and the decline in cinema attendances as television grew in popularity is well documented. Now, around 10 per cent of all British television is occupied by feature films, and the combined audiences for five films screened on television can outnumber admissions to all UK cinemas in one year. There are now both satellite and cable channels exclusively devoted to the showing of movies.

Both the BBC and ITV companies have to fulfil certain programming obligations, which are set out in Government regulations. The basic principle is the notion of public service broadcasting. This places on broadcasters a duty to present programmes of high quality for the public good. Services must therefore inform and educate, as well as entertain, and must reflect a proper balance and range of subject matter. Cable and DBS channels are subject to much lighter regulations, and other satellite television is currently unregulated.

In November 1988, the Government published its White Paper on the future of broadcasting, and announced its intention of putting the viewer at the centre of broadcasting policy, through a greater emphasis on market forces. The White Paper argued that, with the rapid expansion of services, viewer choice rather than regulatory imposition could and should be relied upon to secure the programmes that viewers want. The BBC could continue to operate under the principles of public service broadcasting, but the ITV companies would be subject to lighter regulations. Whether this framework, which has been designed to accommodate the explosion of new television services, will lead to a greater choice of programmes for the consumer, or whether it will result in a lowering of the much vaunted high standard of British broadcasting, has been the subject of fierce debate.

Exercise
Analyse ITV and BBC airtime in any week by programme type (eg. news, quiz show, feature film, etc.). Borrow copies of the *BBC Annual Report and Accounts* and the *IBA Annual Report and Accounts* from your local library, and compare the size of audiences for different types of programmes.

Video

The development of video has transformed television viewing habits. Between 1984 and 1988, households with a video cassette recorder (VCR) increased from 28 per cent to 51 per cent. In the same year, an average of 4.57 hours of television were being recorded by each VCR every week, either for time-shift purposes or for repeat viewing.

Use of pre-recorded videos has shown spectacular growth. Ten years ago, the industry hardly existed, but by 1987 an average of 6.2 million videotapes were being hired each week. The £374 million being spent on hiring videotapes in 1987 was exceeding the total being spent in the same year on all live theatre, concerts, and other arts, and was more than double that being spent on cinema admissions. The home video market is now crucial to the film industry, and it is estimated that around 90 per cent of all pre-recorded videotapes are feature films, the most frequently hired being comedy films. Table 1.1 gives a full breakdown of the types of pre-recorded video tape most frequently bought or rented.

Table 1.1   Types of pre-recorded video tape most frequently bought or rented

	Videos purchased (%)				Videos rented (%)			
	1985	1986	1987	1988	1985	1986	1987	1988
Music (pop or rock and musicals)	34	31	26	25	2	2	2	2
Comedy Films	10	8	9	9	23	24	22	25
Children's Programmes	8	18	27	30	8	8	7	8
Horror Films	7	4	4	2	13	12	16	14
Drama/Thriller Movies	6	9	3	3	18	13	14	13
Sport	5	4	5	4	1	1	1	1
Pornography	4	2	1	–	4	3	3	2
Science Fiction	3	2	2	2	10	8	6	4
War Films	2	3	3	2	6	5	6	8
General Interest & all other categories	21	19	20	23	15	24	23	23
All Categories	100	100	100	100	100	100	100	100

Source: Cultural Trends 1989, Issue 1 (1989)/BMRB (FORTE)*

*The BMRB (FORTE) survey is a continuous survey involving interviews with 30,000 adults in Great Britain each year.

Radio

Like television, radio is poised to develop a whole new range of programme services. The present system has its origins in the 1960s when BBC radio reorganised itself into the four national networks, Radios 1, 2, 3, and 4, and began to develop its network of local radio stations. Radio Leicester was the first, going on the air in November 1967, and there are now thirty-two stations, each on a broadly county-wide basis, covering approximately 85 per cent of the population. In August 1990, BBC Radio 5 went on the air, a national network specialising in educational programmes and sport. The BBC also provides four national regional services – Radio Scotland, Radio Wales, Radio Cymru, and Radio Ulster. The first independent local radio station (ILR) started broadcasting in 1973, and there are now forty-nine stations.

The 1988 Government Paper on the future of broadcasting set out a number of proposals for the expansion of radio. These acknowledged the evidence of demand and potential for additional services, and argued that there was scope for at least three new national services operating alongside the BBC. At a local level, community radio would be introduced, serving smaller areas than those currently served by ILR and the BBC. There would also be scope for some expansion of ILR, and, resources permitting, of BBC radio as well.

A recent survey revealed that there are around seventy million radio sets in the UK, and that the average household owns four radio sets, a fifth claiming to own six or more. Over 90 per cent of the public listen to the radio each week. Although the amount of time the average person spends listening to the radio is only a third of that spent watching television, the decline in radio listening which was recorded between 1982 and 1985 has been reversed. Table 1.2 gives average audiences for a selection of national radio programmes.

Radio has a particularly close relationship with the record industry, on which it depends for a substantial amount of its output. In 1988/89, music accounted for 94.5 per cent, 81.1 per cent, and 76.2 per cent of the output of Radios 1, 2, and 3 respectively, and around 200,000 hours of all radio. There is some tension in this relationship, arising from the different perspectives of the record companies and the broadcasters. The latter resent the £9 million a year they have to pay to the record companies for what they see as free advertising. The record industry argues that not only is it supplying the radio stations at a very economical rate with high quality programme material, but that illegal home-taping of radio programmes is also losing the industry sales.

As with television, the Government is proposing to lighten the rules and regulations for the independent sector. The BBC will continue to operate

Table 1.2   Some typical radio audiences* (millions) 1987/88

Radio 1		*Radio 3*	
Top 40 (Sunday)	4.3	Record Review (Saturday)	0.2
Simon Mayo (Mon–Fri)	3.8	Composers of the Week (Mon–Fri)	0.2
Simon Bates (Mon–Fri)	3.3	Morning Concert (Mon–Fri)	0.1
Dave Lee Travis (Saturday)	3.2		
Steve Wright (Mon–Fri)	2.6	*Radio 4*	

Radio 2		*Radio 4*	
		News 8am (Mon–Fri)	1.8
		Today 8.10am (Mon–Fri)	1.3
		The Archers Omnibus (Sunday)	1.0
Derek Jameson (Mon–Fri)	2.8	Desert Island Discs (Friday)	0.8
Melodies for You (Sunday)	2.0	Any Questions? (Saturday)	0.7
Jimmy Young (Mon–Fri)	1.9	Call Nick Ross (Tuesday)	0.7
Desmond Carrington (Sunday)	1.9	Women's Hour (Mon–Fri)	0.5
Ken Bruce (Mon–Fri)	1.8	The Afternoon Play (Mon–Fri)	0.4

Audience Appreciation
Among programmes achieving a Reaction Index of 80 or above from the Listening Panel were:

Radio 1	*Radio 3*
Nelson Mandela Birthday Concert	Cheltenham Festival
The Beeb's Lost Beatles Tapes	Proms '88
Dave Lee Travis – Weekend Shows	Kathleen Ferrier
McCartney on McCartney	*Taming of the Shrew*

Radio 2	*Radio 4*
Children in Need	After Henry
Desmond Carrington All Time Greats	Desert Island Discs
Friday Night is Music Night	You and Yours
Al Read	1988 Reith Lectures

Source: BBC, *Daily Survey of Listening*, in *1987/88 BBC Annual Report and Handbook*.

*Monday–Friday audiences represent a daily average figure.

on public service principles, at both a national and local level, providing a wide and diverse range of high quality programmes. Independent radio, the new community stations, and any satellite broadcasting channels will be free to respond to market forces, without having to provide the full range of programmes that public service broadcasting demands.

Hi-Fi

Hi-fi is another fixture of the home leisure centre which few households are without. *The British Phonographic Industry Yearbook* (BPI), which is an invaluable and comprehensive guide to the recording industry, estimated that in 1987, 92 per cent of all households had record or tape equipment, and that 77 per cent had both. Audio technology has enabled people to listen to recorded music almost anywhere, in or outside the home, and in 1987 around a quarter of all adults owned either a personal or a portable stereo cassette player, and over a third owned a radio/cassette recorder. Even the Voyager space probe carried a hi-fi system for the benefit of any extra-terrestrial life it encountered!

The network of record shops across the country has remained stable over the past few years at just under 5000 outlets. There are around 2000 specialist record shops, 370 record chain shops (Virgin, Our Price, HMV/Revolver, etc.), and the rest are what is known in the trade as 'multiples'. These are the stores selling a range of goods with branches all over the country. In mid 1988, F.W.Woolworth had the most outlets with over 800, and W.H.Smith, having acquired both the Virgin and Our Price chains, had the largest share of the record retail market. An interesting development has been the arrival of the specialist CD shops, some of them claiming to stock nearly all CD titles available. Despite the cost and the self-destruct scare stories, CDs have now become firmly established in the market, accounting in 1987 for 21.3 per cent of all record retail sales. At the end of 1987, sales of records of all kinds were buoyant, up on the previous year by nearly a quarter, and representing a higher share of consumer expenditure. In addition, the industry claims the market would have doubled were it not for illegal home taping which is costing record shops and artists around 100 million album sales a year.

The *BPI Yearbook* classifies music in the following way:

Type of Music	% Market Share
Pop and Rock	69
Classical	8
MOR/Easy Listening	8
Country Music	3
Childrens' Material and Comedy	2
Jazz and Blues	1
Reggae and African	1
Folk and Irish Music	1
Film and TV Soundtracks	1
Big Band, Brass Bands, and Nostalgia	0.3

It can be seen that Pop and Rock predictably dominate the market, but it should be remembered that the total market is so large that even a market share for a minority interest area, such as Jazz and Blues, means that around 1.5 million units (LPs, cassettes, or CDs) are sold each year. Unlike the film industry, which is dominated by US products, well over half of both albums and singles sold in the UK were recorded by British artists, and only a third by artists from the United States.

At the end of 1987, about 70 per cent of all record sales were made by six companies, often referred to as the 'majors': EMI group, Virgin, Polygram group, BMG, CBS, and WEA. Five of these companies (all except Virgin) not only distribute their own products to retailers, but they also handle distribution for smaller companies such as Chrysalis and Island. This gives them a share of around 85 per cent of the total distribution market.

Despite the domination of both production and distribution by the 'majors', the independent sector, which has an influence far greater than its market share, should not be underestimated. There are probably between 500 and 600 independent labels currently operating, some such as Factory and Rough Trade now quite well known, others being formed as a one-off by musicians in the hope of getting a contract with a 'major'. The independents have a reputation for producing interesting new music which is too risky for the 'majors' to take on. The tradition goes back to the 1940s, when Blue Note became associated with high quality modern jazz, and includes a range of other specialist labels as well as those in the forefront of the Punk explosion of the 1970s. In order that the work of the independents could get through to its market, an independent distribution network was also developed, now operated by companies such as The Cartel, Charly, and Conifer. The problem for many independent labels is keeping their artists. It is not uncommon for independents to succeed in promoting considerable interest in artists, only to find that the artists are offered lucrative contracts by a 'major', with which the independents are in no position to compete. In some respects, the independents can thus be seen to assume the role of unpaid Research and Development departments for the 'majors'.

Books

Despite the growth and popularity of the electronic media, books retain a remarkably strong hold on the public's interest. Like audio cassettes, the experience is portable, and can be appreciated on the bus, the beach and the train, as well as in the home. A Market and Opinion Research Institute (MORI) poll conducted for the *Sunday Times* revealed that over half the population had claimed to have read more than ten books in 1988, and that a third had claimed to have borrowed more than ten books from a public library. Another survey suggests that the number of people buying both hardbacks and paperbacks has been growing steadily since 1981, and that in 1987 a third of the population had bought a hardback in the previous twelve months, and that just under half had bought a paperback. Table 1.3 gives some idea of the most popular subject matter.

Table 1.3   Subject of book being read (%)

	1980	1982	1984	1986	1986 Men	Women
Base: All Readers	891	894	961	931		
Fiction						
Romance	14	17	17	16	1	28
Crime/thriller	14	16	14	12	13	10
Historical	12	7	8	7	4	9
War/adventure	5	5	6	5	9	2
Modern novel	6	8	8	11	8	13
Classic	3	4	2	4	3	5
Science fiction	2	2	3	4	8	1
Horror/occult	2	2	2	3	4	2
Western	3	1	1	1	1	*
Children's	–	*	1	*	*	–
Humour	1	1	2	2	3	1
Other	3	3	3	5	5	5
All Fiction	**65**	**65**	**67**	**69**	**60**	**76**
Non-Fiction						
Encyclopaedia/atlas/dictionary	–	*	*	*	1	–
History	5	6	6	5	7	3
Biography	7	8	7	7	6	8
Educational	6	4	4	3	4	2
Business/technical	2	1	2	1	2	*
Gardening/DIY/leisure	3	2	2	2	3	1
Travel/guides	1	1	1	1	1	1
Religion	2	3	1	1	1	1
Sport	1	1	1	1	1	–
Arts/crafts	1	1	*	*	*	1
Cookery	*	*	*	–	–	–
Other	6	7	7	8	11	5
All Non-Fiction	**35**	**34**	**33**	**29**	**38**	**22**
Don't Know/Can't remember	2	1	*	1	2	1

Source: *Cultural Trends 1989*, Issue 2 (1989).

Figures are for Great Britain.

Whilst the number of public libraries in the UK has been declining, the number of bookshops has been increasing. There were 4549 libraries in 1988, 7 per cent less than in 1980, and between 1984 and 1988 the number of bookshops increased by 7 per cent to 4745, the largest chain being W.H.Smith, which dominated the market with 374 branches. The big chain stationery shops are a crucial outlet for some publishers, and the distribution companies such as Bookwise, which choose the limited number of publications to be supplied to these shops, exercise a significant influence on the industry. However, despite the prominence of the big chains, it can be seen that there are a large number of independent retailers, who fulfil an important function for the public. Books can also be purchased at a diverse range of other retail outlets, such as petrol stations, supermarkets, and department stores. Over two million people are members of book clubs, which account for about twenty per cent of hardback sales to individuals.

On the supply side, the number of titles that continue to be published in the UK each year is staggering. In 1950, it was 17,072, by 1971 it had gone up to 32,538, and in 1988 it was 56,514. The British book trade produces as many titles annually as the United States, with a turnover and domestic market only one-fifth of the size. More fiction and children's books are published than anything else. There has been a spate of mergers and takeovers recently, but the publishing industry in Britain is still small-scale, with many specialist publishers. The forty largest publishing concerns are reckoned to produce about one third of all titles published.

Much has been made of the potential damage caused by the library system to both the publishing and the retail trade. It is interesting to note the results of the MORI poll, mentioned above, which found that instead of providing an alternative to book buying, libraries seemed to supplement it, with book-buyers being more likely to go to a public library than non-book-buyers.

Further details regarding public libraries and the competition from the publishing and retail trade are given in Chapter 2.

Exercise
What do you think are the social and cultural consequences of the development of Home Entertainment?

Going Out

Film and Cinema

The rise and fall of the cinema has been a dramatic feature of the twentieth-century entertainment history. In terms of popularity, it reached its height in 1946, with annual admissions reaching 1.6 billion people. twenty-four years later, in 1970, annual admissions were down to 193 million, a mere 12 per cent of the number of people who had been going to the cinema in 1946. By 1984 the number was down to 53 million, and leisure consultants were predicting that this would drop to 31 million by 1989. However, there has been a sharp upward trend since 1984, and the latest estimates show that 78.7 million were drawn into the cinema in 1987 – an increase of 48.5 per cent on 1984.

The increases in attendance are not due to a corresponding growth in the total number of cinema sites and screens. In the UK in 1988, there were 1316 screens on 661 sites, a situation not significantly different from 1984. The largest cinema chain is Cannon, which, in 1988, following its acquisition of Thorn/EMI Screen Entertainment, Star and Classic circuits, had 380 screens on 143 sites. There were however, an even larger number of independent cinemas – 548 screens on 401 sites. The upward trend in cinema audiences may be due to more popular films, more persuasive marketing, a loosening of the grip of home entertainment, or a combination of all three. The arrival of the multiplex in the UK in the mid-1980s signalled a new, confident approach to cinema provision. By the end of 1988, there were eleven multiplexes in operation, with 105 screens between them, and American Multi-Cinema (AMC) was announcing its intention of doubling cinemagoing in the UK over the next five years. A recent report predicts that there may be as many as one hundred multiplexes, with just under a thousand screens, in operation within the next few years.

US domination has always been a characteristic of cinema in the UK. As early as 1910, only 15 per cent of films screened in the UK were British, and in 1923 the Chairman of the Motion Picture Producers and Distributors of America declared on a visit to Britain: 'We want to Americanize the world'. The British response to this was to introduce in 1927 the screen quota system, whereby all commercial cinemas were obliged to show a percentage of British, (or, since 1973, EEC) films. Up until 1984, films screened in the UK had to be registered with the Department of Trade, and records show that between 1980 and 1984, 1254 films were registered, of which 14 per cent were British, and 52.2 per cent were American. The screen quota system continued until 1985, when it was abolished, along with the requirement to register films with the

Department of Trade. Since the abolition of the import quota, it has only been possible to make an educated guess at the respective percentages of British and American films shown in the UK.

The importance of the film industry to television and video has already been pointed out. These distribution outlets provide a crucial source of income for film investors, for whom huge risks are an occupational hazard. The average Hollywood film cost 27 million dollars to make in 1987, and half of all films lose money. However, because an *ET* or a *Batman* will gross staggering profits, investment in films remains an attractive – if highly speculative – proposition, provided the risks can be spread.

Theatre and Drama

The theatre today is made up of a network of venues and producing managements, both commercial and grant-aided. The term 'commercial' is used to refer to those managements or companies that operate without public subsidy, aiming to make profits on their work through box office sales and associated trading activities. The extent to which artistic considerations are subordinate to the profit motive varies from organisation to organsation, and indeed, some managements would argue that there is no conflict between the two. Conversely, it is argued that, without subsidy, theatres would not be able to present the more challenging plays, and that the higher price of tickets would take the experience of live theatre out of the reach of most people.

Although the character of the commercial sector can thus be significantly different from that of the grant-aided theatres, an increasing interdependence between the two has been a feature of recent theatre history. Commercial managements tour productions to grant-aided theatres, and subsidised companies transfer to the West End. It is also important to remember that the term 'theatre' does not just mean drama: many theatres are increasingly used for a wide range of performance events, including concerts, cabaret, and light entertainment.

As might be expected, there is a greater concentration of theatre buildings in London than anywhere else. The 1988/89 *British Theatre Directory*, edited by A. Holland, lists ninety-six in Greater London, of which around fifty are situated in the West End, the heart of commercial theatre. London also houses the two 'national' companies, the Royal Shakespeare Company (RSC) at the Barbican, and the Royal National Theatre on the South Bank. The *Directory* lists four hundred and eighty-five theatres in other regions of the country, as well as another thirty-six small clubs and lunchtime theatres in London. This list includes some arts centres and civic halls, but there are others to be added, as well as the wide range of venues which from time to time become part of the touring circuit. These can include schools, leisure centres, sports centres, village halls, community centres, outdoor sites and temporary venues adapted for festivals or special performances.

Theatres can be divided into those that have their own resident companies, and those that operate primarily as receiving venues. Almost all of the former receive public subsidy, with the Royal National Theatre and the RSC (in London and Stratford) receiving the most. At the present time, there are also fifty-five building-based, subsidised repertory companies, such as the Royal Exchange Theatre in Manchester. These are essentially concerned with producing work for their own theatres, although from time to time they undertake tours, and occasionally host work from other companies. Some of these companies have studio theatres as well as their main houses, where more 'difficult' work, and in particular new plays, can be presented. Increasingly, repertory companies are also seeking to transfer successful productions to the West End. The advantage to commercial managements is that they are taking on a production with proven appeal, and for the originating theatre, the transfer deal can bring substantial benefits of both cash and prestige.

Exercise
Visit all the theatre venues within a fifteen mile radius of your home. List the names and numbers of performances that have been presented over the last twelve months. Do you consider this to be an interesting programme? If not, what changes would you like to have seen?

The receiving venues, which range from the so-called Number One touring houses equipped to take large scale companies, to the smallest community centre, are serviced either by touring companies or by companies which form for a specific production at a particular venue. A number of commercial production companies, such as the one run by the Albery family, operate in the West End. Investment for productions in sought from 'angels', who will not recoup any of their money until the show has run long enough for it to cover its costs. Once the show goes into profit, the 'angel' starts to make money, and the longer the run the more he/she makes. Conversely, if it flops, he/she stands to lose everything.

Touring companies are classified as large, middle, or small-scale, and are run by both commercial and subsidised managements. Both the National and the RSC undertake some touring, the RSC playing a regular season in Newcastle, and successfully taking its productions into non-traditional venues such as leisure centres and sports halls. At the smaller end of the scale, there are some 300 companies presenting an extraordinarily diverse range of work, from neglected classics to new writing, from performance art to music theatre.

Receiving venues can be privately owned and managed, under local authority control, or operated as independent charitable trusts. Many of them present a wide range of theatre, music, dance and light entertainment, and do not limit themselves just to dramatic productions. This can be seen in the programmes of theatres at seaside resorts, which present a huge volume of work during the summer months, and make a significant contribution to the domestic touring industry. Mixed programmes are also central to the philosophy of Arts Centres, which aim to promote and stimulate interest in a number of different art forms. Over the last two decades, the growth of Arts Centres has been remarkable, paralleling to some extent the growing numbers of small-scale touring theatre companies, which feature prominently in most Arts Centre programmes.

Data on attendances at commercial theatre outside London have not recently been collected, and estimates of admissions to drama performances only take account of the subsidised sector, and London's West End. However, it can be seen from these that the audience for drama grew during the 1980s, from around 13.6 million in 1982/83, to nearly 18 million in 1987/88. In terms of audience volume, the West End towers above everything else, attracting over ten million people, and having a 57 per cent share of the total audience.

It is interesting to note that although the West End and the subsidised theatres are currently earning around the same amount of box office income a year as the cinemas, the eighteen million attending drama performances is only just over a fifth of the number of people going to the cinema. One episode of 'Eastenders' on television will be watched by more than the number of people who go to see live drama in a whole year.

Concerts

As with the theatre, the existence of a subsidised music sector dates only from World War II, when groups of musicians were paid to give concerts around the country to boost the morale of a people under siege. After the war, the newly formed Arts Council of Great Britain continued to support and promote music, but concerned itself only with Western European classical music. The Arts Council's first annual report makes no mention, for example, of the revolutionary music being pioneered in the 1940s by Charlie Parker and Dizzie Gillespie, and which was attracting interest amongst jazz enthusiasts in this country.

Although the arts funding bodies in the UK now recognise jazz as a serious art form and support it in a number of ways, classical music remains the central musical concern of the subsidised sector, and the rest, by and large, has to find its way in the market place. The one major exception is the music of military bands, which is heavily supported by the Ministry of Defence, and in 1987/88 was supplied at a net cost of around £60 million. This is well over twice the Arts Council's combined budget for music and opera. Although there is some statistical information on the subsidised sector, concerts are promoted by such a wide range of organisations in different venues that it is difficult to get a complete picture. There is very little available information on the much larger commercial sector.

There are few concert halls that specialise exclusively in one form of music. The Barbican, home of the London Symphony Orchestra, not only promotes classical concerts, pop music, and light entertainment, but also doubles as a conference centre. The three venues of the South Bank Centre – the Royal Festival Hall, the Queen Elizabeth Hall, and the Purcell Room – all present mixed musical programmes. The Royal Festival Hall also presents some opera and ballet, and the Queen Elizabeth Hall is occasionally used for drama. J. Myerscough's *Facts about the Arts* lists thirty-five venues regularly promoting professional symphony orchestras, and these, such as Nottingham's Royal Hall, also promote a wide range of other events. Most of these venues are owned and managed by local authorities, which often manage small civic halls or leisure centres as well, and these too are used as concert venues. We have already seen how concerts are included in the programmes of many theatrical venues and Arts Centres.

Although there are some large-scale private sector venues that are regularly used for concerts, such as Wembley Stadium and the Earls Court Exhibition Centre, venues in the private sector tend to be more informal, and on a smaller scale. Pubs and clubs are vital to the folk, rock, and jazz scene, and have provided the crucial public performance experience, often in very difficult conditions, for many successful musical careers. Specialist clubs, such as Ronnie Scott's, have acquired an international reputation in their own right. Classical recitals are sometimes promoted in churches and country houses, and open spaces and stately homes have also been used for large scale 'pop' concerts.

The principal UK orchestras can be grouped into the four London symphony orchestras, the five regional symphony orchestras, the five BBC orchestras, and the orchestras attached to the five major opera houses. The London orchestras are the London Philharmonic, the London Symphony, the Philharmonia, and the Royal Philharmonic, and the regional ones are the Hallé, the Royal Liverpool Philharmonic, the City of Birmingham Symphony Orchestra (CBSO), the Bournemouth Symphony Orchestra, and the Scottish National Orchestra. These regional orchestras, together with the BBC and the Opera orchestras, are all 'contract' orchestras – orchestras which engage their players on a permanent basis, rather than concert by concert. Most orchestras cannot afford to do this, and no other British symphony orchestra and only two chamber orchestras – the Bournemouth Sinfonietta and the Northern Sinfonia – are able to do so. The London orchestras do not wish to become 'contract' orchestras as their players prefer to retain the freedom to accept other engagements.

The 1989 *British Music Yearbook*, edited by M. Barton, lists around 150 further symphony and chamber orchestras, over 700 ensembles, and thousands of solo performers. The list gives no indication of how many engagements the artists undertake, and has to be treated with a certain amount of caution. It is even more difficult to assess what is happening in other kinds of music – in rock and pop, for example, or in jazz, folk, country and western, reggae, and African music. There is a huge diversity of promoters, mainly working on a commercial basis and sometimes very informally, about whom there is obviously no reliable statistical information.

Concerts are promoted in a variety of ways, with the private and public sectors often being closely interlinked. Commercial promoters, for example, hire local authority venues, and municipal entertainment departments engage pop groups. Voluntary promoters, such as most jazz and folk club organisers, promote gigs both in pubs and in subsidised venues, and bands frequently promote themselves. There are around 300 members of the National Federation of Music Societies, an association of voluntary promoters which is the mainstay of the small-scale classical music circuit. Unlike the theatre, where runs of several days or weeks are common, concerts are more often than not one-off promotions.

Opera

Full-scale opera performances are notoriously expensive to stage, requiring large orchestras, elaborate staging and huge costs. If an opera house is to be of an international standard, enormous fees will have to be paid to attract the best singers. It follows, therefore, that very high levels of subsidy are required if opera is to be financially viable, and that only a limited number of companies can be maintained.

The major home for opera in the UK is the Royal Opera House (ROH) at Convent Garden, which is shared with the Royal Ballet. The ROH has consistently received the largest single grant from the Arts Council of Great Britain, and the association between the ROH and the Arts Council has always been close. Critics have noted the large number of ROH trustees and directors that have also served as members or senior officers of the Arts Council. The other major opera house, also in

London, is the English National Opera (ENO), based at the London Coliseum.

There are five other opera companies which between them are responsible for most of the work that is seen in the rest of the UK. These are: Scottish Opera, Welsh National Opera, Opera North, Opera 80, and Glyndebourne Productions. They each have 'spheres of influence', or areas of the country, where they concentrate their energies, running touring programmes, developing audiences, and offering educational events. There are also some smaller companies, for example Buxton Opera and the City of Birmingham Opera, which form for a limited number of productions.

Because of the costs involved, opera is very rarely presented without some form of subsidy. An exception is the recent phenomenon of the stadium performance, such as the production of *Aida* which ran for seven nights at the Earls Court Exhibition Centre in June 1988. Staged by rock presenter Harvey Goldsmith, the performances were run on a commercial basis, selling out every night, and demonstrating the enormous popular appeal of opera. Stadium conditions are obviously not comparable to those of an opera house, and have an adverse effect on the quality of the performance. However, the sheer scale of the event gives it an altogether different character, and comparisons are perhaps not particularly meaningful.

Dance

Like opera, full-scale classical ballet is also extremely expensive to produce, and although it is very popular, the subsidy available only allows for the maintenance of five permanently operational companies. Two of these are attached to the Royal Opera House – the Royal Ballet and the Sadlers Wells Royal Ballet. The Royal Ballet is the only company in the UK, classical and contemporary, to have a permanent home, and even this is shared with the opera company. The Sadler's Wells Royal Ballet is exclusively concerned with touring to the receiving theatres, although there are plans for the company to establish a home base at the Birmingham Hippodrome. English National Ballet is also a touring company, as are Northern Ballet and Scottish Ballet, the only ballet companies to be based outside London. The London City Ballet receives some money from the Arts Council on a project by project basis, and there are some companies, such as the Alexander Roy London Ballet Theatre, which manage to operate without subsidy, using recorded music in place of a live orchestra.

The two major contemporary dance companies are the Rambert Dance Company and London Contemporary Dance Theatre (LCDT). A third, the Extemporary Dance Theatre, operates on a smaller scale.

There are also a number of small scale dance companies, some supported by regional arts associations, which are more experimental in their approach, and tour to arts centres, and some schools and community centres. These are the dance equivalent to the small-scale drama companies referred to above, and indeed, with some drama companies drawing on dance techniques, and with dance companies making use of texts, the distinction between the two is often very hard to draw. Companies and soloists drawing on African, Afro-Caribbean, and South Asian traditions have become increasingly prominent on the dance scene. The focus for new dance is The Place Theatre in London, which provides a platform for a wide range of experimental dance companies, and is in fact the only theatre in the country to specialise in dance programmes. None of the contemporary companies has a theatre of its own.

The so-called 'Dance Explosion' reached its peak in the late 1970s, and audiences for both classical and contemporary dance have subsequently declined, though for different reasons. Attendances for performances of classical ballet have remained constant, or even increased, but the total number of performances has fallen considerably. Of the major contemporary companies, LCDT and Rambert Dance, numbers of performances and attendances have declined to one third of the audiences they had ten years ago.

The world of classical and contemporary dance seems far removed from the commercial sector, about which little statistical information exists. It is interesting to note that the Devlin Report on the development of dance in England, commissioned by the Arts Council and published in February 1989, makes no mention at all of this sector. None the less, clubs, holiday camps, seaside resort theatres, and even municipal entertainment departments, all book commercial dance acts.

Cabaret, New Variety, and Other Entertainments

Cabaret and new variety artists are presented in clubs, pubs, and some subsidised venues. There is no available information on numbers of performances and audience trends, although a growing interest in cabaret over the past few years can be discerned, which television companies have both exploited and developed. A number of agencies, such as CAST, specialise in the 'alternative sector', and information on the whole range of light entertainment acts can be found in B. Dunn's *Showcall*, the directory published by *Stage and Television Today*. A selection of categories of entertainment listed by *Showcall*, is illuminating.

Acrobatic Acts	Female Impersonators
Aerialists	Jugglers
Animal Acts	Fire Eaters
Balancing Acts	Flamenco Acts
Children's Entertainers	Floor Shows
Circus Acts	Limbo Dancers
Clowns	Magicians & Illusion
Comedians, Comediennes,	Male Impersonators
& Comedy Duos	Mind Readers/Mental
Comedy Speciality Acts	Old Time Music Hall
Commères and Compères	Outdoor Attractions
Contortionists	Package Shows
Disc Jockeys and Discos	Pickpocket Acts
Drag Artistes	Siffleurs
Entertainers at the Piano	Stag Night Artists
Escapologists	Stunt Performers
Exotic Dancers	Toastmasters/MCs
German Bands	Trick Cyclists
Hen Party Performers	Ventriloquists
Hypnotists Acts	Yodellers
Impressionists	

Source: *Showcall, Stage and Television Today*, 1989.

Amateur and Community Arts

The above sections have been concerned only with the work of professional entertainers and artists, and the organisations and institutions which present this work to the public. However, no survey of provision for Entertainments and the Arts would be complete without reference to amateur involvement in artistic activity, and to the support systems that have been developed.

Facts about the Arts estimated that upwards of one million people participate in amateur music and drama. However, this is a conservative figure, which takes no account of the members of amateur rock and pop bands, of those attending dance classes, of those participating in youth theatre, or of those using the facilities of film and video workshops. The amateur field is in any case difficult to define, and can be stretched to include all those artistic activities which take place in schools, colleges, polytechnics, universities, and adult education classes.

There is a two-way relationship between the amateur and the professional world. Amateurs are sometimes called upon to support essentially
professional events, such as large-scale choral works performed by the
Philharmonia Orchestra, and professionals are sometimes invited by
amateur groups to strengthen, guide or direct their work.

There are also community groups, or animateurs, who aim to
stimulate interest in artistic activity amongst groups and individuals
within the community, and to present work in collaboration with them.
Some artists, or groups of artists, such as Manchester's Community Arts
Workshop, work exclusively on this basis. Others, such as the Grand
Union Orchestra, both tour their own work as well as undertaking
collaborative community projects.

Exercise
Find out about your local amateur music and drama companies.
Who are they? What do they do? How are they financed?

Administration and Finance

Consumer Expenditure

The Entertainment and Arts industry is largely paid for by the consumer.
As we have seen in the above section, parts of it are also supported from
public funds, and although in some areas of the industry, such as live
opera and repertory theatre, more than half of the total income comes
from public funds, across the industry as a whole it is consumer
expenditure which is dominant. The Central Statistical Office (CSO)
provides information on consumer expenditure, and although the
categories used make it difficult to isolate exactly how much is spent
on Entertainment and the Arts, Table 1.4, on page 24, gives a rough
guide. The extent of consumer expenditure on Entertainment and the
Arts puts into perspective funding by the State, estimated at around £819
million in total in 1986/87. Nevertheless, even though State funding of
the Arts in the UK is per capita lower than in most other European
countries there are many cultural organisations that depend upon it for
their existence. State support also has a symbolic dimension to it,
bringing with it prestige, and even a suggestion that the activities
supported are of a superior value to those that are not.

Table 1.4   Consumer expenditure on entertainment and the arts, in £ millions*

	1983	1984	1985	1986	1987
Cinema admissions	124	104	132	142	150
Live entertainments and arts[1]	233	233	267	333	367
Books	620	665	708	811	920
Records and tapes	651	749	898	1060	1357
Radio, TV, musical instruments & other durables[2]	2478	2753	2909	3137	3158
Television & video hire charges/licence fees	2033	2112	2283	2466	2545
Total	6015	6512	7065	7807	8347

Source: *Cultural Trends 1989*, Issue 1 (1989).

*Figures are for the United Kingdom.

[1] The category of live entertainment and arts does not include admissions to museums, galleries, and country houses.

[2] The category of other durables includes photographic equipment.

State funding is either provided directly by central or local government, or channelled through quasi-autonomous non-government organisations (QUANGOs) such as the Arts Council of Great Britain and the British Film Institute. The system is both complex and confusing, and the responsibilities and functions of the organisations concerned often seem arbitrarily divided. The system can best be understood by examining each of the major components in turn.

Central Government

The Office of Arts and Libraries (OAL), headed by the Minister for the Arts, is the government department most concerned with support for the Arts in England, with the Scottish Education Department, the Welsh Office, and the Northern Ireland Department of Education having responsibility for the Arts in their respective countries. The Arts Council of Great Britain, which is funded by the OAL, also channels funds to Scotland and Wales via the Scottish and Welsh Arts Councils. Central government funding is given in Table 1.5.

Table 1.5 Central government main arts funding departments'[1] expenditure on the arts, by country, 1983/84 and 1986/87

	1983/84	1986/87
Arts support	*£ millions*	
England	88.5	131.8
Wales[2]	7.1	8.6
Scotland[2]	12.3	14.1
Northern Ireland	2.8	3.5
United Kingdom	110.7	158.0
Arts expenditure per head of population	*£s per head*	
England	3.58	5.03
Wales	4.84	5.88
Scotland	4.25	5.04
Northern Ireland	4.21	5.17
United Kingdom	3.72	5.08
Arts expenditure as percentage	*%*	
of total public expenditure	0.25	0.28

Source: Cultural Trends 1989, Issue 1 (1989).

[1] The Office of Arts and Libraries, the Scottish Education Department, the Welsh Office, and the Northern Ireland Department of Education.
[2] That proportion of Arts Council of Great Britain grant going to the Welsh and Scottish Arts Councils has been allocated to the central government figures for Wales and Scotland. The grants from the Crafts Council and the British Film Institute to the Welsh Arts Council are shown in the figures for Wales.

Around 85 per cent of the expenditure appearing under the heading 'Arts support' goes to the Arts Council of Great Britain. Most of the rest goes to the small cultural QUANGOs – the British Film Institute, the Crafts Council, the Scottish Film Council, and the Arts Council of Northern Ireland – and to the Public Lending Right Scheme. This scheme was set up in 1982, and gives authors the right to receive payment from a central fund for the use of their books borrowed from public libraries. The fund stood at £3.5 million in 1988/89. The 'Arts Support' heading also includes the Business Sponsorship Incentive Scheme, through which the goverment tries to increase levels of business sponsorship. Under the scheme, for which £3 million was available in 1988/89, the government gives additional funds to those organisations which are successful either in attracting new sponsors, or in getting existing sponsors to increase the amounts they give.

Other central government departments are also involved in Arts support. The Department of the Environment has a responsibility for the 'built heritage', although this is a very broad heading which stretches the definition of the Arts beyond a point which the reader may wish to accept. It includes the National Heritage Memorial Fund, which provides assistance towards the cost of acquiring, maintaining, or preserving land, buildings, paintings and other items of outstanding interest which are important to the national heritage. Items purchased from the fund range from works of art to scientific, industrial, aeronautical and marine objects. The Department of the Environment also supports the Historic Buildings and Monuments Commission for England, more commonly known as English Heritage, which has the responsibility of protecting and conserving England's architectural and archaeological heritage. Other heritage responsibilities of the Department of the Environment include upkeep of the Royal Parks and Palaces, of the Tower Armouries, and of some redundant churches.

The Department of Employment has a long record of supporting arts projects. The employment potential of the Arts is analysed in a report published by the Policy Studies Institute in 1988, which showed that the Arts gave direct employment to 496,000 people, or 2.1 per cent of the total employed population.

Of the remaining central government expenditure on the Arts, the Natural History Museum, now funded by the Department of Education and Science, is a significant item, as is the Ministry of Defence expenditure on military bands, to which reference has already been made.

In total, around £600 million, or £10.60 per head of population, was spent by central government on Entertainment and the Arts in the UK during 1986/87.

Local Government

Our current system of local government has its roots in the late nineteenth century, when the county, district, and parish councils were created, and given legal powers to perform specific functions. By and large, local councillors shared the view that the Arts should take care of themselves, and it was not until 1948 that local authorities were, in fact, legally empowered to provide or support Entertainment and the Arts. It is important to appreciate that local authorities are *obliged* to provide some services and *allowed* to provide others. When the 1948 Local Government Act was passed, all local authorities except Parish and County Councils were allowed but not obliged to spend money on Entertainment and the Arts. With the Parish and County Councils similarly empowered in 1963, and the removal (in theory) of limits to this expenditure in 1972, the legal position has subsequently remained the same.

Both District and County Councils (Regions and District in Scotland) are involved in provision and support for Entertainment and the Arts, and in some, but by no means all areas of the country, the level of co-operation and collaboration between districts and counties is very close. Difficulties are often increased if the county and districts are of different political persuasions, with differing views of what and how much should be supported. This problem does not arise in the metropolitan areas where, since the abolition of the metropolitan counties in 1986, the District Councils have become single-tier authorities, solely responsible for the provision of local services.

Local authorities have a long tradition of owning and supporting museums and galleries, which form a major part of their provision. Most authorities also own other buildings which are used for entertainment, ranging from purpose-built theatres in the larger urban authorities, to village halls in the small rural ones. Some of these buildings, for example many of the repertory theatres, are leased permanantly to independent charitable trusts. Others are managed by local authorities themselves, in which case the authority may present its own entertainments programme, hire the building out to other promoters, or do both. Local authorities also give grant aid to independent organisations, ranging in scale from the large orchestras and repertory theatres to the smallest community festival. The larger grant-aided organisations are often supported in partnership with either the Arts Council of Great Britain or the Regional Arts Association. Management partnerships have also emerged in recent years, an interesting example being the Phoenix Arts Centre in Leicester, which is jointly managed by the City Council and the Polytechnic's Arts Administration Department.

There is a wide diversity of approach to the organisation of entertainments provision within local authorities. Some authorities have Entertainments and Arts departments, others have departments of leisure and recreation. Some put the Arts in the same department as parks and amenities, some put them in with libraries. There are even cases where the Arts are covered by the same department that deals with cemeteries! The Arts can also be supported by education authorities, and there are a number of such authorities which run youth orchestras, theatre in education (TIE) teams, and youth dance schemes. With more attention being given to the contribution the Arts can make to the local economy, arts projects have also been supported by local authority economic development units.

Exercise
What does your Local Authority do in the field of Entertainment and the Arts and which department(s) is/are responsible? Does the Authority have an Entertainment and Arts policy? If so, give your assessment of it, and if not, suggest what you think should be included in it? If you live in a non-metropolitan area, remember to examine both tiers of local government.

The fact that local authority support for Entertainment and the Arts is discretionary rather than mandatory means that there are no minimum levels, or standards, that have to be achieved. The pattern of support is therefore variable, and it is important to appreciate that some authorities are simply not interested, and do not see why public money should be spent on entertainment provision.

The different approaches to the organisation of entertainment provision are reflected in the different ways in which expenditure is accounted for. Thus there is some difficulty in ascertaining, on a comparable basis, how much local authorities are spending on entertainment. As an approximate estimate, of the total local authority expenditure on Entertainment and the Arts in 1986/87 of £218.1 million, the District Councils accounted for well over 85 per cent, and were clearly the main providers.

If local government expenditure is added to the £600 million central government expenditure, total public expenditure in 1986/87 on Entertainment and the Arts (including museums and galleries) amounted to around £819 million, or £14.4. per head of population. Of this, the local government share was just over a quarter.

The QUANGOs

Unlike most of the other Western European countries, there is no Ministry of Culture in the United Kingdom. Instead, responsibility is delegated to a number of independently constituted organisations, which, with the aid of government funding, promote and support cultural activities. Enshrined in this system is the notion of 'the arm's length principle', central to which is the idea that government should not *directly* control the funding. Given that the members of the governing bodies of these organisation are appointed by Ministers, the degree of independence which the organisations enjoy is subject to some debate. It should in any case be remembered that the government has extensive direct responsibility in a number of areas, for example the major art galleries, and military bands. Furthermore, 'the arm's length principle' does not usually apply to *local* government expenditure on Entertainment and the Arts. The structure, functions, and resources of the main cultural QUANGOs are briefly examined below:

The Arts Council of Great Britain

The Arts Council operates under Royal Charter and its aims are:

- To develop and improve the knowledge, understanding and practice of the Arts.
- To increase the accessibility of the Arts to the public throughout Great Britain.
- To advise and co-operate with departments of government, local authorities, and other bodies.

The governing body is the Council itself, which consists of the Chairman and 19 other members, all appointed by the Minister for the Arts. The Council delegates its responsibilities in Scotland and Wales to the Scottish and Welsh Arts Councils respectively. Technically, they remain committees of the Arts Council of Great Britain, but once the budgets are agreed, they operate independently. The Arts Council of Northern Ireland is funded directly by the Northern Ireland Department of Education.

The Arts Council of Great Britain is concerned almost exclusively with professional work, and one of its primary functions is the funding of the major institutions that present this work, such as the Royal Opera House, the symphony orchestras, and the larger repertory theatres. The Council has departments of Dance; Drama; Film, Video and Broadcasting; Literature; Music; Touring and Visual Arts. These departments are responsible for assessing the work of their 'clients', which is the term used to describe an organisation or individual in receipt of Arts Council funds. The activities of the department of Film, Video, and Broadcasting are much narrower than the title suggests: it is a small department, with very limited resources, concerned essentially with the relationship of film and video to the visual arts, and with encouraging broadcasters to bring the work of Arts Council 'clients' to a wider audience.

As well as its departments the Council also has a 'services division', whose responsibilities include assisting client organisations with their marketing, the funding of training schemes, liaison with local authorities and other agencies, and the funding and assessment of the Regional Arts Associations.

Almost all the Art Council's income, nearly £140 million in 1987/88, comes from the Office of Arts and Libraries. Of this, £14.2 million (10.1 per cent) went to the Scottish Arts Council, and £8.8 million (5.6 per cent) to the Welsh Arts Council. Of the £117.8 million spent in England, £32.2 million (27.3 per cent) went to the four 'national' companies – the Royal Opera House, English National Opera, the National Theatre, and the Royal Shakespeare Company. If English National Ballet and the South Bank Centre are added, the share of the 'national' organisations goes up to 37.6 per cent. However, it should be remembered that the Royal Opera House represents three companies – the opera company, the Royal Ballet, and the Sadlers Wells Ballet. The Regional Arts Associations (RAAs), which are examined below, accounted for 23.4 per cent of Arts Council expenditure in England, the next largest share of 11.5 per cent being spent in support of drama.

If we exclude from our calculations the grants to the other funding agencies (the Scottish and Welsh Arts Councils and the RAAs), we will find that well over three-quarters of the Arts Council's funds are spent on the live performing arts. There is a limited engagement with the cultural industries of broadcasting, publishing, film, video, and recording. This is partly historical, in that the Arts Council was not primarily established to intervene in these areas, and partly a reflection of the view that these industries can survive in the market place, whereas sectors of the live performing arts cannot. There is some strength in this argument, but the limited range of the Council's concerns does give it a curiously anachronistic quality, and its grandiose title, implying an involvement in all of Great Britain's Arts, is not entirely appropriate.

The British Film Institute (BFI)

The foundation of the British Film Institute in 1933 preceded that of the Arts Council of Great Britain. It was established as a company limited by guarantee, receiving its Royal Charter in 1983, and it is also a registered charity. Its chartered aims are as follows:

- To encourage the development of the art of the film in Great Britain.
- To promote its use as a record of contemporary life and manners.
- To foster study and appreciation of it from these points of view.
- To foster study and appreciation of films for television and television programmes generally.
- To encourage the best use of television in Great Britain.

The Institute is controlled by a Board of Governors appointed by the Minister for the Arts. Two of these Governors may be the elected nominees of the Institute's members, but these nominations are subject to the Minister's approval. Membership of the BFI is open to everyone, and on payment of a subscription, various facilities and services are made available. The BFI does not have financial responsibilites for film in Northern Ireland; and in Wales, the Welsh Arts Council acts as the

Institute's agent. Responsibilities for film in Scotland are shared with the Scottish Film Council, which is concerned primarily with the development of film exhibition facilities, the promotion of film production, the operation of the Scottish Film Archive, and media education.

Unlike the Arts Council, which is essentially a funding body, the BFI directly manages a number of services and projects. On the South Bank in London, it runs both the National Film Theatre, which shows over 2000 films a year in three auditoriums, and the Museum of the Moving Image, which opened in 1988 with a range of exhibits charting the history of film and television. On the distribution side, it aims to correct some of the shortcomings of the commercial market by arranging deals with distributors and rights holders, and providing tailor-made programming and publicity service to the forty or so independent film theatres. It also provides a service to over 500 educational and film society exhibitors, which require key titles in 16mm, rather than the standard 35mm used for theatrical exhibition.

There is an extensive BFI information service, which acts as a clearing house on all matters affecting film and television at home and abroad. This is provided through the library, the TV unit, the education section (which can provide advice at all levels from primary to higher education), and through BFI publications. These include two periodicals, the *Monthly Film Bulletin* and *Sight and Sound*, as well as a range of books and monographs. There is also a collection of stills, posters, and designs which includes over 3 million black and white photographs, 400,000 colour transparencies, 15,000 posters and 2000 original set and costume designs.

The National Film Archive was one of the earliest BFI initiatives, set up to maintain a national repository of films of permanent value. Its main functions are selection and acquisition, preservation, cataloguing, and the provision of a viewing service. A major programme is underway to have deteriorating nitrate film copied on to safety film.

On the production side, the Institute awards production grants for innovative and experimental film-making, both documentary and feature. It should be remembered that production support is also available from British Screen Finance Ltd (British Screen) and the National Film Development Fund (NFDF), both of which are supported by grants from the Department of Trade and Industry. British Screen is a private company, bringing together Cannon, Rank, and Channel 4, which aims to support emerging talent. NFDF, which is managed by British Screen, provides support for the development of scripts and the production of short films. The BFI often works closely with British Screen in awarding its production grants.

The BFI operates on a much smaller budget than does the Arts Council of Great Britain, but because of the nature of its work, it draws on a wider range of income sources. In 1987/88, its total income was £22.1

million, of which the largest share – £10.0 million (45.3 per cent) – was received as a grant from the Office of Arts and Libraries. The remaining income was generated from membership subscriptions, the sale of goods and services, private donations, and corporate sponsorship.

The Crafts Council

Government support for crafts began shortly after World War II with a grant from the Board of Trade to the Crafts Centre of Great Britain. The grant was repeated annually until 1971, when it was increased significantly and brought within the remit of the Minister for the Arts and the newly formed Crafts Advisory Committee. The Committee became the Crafts Council in 1979, and received its Royal Charter in 1982, with the principle objective set out as follows:

> To advance and encourage the creation and conservation of works of fine craftmanship and to foster, promote, and increase the interest of the public in England and Wales.

There are currently nineteen members of the Council, which is the governing body, and these are all appointed by the Minister for the Arts. Funding of crafts in Scotland is the responsibility of the Scottish Development Agency (SDA) and the Highlands and Islands Development Board (HIDB), both of which are largely financed by the Scottish office. In Northern Ireland, responsibility for public funding of crafts rests with the Local Enterprise Development Unit (LEDU), which is an independent limited company financed entirely by the Northern Ireland Department of Economic Development.

The Craft Council maintains that crafts have certain key characteristics that include:

- the individual maker as dominant at all stages of production
- a sense of innovation in the work
- a design component
- aesthetic content
- a level of technical competence.

It also asserts that the crafts are product-led not market led.

Exercise
Investigate who the crafts people are in your locality. What materials do they work with? How are they supported?

The Crafts Council regards national development, the craft economy, and education as its three priorities. Within its limited resources, and working in partnership with the Regional Arts Associations, the Welsh Arts Council, local authorities and other organisations, it offers a number of different services. It awards grants to craftspeople for training and setting up; offers business advice, particularly in the field of marketing and sales promotion; runs its own shop; runs a touring exhibition service; and it is involved in a range of initiatives to support and promote crafts in schools, in higher and further education, and in the adult education sector.

The Crafts Council, with a total expenditure in 1987/88 of £2.7 million, operates on a much smaller scale than either the Arts Council or the British Film Institute. Three-quarters of its income comes through the grant from the Office of Arts and Libraries, the remainder coming through the proceeds of its shop, exhibition fees, and other trading schemes.

The British Council

The British Council was established in 1934 and granted a Royal Charter in 1940 with the following aims:

- To promote a wider knowledge overseas of Britain, its people and institutions.
- To develop closer cultural ties with other countries.
- To promote a wider knowledge of the English language.
- To administer educational aid programmes.

In pursuing these aims, the British Council employs staff in over eighty countries, and involves itself in a wide range of activities, including running or helping to maintain libraries of British books overseas, provision of English-language teaching, exchange study visits, and some promotion of British Arts. However, the Arts form only a small (though important) part of the Council's work, and the Council promotes the Arts not as a patron but in order to display British artistic achievements overseas. Its work in the Arts is therefore confined to initiating or supporting overseas tours by British companies or individual performers; the promotion of art exhibitions; the distribution of films about the Arts; and the organisation or support of cultural exchange schemes. British Council offices overseas have a certain amount of autonomy in deciding which art to 'export', and policies range from the touring of major companies to the promotion of the most experimental small-scale work.

Out of a total budget of £264.2 million in 1987/88, the British Council spent £3.28 million on the Arts. This was split fairly evenly between drama and dance, film and video, the fine arts, and music and opera.

The Regional Arts Associations (RAAs)

The RAAs were formed between 1956 and 1973 as independent and autonomous organisations for sustaining, promoting, and developing the Arts. There are twelve RAAs in England, three in Wales, but none in Scotland or Northern Ireland. Their general objectives are similar to those of the Arts Council, but their involvement in film and crafts gives them a wider brief, and in practice, the policy emphasis is often very different. The RAAs work closely with the Arts Council, the local authorities, the British Film Institute, the Crafts Council, and many arts and community organisations. The governing bodies of the RAAs reflect this partnership approach, and bring together representatives from the different interests involved. It should be stressed that the RAAs are not regional offices of the Arts Council, nor are they part of local government.

Although each RAA is different, they share a number of features. They all give financial support to both arts organisations and individual artists. Applications for financial support are assessed, usually with the help of an advisory panel, by the specialist officers that the RAAs employ. These officers are also able to give advice to artists, arts companies, educational institutions and local authorities. Few local authorities can afford to employ expert staff in different art forms, and it is therefore argued that employment of such staff on a regional basis is an economical way of doing it.

Many RAAs are increasingly seeing themselves as service and development agencies, planning and co-ordinating arts strategies with local authorities and other organisations. Some are building up their business expertise, particularly in finance and marketing, in an attempt to generate more income both for themselves and their clients. Most RAAs publish their own magazine or newsheet, and some engage in other 'direct promotions', such as the organisation of tours, conferences, and training schemes.

Over the past five years, the responsibilities of the RAAs have grown considerably. There are three main reasons for this. Firstly, the Arts Council has devolved responsibility to the RAAs for a number of clients and activities which can be better managed at regional level. Secondly, following publication of the Arts Council's *The Glory of the Garden* strategy, which attempted to redress the imbalance of funding between London and the regions, the RAAs have received development monies. Thirdly, some of the RAAs have taken on responsibilities previously carried out by the metropolitan counties, which were abolished in 1986.

At the time of writing a question mark hangs over the future of the RAAs. The Minister for the Arts has commissioned a review of the structure and function of the RAAs, and there is speculation that this may result in some 'streamlining', with fewer Associations covering larger regions.

European Regional Development Fund (ERDF)

The ERDF was established in 1975 with the objective of correcting regional imbalance in the European Community (EC). Public authorities in the regions entitled to receive assistance may submit applications for support for either investment in infrastructure or for economic development schemes. Leisure and recreation projects are not eligible unless specifically related to tourism development, and although this severely limits the range of arts schemes that might otherwise apply, the Fund can be seen as a source of arts support. In 1987, £1.7 million went to UK arts projects, mainly heritage schemes.

Private Sources

Advertising

It is important to recognise the role of advertising in radio and television entertainment. Independent TV and radio are almost entirely financed by advertising, and as we have seen, the development of further terrestrial broadcasting services, satellite, cable, and multi-point video is bringing about a rapid expansion of this sector. In 1987/88, the independent radio and TV companies earned a net income from advertising of over £1.5 billion. The enormous power of advertisers, who supply the money to broadcasters in return for the delivery of audiences, have caused some commentators to observe that much of the media could be more accurately described as components of the advertising industry.

The costs of advertising are of course reflected in the pricing of a company's products, and advertising can be seen as another form of consumer expenditure.

Sponsorship

Sponsorship is another form of advertising in which companies engage, and is quite distinct from private or corporate patronage. Patrons, or charitable donors, are not looking for a commercial return or recognition, and while corporate community programmes are concerned about creating a good image, they are not strictly operating as sponsors. Sponsorship is a payment by a business to an arts organisation for the purpose of promoting the business name, products or services. It is a commercial deal between two or more parties, not a gift. As such, the

Inland Revenue will allow a sponsorship payment as a deductible expense in computing profits for tax purposes.

The most well-established organisation specialising in this field is the Association for Business Sponsorship of the Arts (ABSA). Its aim is to encourage the growth of sponsorship of, and participation in, the Arts in the UK by business organisations. Its activities include generating interest in the Arts within the business community, putting its members in contact with appropriate projects to sponsor, lobbying the government for better tax initiatives for sponsors, and administering the government's Business Sponsorship Incentive Scheme. ABSA does not actually find sponsors for arts organisations, but it offers advice and publishes a useful handbook entitled the *ABSA/W.H.Smith Sponsorship Manual*. It also publishes leaflets on sponsorship issues, such as taxation, and runs an annual awards scheme, through which sponsors receive further public recognition for their work. In recent years, a number of agencies have also established themselves, organising a range of sponsorship deals. The 'private' nature of sponsorship arrangements makes it difficult to estimate precisely how much sponsors spend on the Arts in a year. In 1987/88, ABSA calculated the figure to be around £30 million.

Donations

Figures are not available for donations from private individuals or companies. However, a survey of grant-making trusts was recently conducted, and out of a total of £286 million awarded by these trusts in 1987, around £36 million was estimated to have been given to the Arts.

Policy, Planning and Future Prospects

Although Policy, Planning and Future Prospects have been treated separately in other chapters of this book, the policy issues that face those involved in the management of Entertainment and the Arts are so closely related to future prospects, that it makes no sense to separate them in this chapter. With broadcasting entering a new, deregulated era, and the Arts world proclaiming with unprecedented unity that it is on the verge of financial collapse, planning for Entertainment and the Arts becomes even more speculative than usual.

In his famous essay (in the Preface to the *Lyrical Ballads*) written in 1800, William Wordsworth complained that a combination of forces was acting 'to blunt the discriminating powers of the mind and to reduce it to a state of almost savage torpor'. He was writing about the numbing effect of monotonous work, which he identified with the changing nature of employment brought about by the Industrial Revolution. One of the consequences of this, he argued, was a craving for mindless entertainment, and he went on to complain that the great works of Shakespeare and Milton were being 'driven into neglect by frantic novels, sickly and stupid German Tragedies, and deluges of idle and extravagent stories in verse'.

In this essay, Wordsworth articulated a tension between art and entertainment which has been at the centre of an intellectual tradition that has remained highly influential right up to the present day. Art, or the Arts, came to be perceived as an area of imaginative and creative work, far removed from the market place, and of superior moral value. Entertainment on the other hand, was closely identified with commerce. Art stood above industry; entertainment was a product of it.

This tension between art and entertainment, and between art and industry, to some extent accounts for the difficulty in discussing Entertainment and the Arts as a homogeneous area of human activity. The tradition of opposition is so strong that it is difficult even to find a common language in which to discuss the different sectors. There may be very good reasons for this, relating to the different value systems which different sectors reflect, but to pretend that art has nothing to do with entertainment, or that commerce is unconnected with the production of art, is clearly absurd.

First of all, therefore, in discussing questions of cultural policy, it is important to establish broad terms of reference, that take account not only of those arts and entertainments that receive the State seal of approval through official public support, but also of those that are supplied on a commercial basis. This does not mean the suspension of critical judgements, or a refusal to say that one activity might be more valuable than another, but it does mean a recognition of the enormous range of activities implied, and that State approval is not necessarily the arbiter of either quality or value.

If we accept these terms of reference, our examination of cultural policy will take account of the diverse range of activities considered in the first section of this chapter. The dominant idea that emerges is that of the home as leisure centre, constantly bombarded with home entertainment products by the expanding cultural industries of broadcasting, video, recording and publishing. This is powerful competition for those that seek to attract people into public venues.

In looking at the industry as a whole, three dominant policy issues, all concerning the nature and extent of State intervention in cultural matters, stand out at the beginning of the 1990s. Firstly, apart from broadcasting, the cultural industries are largely left to the free market. Does this provide the best operating conditions for these industries, and how well does it serve the consumer? Secondly, with broadcasting services expanding, the government is proposing to impose a lighter regulatory framework. Does this herald, as Mr Rupert Murdoch argues, a new age for broadcasting with more choice and higher standards, or will the competition for advertising revenue result in a new uniformity? Thirdly, what are the implications of pegging public subsidy for the Arts at standstill levels?

Cultural Industries

The industries of broadcasting, publishing, film, video, and recording represent the dominant force, both economically and culturally, in UK arts and entertainment. Put simply, these industries supply the cultural products that people spend most money buying, and most time consuming. They control the production and distribution of the words, sounds, and images with which we make sense of our lives and the world we live in. They operate on an entirely different scale from what might be called the cultural institutions – those organisations which promote the Arts with the support of public funds.

Given the power of the cultural industries, it is important to examine the principles on which they operate. There will always be exceptions to any general set of observations, but with this qualification, a number of common characteristics can be identified. The most important is that a cultural industry, like any other industry, is in business to sell products, and the level of demand for its products is therefore critical. The requirements of the consumer are paramount. There is no public subsidy safety net, and if demand falls, the company will go out of business. If the company is going to engage in any non-commercial activity, it will have to be paid for out of its profits.

Cultural industries have developed a number of strategies to keep demand buoyant. These are necessary because of the essentially high-risk nature of the cultural product. Demand for the cultural product is highly volatile, with relatively small changes in income levels (through, for example, higher interest rates) leading to large changes in the demand for cultural products. In other words, if money gets short, it is the luxury purchases that are the first to go.

This volatility of demand is also reinforced by the fact that the same cultural product is rarely bought twice. The consumer sees only a very small percentage of films more than once in the cinema or on video, and he/she hardly ever buys the same record or book twice. Thus, there must be constant variety and diversification, and each new product is to a certain extent an unknown quantity. Just because the last record, film, or book was popular, there is no guarantee that the next one will achieve a similar popular success.

Once this volatility of demand is recognised, the marketing strategies of the cultural industries become more easily understood. The first and most obvious is the operation of the *star system*. Producers do not know in advance whether a new cultural product will be popular, but if they know that consumers have an emotional attachment to a performer, the use of that performer will help to stabilise demand. Hence film stars come to be referred to as bankable commodities.

Another strategy is the development of the *prototype*. If a formula is found to work, it will be applied again. This can lead to a series of products in the same medium, such as the continuing development of the James Bond films, or related projects in different media. These are represented as the film of the book, the book of the film, the record of the film music, and so on.

The exploitation of successful products across different media is facilitated if the originating company has interests in a number of media. This leads to the centralisation of cultural power in a small number of multinational corporations, such as Thorn EMI and CBS, whose interests range across film production, broadcasting, publishing, and record production. Some companies also maximise their advantages by expanding not only across different media, but also within different sectors of the industry. Thus, there are record producers with interests in manufacture, distribution, wholesaling and retailing.

Another response to the volatility of demand can be seen in the conservatism of much cultural production. It is safer to supply older tried and tested forms than to take the commercial risks involved in experimentation. Soap operas have an enduring popularity, with the added advantage of another built-in marketing strategy. Incorporated into the structure of the soap opera is the stimulus for constant re-consumption: each episode will usually conclude by arousing a curiosity that can only be satisfied by watching the next episode.

Exercise
Choose a film, record, TV programme, or book that has enjoyed outstanding commercial success. Can you identify any key production or marketing decisions that you think might have contributed to this success?

The operational imperatives of the cultural industries, which demand a constant drive to increase consumers and sell more products, raise important issues for all those interested in the provision of Entertainment and the Arts. On one hand, these industries provide a plentiful supply of inexpensive cultural products, which provide entertainment and stimulus to people across the whole range of age, sex, and class. Furthermore, those dissatisfied with the products of mass entertainment will find that the cultural industries are also meeting many of their more specialist cultural needs. Both the publishing and record industries cater for a wide range of minority tastes. The cultural industries also provide instantaneous communication of information, and have created what has been called the 'global village'. There has been a massive extension of the possibilities of employment for artists of all kinds.

On the other hand, it is argued that although minority tastes are catered for within the cultural industries, the dominant concern is the selling of cheaply-produced products to mass audiences and that this leads to what a former Secretary-General of the Arts Council described as 'giving the public what it can be most easily persuaded to accept'. This, he considered, was a more accurate description of the process than the more commonly expressed notion of 'giving the public what it wants'. Harsher critics see in the cultural industries a disturbing concentration of power in too few hands, a narrowing of choice for the consumer, a deepening of sexist and racist prejudices, and a fostering of the cult of violence. On an international level, it has been observed that advanced industrialised nations produce cultural products, and that developing countries receive them. This has been described as a form of cultural imperialism.

These issues are extremely complex, and consideration of the role of the State in either the regulation or support of the cultural industries has to be related to a view of both the consumer and of the so-called free market. Does the free market respond to what consumers want, or are tastes shaped by a cynical industry interested in maximising profits? Does the consumer have adequate cultural choice, or is this prohibited by the economic imperatives of the cultural industries? Is the consumer the best judge of quality?

Whatever answers are given to these questions, which will partly be informed by the reader's political views, consideration should be given to three possible areas of State intervention. The first concerns ownership. In the 1988 White Paper on Broadcasting, it was stated that the government was determined that ownership in the independent sector should be widely spread. It set out a number of suggestions, which included the prevention of non-European Community companies from holding independent TV franchises, and restrictions on cross-media ownership of press and broadcasting. Consideration should be given to similar measures across all the cultural industries, in order to keep the market open for newcomers and to prevent any tendency towards cultural uniformity.

Secondly, the research and development function of the 'independent' record companies and of the small publishers should be recognised. Appropriate methods of support should be considered for independent distributors, and to encourage locally owned and managed bookshops and record shops. The aim should be to increase local choice. Thirdly, the levels of State investment in the film industry, and the effects of the abolition of the screen quota system, should be reviewed. UK government investment in film production is significantly lower than in France, West Germany, or Spain, where the number of feature films produced per year is consequently much higher.

The Regulation of Broadcasting

The characteristics of cultural industries outlined above apply equally to broadcasting. But it is on account of the power to influence that broadcasting has been singled out for government attention, and has been subject to strict regulation ever since the BBC was formed in 1922.

The current system of regulation is based on a principle of public service broadcasting, which has informed the work of both the BBC and independent television and radio. Public service broadcasting is understood to imply an obligation to inform and educate as well as to entertain, and to reflect a proper balance and a wide range of subject matter.

The notion of public service is enshrined in the BBC's Royal Charter and its work is overseen by a Board of Governors. The Independent Broadcasting Authority (IBA), whose members are appointed by the Home Secretary, is responsible for providing independent television and independent local radio, and is also required to provide public service broadcasting. Its responsibilities have been spelt out in a succession of Acts of Parliament, the latest being the 1984 Broadcasting Act. Essentially, it has four main functions: it selects the independent programme companies to operate in each area, and awards the licence or franchise; it owns and operates the transmitters for ITV and local radio; it controls programme scheduling; and it controls advertising. In 1984, it was also given powers to award the franchise for a satellite service, which would be exempt from the public service obligation to provide a wide range of subject matter. Cable channels operate under a lighter regulatory framework, supervised by the Cable Authority. As we have seen, low- and medium-powered satellite services, such as Sky, are currently unregulated.

The 1988 White Paper signalled that there were soon to be sweeping changes in the organisation of UK broadcasting. The details of many of these changes are still to be determined, but the broad principles are clear. The proliferation of new programme services both in television and radio, which has been made possible by technological advance, has rendered the existing system of regulation obsolete. Statutory measures are necessary to ensure a balance of different programmes when there are only a small number of channels and stations to choose from, but when the services multiply, consumers can increasingly sort this out for themselves.

In the immediate future, the BBC will continue to be financed primarily through the licence fee, which will be linked to the Retail Price Index (RPI). However, the government has served notice on the BBC that after 1991 it will be looking to set the licence fee increase *below* that of the RPI. This is designed to provide the BBC with an incentive to raise income through subscription, which the government sees as an alternative to the licence fee. The BBC will continue to keep out of the advertising market, but there will be a relaxation of sponsorship restrictions. It can be seen, therefore, that the White Paper proposals seek broadly to retain the BBC's current role, and at the same time, to introduce new methods of financing it. The government has taken the same kind of approach to Channel 4. It believes that the current role should be maintained, but that there should be changes to the structural and financial arrangements. At the present time, Channel 4 is a subsidiary of the IBA, paid for by a subscription from the ITV companies, which raise the major part of their revenue from the sale of advertising on ITV and Channel 4 in their area of operation. Three structural options are under consideration. Firstly, services on the fourth channel could be provided by a private sector company, licensed and selling its own advertising like any other ITV company. Secondly, Channel 4 could remain a non-profit-making body, but be given freedom to raise funds through advertising, subscription, and sponsorship. To avoid Channel 4 being wholly dependent on these sources, and to provide a safeguard against any erosion of the remit which might arise as the competition for advertising intensifies, a minimum level of income could be guaranteed and paid for by a levy on the ITV companies. Thirdly, there could be a special link between Channels 4 and 5, with the former pursuing its special remit, and the latter being subject to the more commercial regime. The Government believes that the ITV companies should continue to finance the Welsh fourth channel, which would not be able to cover its programming and transmission costs through sale of advertising.

The proposals for independent television and radio are far wider reaching, and it is in these sectors that the government's express aim of putting the viewer and listener at the centre of broadcasting policy is most apparent. In view of the number of new TV and radio stations coming on stream, the government proposes to introduce lighter regulations, supervised by a new Independent Television Commission and a new Radio Authority.

The essential difference in the new lighter regulations will be the removal of the obligation on all independent broadcasting companies to provide the full range of programmes demanded by public service broadcasting. All programme services will have to meet certain consumer protection requirements, but beyond these the regulations will be much more flexible, and will allow different approaches.

The consumer protection requirement will be as follows:

- Nothing should be included in the programmes which offends against taste and decency or encourages crime or disorder or is offensive to public feeling.

- Where news is presented, it should be impartial and accurate.
- Programmes should omit all expressions of the views and opinions of the persons providing the service on religious matters or on matters which are of political or industrial controversy or relate to current public policy.
- Due impartiality should be preserved in dealing with such matters.
- The content of advertisements should be subject to the same requirements, where they are relevant.

Low- and medium-powered satellite services, local television services supplied by cable and MVDS (see page 5), and independent local radio stations will be subject to no further programme requirements. DBS services (see page 4) will have only to comply with the additional requirements of commissioning 25 per cent of their programming material from independent producers, and of presenting a 'proper' proportion of programme material of EC origin. These requirements will apply also to Channels 3, 4, and 5, which will be further obliged to provide a diverse programme service that includes news and current affairs. The requirement to provide educational programming will apply only to Channel 4. The new national radio services will not be required to provide a news service, but they will have to present a diverse programme service, and not limit themselves to a narrow format.

The new approach to regulating broadcasting will be reflected in the functions of the Independent Television Commission (ITC) and the new Radio Authority. Firstly, the ITC will not assume responsibility for the detailed approval of television scheduling, or for the prior clearance of particular programmes. This is currently undertaken by the IBA, but when the new arrangements come into force following the expiry of the current franchise licences at the end of 1992, it will be up to the broadcasting companies to decide what to show and when to show it, subject only to the regulations applicable to the type of service they are providing. The government believes that the greater strength of the viewer in broadcasting will promote programme quality as well as increased diversity of choice. Secondly, the ITC will be required to draw up new codes on advertising and sponsorship. The government envisages that these will result in a more flexible and liberal approach than is currently possible under the 1981 Broadcasting Act. The government itself intends to reserve the right to approve any maximum limits on advertising minutage, and to adjust this limit should it be necessary to 'allow relief to be brought to the advertising market'. Thirdly, both the ITC and the Radio Authority will operate a new system of awarding franchises to Channel 3 and Channel 5 programme companies, to the new local television services, and to the new national radio stations.

The most novel element in the proposed new franchise system is the introduction of competitive tendering. Under the current system, the IBA invites applications for ITV franchises every eight years or so, and awards the licences to those applicants who submit the best proposals. Successful companies which go on to make sufficient profits pay a levy to the IBA. The system of awarding the franchises has been widely criticised as arbitrary and opaque, and the government sees advantage in introducing a more objective, commercial set of criteria. It is proposed that the ITC should operate a two-stage procedure. In the first stage, applicants would have to pass a quality threshold, and convince the ITC that they could meet the appropriate programming requirements. They would also have to meet whatever ownership tests are imposed. All applicants passing this threshold would then go on to the second stage in which they would offer financial tenders for the licence. The ITC would be required to select the applicant for each licence who had submitted the highest tender.

The ITC would be responsible for monitoring the performance of the licence holders, and would undertake formal reviews of performance. If, after a review, it was deemed that the company was failing to meet its licence conditions, the ITC would have the power to issue a formal warning (a yellow card) and to remove a licence (a red card) one year later if performance remained unsatisfactory.

A licence would be issued for a fixed term of, say, ten years but it would be open to licensees during the final years to apply for licence renewal for a further fixed term, without having to go through the competitive tendering system again. However, the company would have to pay a licence renewal fee to the ITC. In addition, all programme companies would have to pay a levy in the form of a percentage of advertising revenue at progressive rates.

These proposed changes in the structure and organisation of broadcasting have met with a wide range of responses. For Mr Rupert Murdoch, they are a step in the right direction, but they do not go far enough. In his keynote address to the 1989 Edinburgh International Television Festival he argued that in fifty years' time today's television regime will appear extraordinary primitive, not dissimilar to the system of control which governed the printed word for many decades after the invention of the printing press. He compared the current moves towards deregulation to the English Parliament's abolition of pre-publication censorship of the printing presses in 1694. He confessed to never having heard a convincing definition of public service broadcasting, and argued that much of the so-called quality television was no more than 'the parading of the prejudices and interests of the like-minded people who currently control British television'. He considered them an elitist group, desperate to defend their own stronghold and unwilling to allow others in.

For others, it is precisely the subjection of broadcasting to a different value system that causes so much alarm. Critics point to the values reflected in Murdoch's most popular newspaper, *The Sun*, and ask if the television and radio equivalent is really what we want our airwaves used for. They point to the careful development over the years of a highly responsible system of broadcasting, which, they argue, is internationally regarded as the best in the world, but which is now threatened by indiscriminate commercial interests.

These are, of course, polarised positions, and in them we can see the old conflict between art and industry. The issues are further obscured by the speculative nature of the government's proposals. For example, when a company is required to present a 'diverse programme service', what does it actually mean? How will this be interpreted by the ITC?

The full impact of the restructuring of broadcasting will only become clear once the details have been worked out and the system is in operation. As always, the theory will be judged on the practice. However, even at this stage, a number of observations can be made, and attention drawn to future problem areas.

The first concerns the fundamental principle of putting consumers at the centre of broadcasting policy. It is a sentiment with which few would disagree in theory, but it has to be qualified by two factors. Firstly, consumers influence broadcasting policy by making choices on what to see and listen to. The degree to which this role means anything depends upon the range of real choices available. Secondly, consumers are only at the centre of broadcasting policy if account is taken of *all* consumers, of the minority as well as the majority.

Programme diversity and increased choice are therefore essential to the concept of consumer supremacy, as the government itself recognises. The question remains as to whether a greater emphasis on market forces will produce this diversity. As we have seen, the independent sector is largely paid for by advertising, and the greater the number of viewers, the greater the income from advertising sales. Thus the financial incentive is to present those programmes which will attract the largest audience. These are the 'economies of scale' in broadcasting, which are likely to become even more important as competition for advertising increases with the growth of new programme services. It remains to be seen whether there is suffcient advertising revenue available to sustain the whole range of services being proposed.

It has been suggested that in future further financial pressures will be put on independent television and national radio operators by the sheer scale of the bids that will be necessary to win franchises. It is argued that all these financial pressures will force the operators to cut programme costs as far as possible and to devise the cheapest possible ways of maximising advertising revenue.

It can be seen from these arguments that there is a tension between an increasingly competitive environment and a commitment to quality and programme diversity. This tension is increased by the government's decision to drop qualititive criteria from the final stage of the franchise award procedure, which compels the ITC to give the licence to the highest bidder, regardless of other considerations. The ITC's role in monitoring programme standards will therefore be critical, particularly as it will not have the powers, currently held by the Independent Broadcasting Authority, to block takeover bids.

Increased competition will have a knock-on effect on the BBC. As we have seen, the government has already acted to reduce the BBC's dependence on the licence fee, and looks forward to its eventual replacement by subscription. It is anticipated that some independent companies will also begin to raise income from subscription. If the BBC enters the commercial market in this way, the era of public service broadcasting, as it is currently understood, will finally be over.

Funding the Arts

Central government revenue expenditure, from its main arts funding departments, increased in real terms by 16.3 per cent between 1978/79 and 1983/84. Between 1983/84 and 1987/88, it increased by 4 per cent. These figures exclude the funding responsibilities taken over by central government following the abolition of the metropolitan counties in 1986, which reflect a transfer of funds, and not an increase in the amounts available. It can therefore be seen that growth in the main central government funding of the arts has slowed down in recent years. In calculating the level of this growth, allowance has been made for the general level of inflation, but if inflation in areas of the arts is higher than average, as some economists argue, then the real growth is even lower. The experience of most arts organisations funded by the Arts Council and the Regional Arts Associations in recent years is that by the time the grants have filtered their way down, levels have been well below the rate of inflation, often at cash standstill or below. The restrictions on local authority expenditure has also made an impact on the levels of arts funding. Table 1.6 illustrates the effect that all these changes have had on the relative proportions of income generated by arts organisations from different sources.

Arts-promoting organisations have developed a number of strategies to deal with this situation, and it can be seen from Table 1.6 that the major effort has gone into increasing box office income. This has had a number of implications.

Arts organisations perform a delicate balancing act, with market-led pressures on the one hand, and product-led pressures on the other. If they become too dominated by market considerations, there is a danger that they will stop taking risks, avoid experiment, and thus cease to fulfil the research and development function that is one of the essential justifications of a subsidised sector. Put simply, if arts-promoting

Table 1.6   Sources of income of selected arts organisations in England and Wales, 1983/84 and 1987/88, as percentages of total income

	Arts Council of Great Britain	Local authorities/ other public sources (inc RAAs)	Earned income	Sponsorship/ donations
National companies:[a]				
1983/84	54	3	39	4
1987/88	46	2	46	6
Other opera:[b]				
1983/84	65	7	22	6
1987/88	64	7	24	5
Dance:[c]				
1983/84	40	21	35	4
1987/88	41	15	39	5
Contract symphony orchestras:[d]				
1983/84	30	22	43	6
1987/88	32	16	47	5
London orchestras:[e]				
1983/84	11	6	71	12
1987/88	11	–	78	11
Repertory theatres:[f]				
1983/84	32	23	43	2
1987/88	30	21	48	1
Touring drama:[g]				
1983/84	57	11	31	1
1987/88.	59	5	35	1
Galleries:[h]				
1983/84	49	14	32	5
1987/88	39	23	25	13
English festivals:[i]				
1983/84	14	8	47	31
1987/88	10	9	49	32
All art forms:[j]				
1983/84	44	10	41	5
1987/88	39	8	47	5
Welsh festivals:[k]				
1983/84	23	22	39	16
1987/88	22	17	39	22

Source: *Cultural Trends 1989*, Issue 1 (1989).

[a] The four national companies are the Royal Opera House Covent Garden, English National Opera, National Theatre and the Royal Shakespeare Theatre.
[b] Five revenue-funded opera companies.
[c] Four revenue-funded medium-scale dance companies.

Table 1.6 (*cont*).

d English contract orchestras and chamber orchestras.
e The four London orchestras.
f Twenty-one regional building-based drama companies and eight building-based companies in London.
g Fourteen revenue-funded non-building-based drama companies.
h Four revenue-funded galleries.
i Three major music festivals.
j All organisations included in (a) – (i) above.
k Five major music festivals.

organisations can only present what they think is going to be immediately popular, they create a climate in which artistic development is stifled.

There is evidence to suggest that the balance has shifted too far towards market forces in recent years, and that the subsidised sector has become more susceptible to the dangers associated with a consumer-centred policy. This has resulted in pressures to programme the work which will draw the largest audiences, to avoid the difficult and the unfamiliar, and to pay less attention to minority interests.

Adminstrative as well as artistic policies have been affected. In 1984, the Arts Council of Great Britain, under the chairmanship of Lord Rees-Mogg, published the quaintly-titled strategy document, *The Glory of the Garden*. In his introduction to the document, Lord Rees-Mogg drew attention to the original aims of the Arts Council, outlined by its first chairman, Maynard Keynes. These were to 'make London a great artistic metropolis' and 'to decentralise and disperse the dramatic and musical and artistic life of this country'. 'Nothing', Keynes robustly declared, 'can be more damaging than the excessive prestige of metropolitan standards and fashions'. Lord Rees-Mogg went on to argue that the Arts Council had been successful in its aim of rebuilding the cultural life of London, but that there was still much to be done in the regions. The evidence for this had been clearly provided by Robert Hutchison's 1982 report, *A Hard Fact to Swallow*, which concluded that provision for the Arts in the South-East of England was far more comprehensive than anywhere else in the UK, with around half of the Arts Council's expenditure on the Arts in England subsidising activities in London. The declared aim of *The Glory of the Garden* strategy was to go some way towards rectifying these imbalances. 'The British garden of the arts' pronounced Lord Rees-Mogg, 'has great beauties throughout, and a magnificent display at the centre, but there are empty beds and neglected shrubberies. We would like to see the whole garden in bloom, and all the people walking through it to enjoy the flowers'.

It is, of course, extremely difficult to realise a policy of this kind without a substantial increase in resources. Without extra funds, the only option is to redistribute funds from the centre to the regions, or 'robbing Peter to pay Paul' as it has been described in the press. Regional arts managers may complain of the large proportion of Arts Council funds that are consumed by the national companies, but if pressed, few actually would want to see these organisations damaged in order to allow growth elsewhere. The Arts Council, certainly, does not wish to see London's cultural institutions deteriorate (nor would the government allow it), and so without more resources the imbalance between London and the regions remains. In 1987/8, the disparity between London and everywhere else was even greater than at the time of the publication of *The Glory of the Garden*.

The Arts Council has seen improved regional provision as a key element in its strategy for achieving one if its chartered objectives, that of improving accessibility to the Arts, and its funding of the Regional Arts Associations has been a major part of this strategy. The restrictions on public expenditure have not only put a brake on this process, but have also affected the other strategy for increasing accessibility, that of keeping ticket prices within the reach of everyone. The increase in earned income shown in Table 1.6 is partly explained by increased attendances and other trading activities, but it has also been generated by increasing the price of tickets. *Cultural Trends 1989*, Issue 1, shows that compared to both average earnings and retail prices, ticket yields have increased faster overall for the period 1979/80–1987/88, in all categories of admissions. Audiences have not yet been surveyed on a sufficiently consistent basis for it to be possible to know the effect that this has had on the social profile of arts audiences.

It has already been noted that UK levels of arts subsidy compare badly with those of other Western European countries, particularly West Germany, France, and the Netherlands. The prospect of a single European Market in 1992 has focused attention on Europe, and the possibilities of greater creative collaboration. These can only be satisfactorily pursued on equal terms, and if UK arts companies are poorly resourced, they will continue to experience difficulties in working with their European partners.

Thus it can be seen that the changing climate of public expenditure on the Arts has direct implications for the future production of experimental work, regional development, ticket prices, and the possibilities of European collaboration. It also makes it increasingly difficult for newcomers to enter the market, and to achieve the security of 'revenue funding' – the term used to denote a commitment from the Arts funding organisations to support a project on a long-term basis.

However, the changing climate has also done much to erode what has been described as a 'welfare state mentality in the arts' – a tendency to rely on public subsidy rather than to go out into the market place and earn money. It must be said that there are many arts organisations that have always operated in a businesslike and efficient manner, on extraordinarily tight margins. They have resented what they see as condescending suggestions from inexperienced Arts Council or Regional Arts officials that they have much to learn from commercial industry. On the other hand, there are others that have benefited from a more competitive climate. With the help of training programmes and consultancies, many have taken the opportunity to learn and apply new marketing and financial skills.

Greater energies have also gone into attracting business sponsorship, which, as we saw earlier, stands at around £30 million a year. These additional resources are welcomed by arts organisations, but it is the larger prestigious companies and events that represent the most attractive proposition to sponsors. Some arts administrators have complained that the time and energy required to raise business sponsorship is disproportionate to the results achieved.

The one area in which there is perhaps the greatest need for increased efficiency and better use of resources is in the system of arts funding itself. While the arts-promoting organisations have to earn money to survive, and pay themselves out of what they earn, the Arts Council and the Regional Arts Associations are insulated from market forces, and funded almost exclusively from public sources. The operating costs of these organisations, which include salaries attached to recognised pay scales, are fixed costs which must be met before any increase in grants to 'clients' can be considered. This is not to suggest that the staff of arts-funding organisations should not be employed under proper conditions, but rather to point out that there is a two-tier system of employment in the Arts. Only the major national and regional promoting organisations can afford to offer anything like the same kind of employment conditions as the funding bureaucracies, and even then, they have to earn a substantial proportion of their income to do so.

The answer may lie in a 'streamlining' of the funding system. Is it necessary to have twelve Regional Arts Associations as well as three Arts Councils and the local authorities? Does the system give value for money, or does it place unacceptable strains on the work it exists to support and sustain? It may be that the 'arm's length principle' has also had its day, and that when organisational changes are made, as they surely must be, the pretence that arts funding exists outside the political arena will finally be dropped. If this is the case, we can expect to hear with added force the arguments for a Ministry of Culture, headed by a Cabinet Minister, which recognises the range of work discussed in this chapter.

Further Study

Choose a cultural organisation in which you are interested (for example, an arts centre, a record company, or a publishing house). Find out as much as you can about it, and if possible arrange an interview with a senior member of staff. Try and obtain information on the following, and analyse it:

● The historical development of the organisation.
● Its artistic policy.
● Its marketing policy.
● Its financial policy.
● The relationship between these three strands of policy.
● The management and staffing structure of the organisation.
● Its present position in the industry sector (for example, how does it compare with its competitors?).

Questions
1. Can you identify factors that are common to all sectors of the Entertainment and Arts industry?
2. What is the justification for public subsidy of Entertainment and the Arts?
3. What do you think will be the effect on television programming of the government's proposals for the lighter regulation of broadcasting?

References

Arts Council of Great Britain, *Annual Report and Accounts* (Published annually).
Association for Business Sponsorship of the Arts, *Annual Report and Accounts* (Published annually).
Association for Business Sponsorship of the Arts (1989) *ABSA/W.H.Smith Sponsorship Manual*, ABSA.
M. Barton (ed.) *British Music Yearbook*, Rhinegold Publishing Ltd (Published annually).
A. & C. Black, *Writers' and Artists' Yearbook* (Published annually).
British Broadcasting Corporation, *Annual Report and Handbook* (Published annually).
British Broadcasting Corporation, *Daily Survey of Listening*, 1987/88 *BBC Annual Report and Handbook*.

The British Council, *Annual Report and Accounts* (Published annually).
The British Film Institute, *Film and Television Yearbook* (Published annually).
British Phonographic Industry, *BPI Year Book* (Published annually).
R. Conway and D. McGillivray (eds), *British Alternative Theatre Directory*, Conway McGillivray Publishing House Ltd (Published annually).
The Crafts Council, *Annual Report and Accounts* (Published annually).
The Devlin Report (1989) *Stepping Forward – some suggestions for the development of dance in England during the 1990s*, Arts Council of Great Britain.
A. Doulton (1989) *The Arts Funding Guide*, Directory of Social Change.
B. Dunn, *Showcall*, Carson & Comerford Ltd, Stage and Television Today, (Published annually).
A. Feist, and R. Hutchison (eds) (1989) *Cultural Trends 1989*, Issues 1 and 2, Policy Studies Institute (published quarterly).
L. Fitzherbert, and M. Eastwood (eds) (1989) *A Guide to the Major Trusts*, Directory of Social Change.
A. Holland (ed) *British Theatre Directory*, Richmond House Publishing Co. (Published annually).
R. Hutchison (1989) *A Hard Fact to Swallow*, Policy Studies Institute.
J. Myerscough (1986) *Facts about the Arts* 2, Policy Studies Institute.
Regional Arts Associations, *Annual Reports and Accounts* (Published annually).

Further Reading

M. Field (1986) *The Publishing Industry – growth prospects fade*, Comedia.
Home Office (1987) *Radio: Choices and Opportunities*, HMSO.
Home Office (1988) *Broadcasting in the '90s: Competition, choice and quality*, HMSO.
G. Mulgan and K. Worpole (1986) *Saturday Night or Sunday Morning – new forms of cultural policy*, Comedia.
J. Myerscough (1988) *The Economic Importance of the Arts in Britain*, Policy Studies Institute.
J. Qualen (1986) *The Music Industry – the end of vinyl*, Comedia.
R. Shaw (1986) *The Arts and the People*, Jonathan Cape.
G. Wade (1985) *Film, Video, & Television – Market forces, fragmentation, and technological advance*, Comedia.

The New Reading Room, British Museum
(*reproduced courtesy of the Illustrated London News Library*)

2 Libraries

Graham Nicholson

Reading continues to be one of the major leisure pursuits in the UK. Despite the competition from television, radio and recorded music, around half the population claim to read books with some degree of regularity. Many more read newspapers and magazines.

By no means all of this demand is met by libraries. Publishing and retail bookselling are big business. In Britain alone some 50,000 titles are published each year. Books, newspapers and magazines can be bought through all manner of outlets including supermarkets, railway stations and airports. Mail order and book clubs, as well as traditional book-shops and newsagents all seem to flourish.

The alternative to buying is borrowing. People pass on books and magazines to each other in an informal way. But if one wants a wide selection from which to choose, or has a particular title in mind, there is no alternative to a visit to a public library. In the past, there were private subscription libraries, such as W.H.Smith's and Boots', but they could not withstand the competition of free public libraries. From the middle of the nineteenth century, a network of libraries was gradually set up, until in 1964 the Libraries and Museums Act imposed a duty on local authorities to provide a 'comprehensive and efficient' free library service.

The public library service is thus in the unusual position among leisure services of having a virtual monopoly of provision and a statutory duty to deliver a high-quality service.

Much of what libraries do cannot be categorised as leisure provision. For instance, they provide all manner of business, technical and community information. They have an important back-up role in education, carrying materials to support the curricula of schools and colleges, and help people from all sections of society to educate themselves. Many librarians, through their training and cultural out-look, see information and education as the library's most valuable contribution, and feel less comfortable with a leisure orientation.

Libraries none the less do play an important role in leisure provision. Each year some 450 million books are borrowed from British libraries: 270 million of those are fiction, while another 80 million are children's titles. Many of the non-fiction books are borrowed for a leisure interest, be it gardening, DIY or history. Library services now offer materials such as records, cassettes and the increasingly popular compact discs and videos.

Though they have few direct competitors, libraries face intense competition for leisure time. Home entertainment offers far more choice today than in the past. The population is mobile, and can choose alternative leisure pursuits. Book issues are declining – down 10 per cent or more in the past decade – but this is partly made up by greater use for information and study, and by the lending of non-book materials.

Libraries face the future with many advantages. The public is solidly in support of the free library principle. A national network of branches puts libraries within everyone's reach. There is a large membership and everyone accepts the educational and social value of the service. Yet changes in leisure patterns provide the library service with new challenges. Can libraries still appeal to a broad public and avoid becoming the preserve of the middle class and the retired? How far should libraries diversify away from their traditional concentration on books? How can they survive and prosper despite the continuing squeeze on public sector spending?

Provision and Facilities

A good library is one that meets the needs of its users. As people and communities differ, so libraries must differ also. Some libraries specialise in one kind of material, others carry a broader range, some a large selection of popular reading. Together they should add up to something approaching a comprehensive service within that area.

Hierarchy of Provision

The major reference libraries are a race apart from the rest. Much bigger than the average neighbourhood library, they can cope with virtually any enquiry or line of research. Their users are principally students, professionals and business people. Information rather than recreation is their major role, though they may well be good places to find out about leisure opportunities.

Most towns have a central library with a large lending stock. Its very wide range of fiction will range from established classics, through modern 'literary' novels of the kind that win Booker Prizes, to romantic stories, and books written specially for children and teenagers. Of the non-fiction, some will be quite technical, such as electronics or management for students and professionals, but much will be of more general interest, such as illustrated books on arts and crafts, and history and travel.

More locally, in the suburbs or outlying villages, one will find a branch library. Good librarians will know their readers, so its contents will reflect the tastes of the local population. The reading matter will probably be more general and popular than in the central library. A good branch library should cope with a school pupil's requirements for background reading up to GCSE or possibly A level.

Small centres of population are typically served by part-time libraries. Inevitably, the stock they carry is mostly light, recreational reading. It is simply not economic to have a wide selection of books available at each small service point. An alternative is a mobile library. The purchase and upkeep of a specialist vehicle is not cheap, but it can make sense, especially in rural areas. A vehicle will spend about half a day at each stop, ideally plugged into power for heating and lighting at a prepared parking site. In this way a mobile library can serve twenty or more communities in a regular cycle of visits. It makes intensive use of its book stock, whilst saving on premises and staffing costs (see Table 2.1 over).

In this hierarchy of provision the fullest service is available only from the largest libraries. Yet readers at very small libraries have access to huge resources through the system of book reservations. For a nominal reservation fee, it is possible to request any book. A library service will transfer the book from another service point, or buy a copy of the work if it thinks it will be of interest to other readers. Failing that, it will borrow a copy from another library service. If all else fails, the British Library Lending Division, based at Boston Spa in Yorkshire, will supply the local library with virtually any printed material from its comprehensive collection. This system, quite simple but effective, is a good example of the co-operation that exists between all the public libraries in the United Kingdom.

Audio-visual Loans

Most libraries now lend other media. Records have been the most common, but libraries are passing on to other formats which are less prone to damage. Pre-recorded cassettes now outsell records, and they are popular too with librarians who find them easy to store and display. The near future probably lies with compact discs which are ideal for lending because they are virtually undamageable. Most libraries make a charge for the loan of recorded music, usually enough to cover the direct costs of the service.

Videos can also be borrowed. There is direct competition here with the private sector. Some libraries meet the competition of High Street videos head-on and lend popular feature films and children's titles. This can be

Table 2.1 Library service points – by hours open to the public

Year and number of libraries	Over 60 hours p.w.	30–59 hours p.w.	10–29 hours p.w.	Less than 10 hours p.w.	Mobiles	Homes, Hospitals, etc.	Total
ENGLAND AND WALES							
1977/78 (120)	117	2212	1072	756	586	9193	13936
1978/79 (118)	92	2212	1068	670	588	9562	14192
1979/80 (120)	85	2203	1124	608	574	10161	14755
1980/81 (118)	69	2126	1157	527	569	10188	14636
1981/82 (119)	51	2135	1189	488	558	10713	15134
1982/83 (119)	48	2121	1221	476	553	11208	15627
1983/84 (119)	43	2127	1222	433	556	12226	16607
1984/85 (115) (+1)	33	2093	1230	448	545	12036	16385
1985/86 (117)	36	2090	1236	407	544	13901	18214
1986/87 (110) (+9)	38	2130	1271	439	545	15266	19689
5-year difference 1982/83 to 1986/87	−20.8	+0.4	+4.1	−7.8	−1.5	+36.2	+26.0

Source: M. Donoghue and P. H. Mann (1988) *Public Library Statistics 1977–87: A Trend Analysis.* Data is for England and Wales, taken from CIPFA Actuals with additional data collected by the author.

quite a profitable service. Others have decided not to duplicate what is on offer elsewhere, and concentrate on educational videos, especially the sort that teach you how to cook, play tennis, or use a computer. They may include classic movies from the past, and films of books that are on examination syllabuses. This is an example of niche marketing which has proved quite successful.

By comparison, the lending of works of art by libraries has never really taken off. It has usually been seen as a frill, and therefore starved of funds and development. Mostly libraries have offered framed reproductions of popular paintings. Original work hardly gets a look-in, and librarians generally seem happy to leave promotion of the fine arts to others.

Libraries have an important facilitating role in leisure provision. By supplying multiple copies of plays or music the library enables amateur groups to choose, rehearse and finally perform new works. Books on DIY, car maintenance, flower-arranging and other hobbies are essentially helping the reader to make their own leisure opportunities.

The library service collects information about the community and its activities. Thus it can point enquirers to musical societies, environmental groups and rambling clubs, and it will have literature about places to visit. It should have details of meeting rooms for hire and know about leisure venues and their programmes. Its collection of travel guides, and even its set of bus timetables, can help people to use their leisure time more effectively.

Libraries are willing to display posters and to circulate leaflets about local activities. It is normally enough to deliver a single consignment of publicity material to the library headquarters or central library. The service will then circulate it to all its service points.

Exercise
Go to your local library and find out which leisure activities are available to the community. How comprehensive is the information? How might libraries communicate this information more effectively?

Meeting Special Needs

There is much that libraries can do for people with physical or sensory handicaps. Perhaps the most effective provision is a good selection of large-print books for those with poor sight. For the blind and partially blind there are 'talking-books' (cassette recordings). Some titles are commercially available, but libraries can use volunteers with a good reading style to make their own recordings. New technology is coming to the aid of the blind in the shape of the Kurtzweill machine. This computer-driven device reads aloud printed books in a synthesised voice.

The deaf have no special difficulties with printed materials, but they can have difficulties in making their enquiries known. Many libraries have undertaken staff training to assist those with hearing difficulties. A few stock specially sub-titled videos and have Vistel terminals – telephones for the deaf which transmit typed messages.

Access to older library buildings is generally rather poor, and librarians accept that improvements have to be made. Ramped entrances, chair lifts or passenger lifts are much more common than in the past, but adaptations to existing buildings can be very expensive and there is still much to do.

Older people are major users of libraries. They include avid readers who get through six or eight novels in a few days. For some, the visit to a library is a social event to which they look forward. They are sure of a friendly welcome, in a warm building where there is no obligation to spend money. The staff come to know their regulars, and try to find time for a chat. In recent years librarians have made positive efforts to move away from the idea of libraries as echoing chambers of books in which all conversation is to be avoided. They have carpeted the rooms, installed comfortable chairs and tables, and organised coffee mornings to emphasise that the public is welcome to linger and socialise.

Unfortunately, a growing number of older people are no longer able to get to the library. For them, books delivered by a home-service vehicle are a lifeline. The regular contact made with the housebound is invaluable, and libraries need to work closely with Social Services departments, as each can help the other by identifying need or distress. Voluntary organisations such as the Red Cross and Women's Royal Voluntary Service (WRVS) are often willing to assist in the service.

Library services have tried to respond to the needs of ethnic minorities, and are committed to multicultural provision. Many of those from the Indian subcontinent in particular, are unable to read English. The first hurdle for libraries to overcome has been the lack of staff with knowledge of the languages and cultures concerned. The Home Office has given grants to library authorities to employ trained librarians with the necessary skills, though there is still a shortage of such people.

Libraries and Local Culture

In their early days, public libraries contained rooms for recreation and social activities. The Institute of Saltaire, Bradford, the gift of a Victorian philanthropist, contained not only a library, reading room and lecture hall, but a billiards room, smoking room, bagatelle room, gymnasium and rifle room. Present-day libraries have largely abandoned this approach. Meeting rooms have become book stores, the conversation and games rooms given over to additional shelving. Meanwhile local authorities have hived off their recreational provision into sports and leisure centres. It is surely unfortunate that libraries have been separated from recreational departments. It has led to the piecemeal development of facilities where there might have been some useful integration.

Despite this, libraries have retained a wider cultural role. Many have a gallery or exhibition space for the work of local artists. The same space may double as a small-scale concert venue or lecture room, which can be the home of local societies or a writers' workshop. A writer in residence is a good way of encouraging the creativity of local people.

More and more people are interested in local history. Some want to trace their ancestors, others to discover the history of their house. Older people are often fascinated by the days of their own youth. For all these, the library and the local archive are indispensable. Archives preserve unprinted materials – such as letters, diaries and company records. They preserve public records including registers of births, marriages and deaths, which are the raw material of family history research. Local history collections contain printed documents, newspapers and books as well as maps, old prints and drawings.

There are some lucrative opportunities for libraries to exploit their local history collections. Old photographs, framed or reproduced in picture history books, are in demand. Picture libraries and publishers will pay fees for the use of really interesting subjects. Libraries can also act successfully as small publishers, specialising in local interest books, to sell through their branches and local shops. Reminiscences of life in the not-so-distant past, with a nostalgic appeal for the older generation, sell particularly well.

Exercise
Many young people seldom (or never) visit a library. Why? Can you suggest what should be done to attract a greater number of youngsters into libraries? Do the design and layout of libraries need to be changed?

Administration and Finance

Public libraries are administered locally, but they share many procedures and work together extensively. They are all subject to the same statutory requirements and, in theory at least, are subject to the scrutiny of the Minister for Arts who has a duty to ensure that they are providing a satisfactory service. It is not surprising, therefore, that users may feel they are using a national service.

The library authorities in England are the first-tier local authorities: the shire counties, the metropolitan districts and the London boroughs. In Scotland, by contrast, the District Councils rather than the Regional Councils are the library providers. It is different again in Wales where the County Councils provide the service unless individual districts apply to the Secretary of State for library powers, as a number have done. Finally, in Northern Ireland the service is provided through five Education and Library Boards.These variations have management implications. Small is not necessarily beautiful where library services are concerned.

Until the local government reorganisation of the early 1970s, libraries often stood as separate departments led by a Chief Librarian. The trend since then is to combine libraries with museums and arts in a cultural services department, or to put them into a comprehensive leisure services department. Librarians are divided over the benefits of the new structures. Some see new management techniques threatening their professional approach and a 'fun and fitness' philosophy undermining their educational values. Others see benefits in the sharing of resources and expertise, and welcome the integration of service delivery.

Management and Staffing

Whatever the top management structure, public library services depend on the work of professional librarians. There are over 7000 practising professionals in the United Kingdom. They receive training either by taking a degree in librarianship, or by postgraduate study, followed by two years' employment during which time they complete a number of assignments. On successful completion they become chartered librarians, and are Associates of the Library Association, the professional body. They will have a good grounding in library skills and some management awareness, on which they will build by further experience. The quality of training is high, and though pay is modest, able people are attracted and retained within the profession. Women considerably outnumber men.

In traditional library management a librarian is assigned to each major service point, and becomes the all-purpose manager. He/she supervises the staff, takes responsibility for the building, is the public relations officer, as well as undertaking the professional tasks of maintaining the quality of the bookstock and meeting requests for information. He/she may be helped by one or more junior librarians (depending on the size of the library) as well as by 'non-professional' library assistants who undertake the more routine work.

This arrangement has some real strengths. The librarian gets to know his/her local community very well, and can mould the service to its needs. He/she can give close personal attention to the quality of every aspect of the library. But there are drawbacks too. One or more professional librarians to each main service point adds up to a large staff complement. Those librarians tend to be generalists covering a wide range of duties. The service can find itself short of in-depth subject knowledge. There is a danger that the librarian will be bogged down in routine administration and staff supervision, which, while important, is not necessarily the best use of a professional's time.

An alternative, now widely adopted, is team librarianship. A number of libraries are grouped together and managed by a team of librarians. Each of the team develops a speciality. One librarian, for example, may concentrate on children's books, and another on adult non-fiction. They employ this expertise in all the libraries in the group. When this works well it can result in a better choice of books and some economy in staffing costs.

Critics of team librarianship dislike the fact that it can lessen the identification of a librarian with a local community. One remedy is to give the team librarian pastoral responsiblity for a particular library. Thus while the flexible use of professional skills is retained, responsibility for community liaison and the overall standard of service remains with an identifiable person.

To be effective, team librarianship needs reliable back-up by senior library assistants – the non-commissioned officers of the library service. These are people who are not formally qualified as librarians, but have learnt the business of running a library on the job. The wise librarian delegates supervision of library routines, carried out by the 'non-professional' assistants, to his/her senior library assistant, who ought to carry a status and grading that reflects his/her value to the service.

The main library workforce is made up of library assistants who are overwhelmingly female. They are the front-line staff, and they are busy people. At the counter they issue and receive back books and other loans, record fines and charges. They return books to their proper places on the shelves. Anything that involves the carrying and rearranging of books is surprisingly physical work, and not the genteel occupation that is commonly imagined. Off the counter, assistants prepare books for issue, and undertake minor repairs and rebinding. They are the people the public see, whom they ask for information, for help with the catalogues and advice on books to read.

So it is imperative that library assistants know the library and its resources well, are articulate and friendly in their approach. It calls for good selection of intelligent, well-motivated people, and a thorough training programme.

Sources of Finance

It is difficult to provide a comprehensive service on a small budget. Bigger services, such as those in the English shire counties, can afford a really wide range of reading materials, and have enough members to make the acquisition worthwhile. They employ a force of professional librarians, who can implement effective systems on a broad scale. To give an example, the process of choosing, purchasing and cataloguing books is a major overhead cost. It requires professional knowledge and judgement, ordering and computer systems, and clerical back-up. This is the case whether the library authority has £200,000 or £2 million to spend on books each year. The process will therefore cost less, proportionately, in the larger library service. The lowest costs per head of population for library services are achieved in the English shire counties, most of which have a population of around a million.

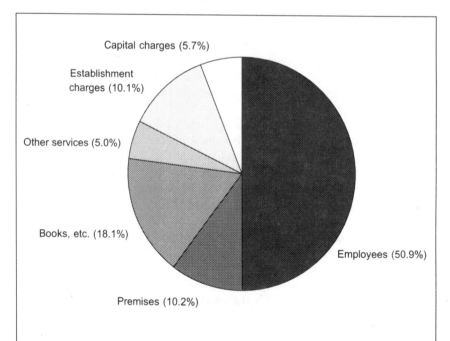

Figure 2.1   Components of total expenditure as a percentage of total

Source: CIPFA (1988) *Public Library Statistics 1987–1988 Actuals*, Institute of Public Finance and Accountancy.

The cost of public libraries in the United Kingdom (after deduction of income from fees and charges) is around £500 million a year, or nearly £10 per head of population. Half of that relates to staff costs, while another 16 per cent is spent on premises and debt charges. Only 18 per cent goes on books and other library materials, a figure that has hardly changed over a number of years. Price inflation on books has considerably outrun the general level of inflation, and the implication is that libraries are spending less money than before on books. Unfortunately, the book fund is an easy target when economies have to be made, as it is easier to cut than staffing or opening hours. In the long run, fewer books bought must mean a poorer service and librarians do well to defend their book funds as essential to an efficient and cost-effective library (see Figure 2.1).

All this has to be paid for. The law prohibits libraries charging for their main activities; they must lend books and provide them for reference free. They can charge for late return of books and for lending non-book materials, and they make some income from publishing and sales, from photocopying and use of computer databases. Libraries typically raise around only 6 per cent of their overall costs in these ways. Many are seeking ways to improve their income, but for the foreseeable future most library expenditure will come from public funds (see Table 2.2 on page 66).

Policy and Planning

This is not an ideal world, and resources are always limited. So libraries have to make choices about the services they deliver. In making those choices, librarians need to recognise that patterns of use are changing. For example, the lending of fiction for adults is declining, but the demand for video recordings is growing. Librarians must also understand that the environment in which they work is changing too. Information has become the most significant commodity of all, while the potential of new technology for libraries is huge. More elderly people and fewer school children will make up the population in the next decade. Meanwhile the government is nudging libraries towards more co-operation with the private sector, towards generating more income and towards contracting out services. So libraries need to review past policies, and have their long-term plans for the future in place.

Exercise
How could libraries generate more income? What are the advantages and disadvantages of libraries becoming more commercial?

Table 2.2 Public libraries' earned income

	England & Wales				Scotland			
Year	Libs	£	Percentage incr. p.a.	Percentage of expend.	Libs	£	Percentage incr. p.a.	Percentage of expend
1977/78	120	7 146 817	20.2	3.9	36	457 617	*	2.6
1978/79	118	8 479 401	18.6	4.1	38	438 961	−4.1	2.1
1979/80	120	10 082 202	18.9	4.2	38	632 893	44.2	2.4
1980/81	118	12 476 922	23.8	4.5	37	650 063	2.7	2.7
1981/82	119	14 302 897	14.6	4.7	39	985 229	51.5	2.7
1982/83	119	16 129 267	12.8	4.8	40	1 166 633	18.4	2.8
1983/84	119	18 310 393	13.5	5.1	40	1 130 109	−3.1	2.5
1984/85	115 (+3)	19 428 833	6.1	5.2	38	1 319 602	16.8	2.9
1985/86	120	22 487 091	15.7	5.6	41	2 769 397	*	5.5
1986/87	110 (+9)	25 885 354	15.1	6.1	40 (+1)	2 997 768	8.2	5.7

* Figure not available.
Source: M. Donoghue and P. H. Mann (1988) *Public Library Statistics 1977–87: A Trend Analysis.* Data taken from CIPFA Actuals with additional data collected by the author.

Service Planning and Delivery

Nothing would seem simpler than to have the libraries in the right places. Yet this is very often not the case. For one thing, the public library service has a legacy of buildings, including many civic landmarks which are more impressive than practical. Populations change or move away, particularly in the inner city areas. New suburbs spring up and grow. Moreover, it is a political fact of life that local councillors have pet schemes for new libraries in their own patch and are reluctant to close under-used branch libraries. Therefore, it is vital the library service has a rational and long-term plan for its library sites. It should know which are the main libraries, possibly to be further developed. It should identify any that need to be relocated, or even closed, and whether there are significant areas without any library provision.

In planning a library, or extending services, the key to success is to know the local community. Librarians sometimes speak of 'community profiling', by which they mean assessing the area and the people to be served. The librarian will want to know the patterns of age, education, employment, and ethnic origins of the population as a guide to the mix of services that would be appropriate. An area with many professional people and students will have different needs from those of an area with high levels of unemployment and an ageing population.

Selection of Material

There was a time, not so many years ago, when library committees would regularly vet the list of books chosen for libraries. Fortunately that no longer happens, and library staff select materials following agreed guidelines. The main basis for choice is public demand. There is absolutely no merit in having unused books on the shelves, however worthy they may be. Librarians will respond to requests from readers, and use their own knowledge and judgement of what will be read. They may draw management information from new technology library systems about which classes of books are in heavy demand. However, they will bear in mind that the population is made up of many minority interests, and so will balance the very popular types of books with a variety of less popular material.

Pressure can be exerted on librarians to exercise a censorship role. Some members of the public become upset because the library contains literature with explicit writing or language. Judgement of what is in good taste is notoriously a personal thing, and librarians are wise to leave any banning to the courts. Political pressures are more difficult to resist. Councils have been known to ban material favouring the Campaign for

Nuclear Disarmament, while many prohibit materials published by the South African government. The Library Association, the professional body of librarians, has tackled this point in a recent pamphlet directed at local government members:

> It is not the role of the library to suppress information and opinions – whether of a religious, political, or any other nature. Side by side on the library shelves there should be publications presenting different views, thus allowing members of the public to exercise their own choice and to reach their own judgement after having read all the relevant facts and figures.

Information Technology

Libraries and information work are ideally suited to the application of new technology. Early computerisation, in the 1970s, was a matter of recording issues and returns of books, and of holding the library catalogue. These systems were mostly dependent on the local authority mainframe computer. The modern approach is to use 'stand-alone' systems which operate on their own mini-computer. Another term for these systems is 'integrated', which is to say that all the functions of the library are controlled by the system simultaneously. To give an example: when a book is borrowed, the transaction is recorded not only against the borrower's name, but against the catalogue entry for that book. Thus if another reader requests the item, perhaps in another service point, the counter assistant immediately knows that the book is on loan, when it is due for return, and whether there is an identical copy elsewhere in the system. The librarian can then instruct the computer to print automatically a reader's notification when a copy comes available. Integrated systems simplify the processes of ordering and cataloguing books, and provide much better management information about the performance of the service. A single example again: the computer can record precisely the volume of library borrowing by hour, day or week, for each service point. This is invaluable information for planning the best opening hours and deployment of staff.

Such sophistication does not come cheaply. There is a danger of buying an expensive system for its own sake. As with any major development, there are two essentials at the outset. One is a person responsible for the successful management of the project. That person will co-ordinate the input of the library's own staff, of advisers (such as the local authority's computing department), and of systems suppliers. Secondly, and crucially, objectives need to be clear at the outset. In general terms they will be to provide a better standard of service to the public. More specifically they will include targets such as the speed of service, improved availability of library materials, better information for library users, and staff savings. Precise requirements must be set out in a clear and comprehensive specification otherwise system suppliers will wriggle off the hook of their fine promises about what their system will do.

There will be a tendering process. Would-be suppliers will quote against the specification and detail how they will achieve the end results. This is not an area in which the cheapest tender will automatically be accepted. Librarians will want to evaluate the two or three best tenders in some detail. That will include seeing the systems operating in real life elsewhere. It will require the background of the companies, including their financial status, to be investigated. Their ability to provide back-up maintenance over an agreed period is vital. Legal advice must be taken over the forms of contract. There may well be some hard bargaining to be done over details of the system and costs. One must not forget the impact that the new systems will have on staff, and the unions should be fully informed and consulted on the proposals.

Once the decision has been made, and a system purchased, implementation begins. It may be fashionable to speak of 'turn-key' systems, but in reality implementation will be a lengthy process. The equipment (the hardware) and the programs (the software) must be tested in detail against the specified performance. They are only accepted – and paid for – when working completely satisfactorily. A great deal of data will need to be fed into the system, and this process must be managed effectively. Training of staff is of the utmost importance.They need to learn how to use the system, but equally they must be persuaded of the benefits of it, both for themselves and for their customers. If they believe in the system, staff will make light work of the inevitable teething problems.

Exercise
Next time you visit a library make an assessment of how Information Technology may have improved the quality of service offered.

Future Developments

Early in 1988 the Government put forward a Green Paper on the future of libraries. While it stood by the principle of a 'free basic library service' it suggested that library authorities should be able to charge for a wider range of services, and should be encouraged to develop new 'market-led' services and joint projects with the private sector. It seems that the government was unprepared for the deluge of criticism from the public and the profession and for their tenacious support for the free library principle.

The Government backed down and diluted its proposals. None the less, the Green Paper stimulated some fresh thinking while the introduction of the Community Charge and the worsening financial difficulties of local authorities in the 1990s are forcing libraries to look for ways to increase their earned income. Some are appointing commercial officers with a remit to exploit every revenue opportunity. For instance, space is an asset that can be exploited. Exhibition and meeting facilities are marketable, particularly as many libraries have central locations and prestigious buildings. Library shops are appearing, specialising in local publications, cards, stationery and memorabilia. Some can make money out of catering, and wall space can be sold for advertising.

In addition, libraries are looking for ways to exploit their information sources. New computer systems give them the possibility of running their own 'view data' systems. This can be a way of disseminating local information out of the traditional reference library to wherever there happens to be a screen. There is scope here for collaboration with commercial interests in selling space and advertising on the screens. As history researchers, especially beginners, can make very time-consuming demands on librarians, so a number of libraries are now offering fee-based genealogical and historical research services.

Libraries under Threat

The core business of libraries, the lending of books, is in a modest but definite decline. One danger is that libraries are being marginalised as people's leisure and shopping patterns change. Retailing has diversified from high streets to shopping arcades, to supermarkets and now to out-of-town hypermarkets with built-in leisure facilities. Meanwhile, libraries are still largely following the pre-war pattern of village high streets and corner-shops. One would like to see more attempts to plan libraries as part of new developments, catering to the car-borne family group.

Another danger is that libraries will lose the custom of the next generation of readers. Children who have been avid readers tend to give up the library as teenagers. They describe it as boring and as having nothing for them. Research has shown that these young people do read, but not the sort of materials that libraries contain. Here and there special teenage libraries are being opened. The environment is untraditional, there is an emphasis on records, videos, computer games, magazines and youth culture generally. The approach is having some success and looks likely to spread.

Looking ahead, prospects for the recruitment of library staff are beginning to appear difficult. Libraries have never paid well, but there have been enough school leavers and young trained librarians to fill the posts. Now there are fewer young people coming onto the job market. Libraries (like many other employers) will have to become very flexible, encouraging job-sharing and part-time working. They will need to re-recruit, and perhaps retrain, older staff with experience.

The history and tradition of the library service is a strength for the future. But this must not be an impediment to change and renewal. There is evident need for diversification of the service, and for a positive approach which responds to the changing demands of society. The continuing shortage of resources, particularly as a result of the Community Charge and the 'capping' of local authority spending, means that librarians must be willing to make choices and have well-thought out plans for the future.

Further Study

You might like to visit a public library, preferably a large one, and consider how user-friendly it is.

You would need to make a check list of all the factors to consider, and there would be quite a number and variety. For instance, how accessible is it by public transport, or by private car? Is there convenient parking? How far would a visit fit in with other activities such as shopping? Is it accessible in the sense that disabled people, or a person with children, can get into and around it?

How good is the signing – is it clear, simple, and accurate? Can you find the books you want easily, by using the catalogues or by asking the staff? Is there well-displayed community information, and details of forthcoming events?

Are there adequate arrangements for study, are the chairs comfortable, and the tables spacious? Is the lighting good for reading? Are there refreshments and toilet facilities?

What image does the library project, in its appearance, layout, publicity materials, etc.? How do the staff react to difficult questions? Do they appear eager to help? How good are they at giving information over the telephone?

It would probably be useful to do a similar analysis of a large bookshop to see whether there were significant differences in approach, and whether there are lessons that might be applicable to a library. However, in doing that you should first consider what the differences between a bookshop and a public library are.

If you were the librarian in charge, what would be your priorities for improvements in the service offered to users, and why?

Questions
1. Do library services compete with, or complement the retail book trade?
2. What factors should influence the choice of books and other materials for libraries?
3. 'A library is still fundamentally a place where there are a lot of books – but today it should be more than that.' What, beyond books, are the essentials of a good library service?

References

CIPFA (1988) *Public Library Statistics 1987–88 Actuals*, Chartered Institute of Public Finance & Accountancy.

M. Donoghue, and P. H. Mann (1988) *Public Library Statistics 1977–87: A Trend Analysis*, LISU, Loughborough University.

HMSO (1988) *Financing our Public Library Service: four subjects for debate*, London.

The Library Association (1988) *The Public Library Service*, The Library Association.

Further Reading

Anon (1986) *Ex Libris*, The Adam Smith Institute. A radical view of the pattern of public library provision.

T. and E. Kelly (1977) *Books for the People: An Illustrated History of the British Public Library*, André Deutsch.

W. J. Martin (1985) *Community Librarianship*, Library Association.

J. E. Rowley (1985) *Computers for Libraries*, 2nd edition, Clive Bingley.

B. Totterdell (ed.) (1978) *Public Library Purpose*, Clive Bingley.

B. Usherwood (1981) *The Visible Library: Public Relations for Public Librarians*, Library Association.

**Vision of the past: a visitor to the exhibition encounters
Tyrannosaurus Rex**
(*photograph by Michael Powell*, The Times)

3 Museums

Anne Partington-Omar

Museums are increasingly popular places. There are currently over 2500 in the United Kingdom, in all counties and in communities of all sizes. They have a long tradition of scholarship, education and public service. They encourage enquiry and vision, and contribute greatly to our intellectual and cultural life.

Millions of people visit museums each year, seeking knowledge, enjoyment and a greater understanding of other times, other people, other places. Museums boost the morale of the communities that they serve, giving a sense of place and pride. As cultural amenities they help attract business investment and encourage tourism. As educational resources they offer unique opportunities for contact with original material.

Museums also represent a wider set of values. There is an increasing commitment to preserving, caring for and learning about the artefacts and customs of our heritage. There is a new enthusiasm for collecting, for the acquisition of items that have a personal meaning or that represent disappearing traditions or skills.

Currently museums in the UK are in a paradoxical situation: a period of diminishing finance has seen a corresponding increase both in the number of museums and in government reports recommending additional funding. The last decade has seen the total number of museums grow at the rate of one every fourteen days.

There can be no doubt that there is national recognition of the important role played by museums, not only in preserving key aspects of the nation's heritage but as a public service, as a contribution to the quality of life and as an influence on the economy of the country. Through their collections museums offer rich encounters with reality, with the past, with what exists now and with what is possible. They stimulate curiosity, give pleasure, increase knowledge, acquainting us with the unknown and imparting a freshness to the familiar.

The recent emergence of interest in 'heritage' matters has focused both public and museum concern on the protection of the museum's unique role in caring for and interpreting the objects in their safekeeping.

Provision and Facilities

There are three broad categories of museums in the United Kingdom: national, local authority and non-public/private sector.

National

This term is used here to denote those museums which receive direct funding from central government. There are seven government departments mainly concerned with museums and related functions and they fund institutions as diverse as the international treasure trove known as the British Museum; the National Museum of Science and Industry with its themed outstations at York (National Railway Museum) and Bradford (National Museum of Photography, Film and Television); the 100-acre open-air site displaying relocated Welsh buildings at St Fagans, Cardiff; and a plethora of regimental museums and specialist institutions such as the Army Physical Training Corps Museum at Aldershot.

Local Authority

The Local Government Act, 1972 gave concurrent powers to metropolitan and shire counties, cities, metropolitan and shire districts, parish and town councils, to act as museum authorities.

With the demise of the metropolitan counties, the major services they ran have been taken over by appropriate authorities; for example, the Merseyside Museums became national and therefore funded by central government; Tyne and Wear formed a Joint Museums Committee. The shire counties range in provision from countrywide comprehensive services (as in Leicestershire, Hampshire and Norfolk, with museums strategically placed at large centres of population), down to Essex and Suffolk with no direct provision. The city museum services range from the giants such as Glasgow and Portsmouth, to more modest but significant provision in Nottingham and Hull, down to the Town Hall Plate Room in Oxford and no provision in Cambridge.

Metropolitan councils such as Kirklees and Bradford run major services spread throughout their geographical area, with Tameside, Stockport and Bolton running more localised provision. Shire districts and boroughs range from significantly major provision in Brighton through to well-established services in Reading and Blackburn, and eighteen of the London boroughs have at least one museum. But there is no provision in the remoter districts or those where adequate provision is made in one of the other sectors.

Non-Public/Private

Covered in this sector are private companies, national industries, educational institutions, charitable trusts, voluntary associations and private individuals.

The sector is as diverse as its source of funding, and contains those museums which cannot currently be regarded as bona fide museums under the current national registration scheme, as they are either the property of an individual or family, or are not separated from a profit-making company.

Small voluntary association museums, like the Woolpit Byegones Museum in Suffolk, rub shoulders with the independent charitable trust giants like Telford's Ironbridge Gorge Museum. The latter incorporates several museums including a 50-acre open-air industrial museum along with the famous iron bridge and its tollhouse, a Quaker burial ground, the Coalport China Museum and Jackfield Tile Museum, a tar tunnel, and Teddy Bear Shop and Museum. Other 'giants' include major educational institutions exhibiting fine arts at the Sainsbury Centre within the University of East Anglia in Norfolk, and Edinburgh University's Russell Collection of harpsichords and clavichords. There are also private company museums illustrating the history of brewing (Bass PLC, Burton-on-Trent) or shoe-making (C & J Clark Ltd, Street, Somerset). The fanatical interest of private owners in mechanical music (Cotton, Suffolk) or automobilia transport (Hebden Bridge) are dwarfed by the monuments to national industry such as British Telecom's Technology Showcase, in London.

Just over half of all the museums in the UK are the direct result of the need to find a home for an existing collection, perhaps due to the decease of the original collector or the loss of interest in a society's private collection. The majority of museums, particularly in the public sector, established before the Second World War, were based on collections from the traditional areas of fine or decorative art, archaeology, or natural sciences.

The rise of private sector (independent museums) since the early 1970s has seen a shift towards collections based on social history (particularly rural history), industrial archaeology (particularly site museums) and technology and transport (see Table 3.1). There was, not surprisingly, a significant increase in the collection of military and service material in the period following the two world wars, resulting in the growth of regimental and military museums.

Table 3.1   Attendances at independent museums in 1988, by type of collection

	Attendances (thousands)	Percentage of total attendances	Number giving information on attendances	Average attendance (thousands)*
Local history	1 857	15	96	19.3
Transport	2 866	23	44	65.1
Industrial	3 486	27	62	56.2
Art	528	4	11	48.0
Military	1 241	10	17	73.0
Specialist/other	2 700	21	35	77.1
Total	12 660	100	265	47.8

Source: *Cultural Trends 1989*, Issue 4 (1989).

*Based on the 265 museums responding to this question.

Exercise
Find out what national, local authority and non-public or private sector museums exist in your locality. Try to visit a variety of museums and note whether they charge for admission, what they display, the services offered, and any contrasting features of policy and management.

Every county in the UK has some form of museum provision but the distribution is remarkably uneven. There is a concentration in the South of England (over 47 per cent of the total number of museums) while the heavy industrial areas of the North-West of England, South Wales, and Strathclyde have very poor provision. Around three-quarters of the current museums have opened since World War II, nearly half of them since 1971. There has been a major increase in the non-public sector with the majority founded by voluntary associations or private individuals, mostly in the South of England.

What is a Museum?

The majority of museums are now in the non-public sector, with the largest single category being the voluntary associations. Within the public sector, the largest single class of governing body is that of the local authority, predominantly district councils.

Given this wide disparity of provision, provider and product, it is perhaps not surprising that there is difficulty in reaching a common definition of a museum. Prior to 1984, the Museums Association (the professional body for museum employees) adopted the world definition which currently reads:

A museum is a non-profit making, permanent institution in the service of society and its development, and open to the public, which acquires, conserves, researches, communicates and exhibits, for the purposes of study, education, and enjoyment, material evidence of people and their environment.

In 1984 this changed to:

A museum is an institution which collects, documents, exhibits, and interprets material evidence and associated information for the public benefit.

This has been seen to reject the charitable and altruistic motive of the museum and the unambiguous dedication of the museum movement 'to the service of society and its development'. There is a significant move to look again at what a museum is, should be, and should stand for. This will be especially relevant in the light of the Audit Commission's 'value for money' assessment and comparative costs of museums in metropolitan districts and shire districts in England and Wales in the early 1990s. It will be important to ensure that the basic definition of each museum's fundamental responsiblities and objectives is fully taken into account. The result of this assessment will be difficult enough to compare, due to the disparity of the operational programmes of museums and galleries, both within their base (for example, the existence or otherwise of lively exhibition and education services), and outside (for example, the provision of outreach services beneficial to the community, such as ecological databases, archaeological or oral history survey programmes, or work with ethnic minority and other community groups). But further difficulties will arise over disparity in buildings, with a museum in which the building itself is a major historical monument (and exhibit) requiring massive and continuing high-cost maintenance, spending far more on premises than one in low-cost accommodation.

The 1984 definition of museums did allow for the distinction to be drawn between them and the newly-sprung 'heritage centres'. The key difference is in the use of the words *material evidence*, *material* because it is something tangible, and *evidence* guaranteeing the authenticity, the 'real thing'. It is in the interpretation of this material evidence that museums both have the most to learn from, and to contribute to, the heritage movement.

It is only too easy to point to the apparent success stories, the huge heritage trail-blazers, who so competently involve their audiences and part them from their money. Regretfully, it is very difficult to find one which is truly a museum and carries out all the responsibilities associated with such an institution without compromise.

The emphasis on heritage has boomed. Robert Hewison, in his book *The Heritage Industry*, argues that it is to history's detriment. He states that we are manufacturing heritage, a commodity that no one seems able to define but which everyone is eager to sell, in particular those cultural institutions that can no longer rely on government funds as they did in the past, and these include museums.

The President of the Museums Association, in his presidential address in 1989, described the idea that museums are part of the leisure industry as 'a heavily promoted heresy' and attacked the current obsession with 'The Heritage', which he characterised as 'a highly romanticised series of modern mythologies, deodorised and sanitised and, above all, class-orientated. With the upper and middle classes living out their heritage in the decorative arts museums and the working class in the social history museums and never the twain shall meet'.

So what is it that museums do that distinguishes them from the other heritage providers? The primary duty of a museum is to preserve unimpaired for the future, the significant material that comprises the museum collection. Subject to this, there is a responsibility to use the collections for the creation and dissemination of new knowledge, through research, educational work, permanent displays, temporary exhibitions and other special activities.

The way that the museums carry out these duties should be in line with written policies and should not compromise either the quality or the proper care of the collection. The information in the displays should be honest, objective and impartial, avoiding the perpetuating of myths or stereotypes. These principles do not sit easily with the mass heritage attraction whose long-term future is doubtful, and whose marketing-led storylines not only perpetuate but enhance myths.

The Museums Association (MA) has provided a code of practice for museum authorities (boards of trustees, local authorities, museums committees, etc.) and a revised version of the 1977 Code was adopted in 1987, which is the basis of the museum registration scheme being implemented by the Museums and Galleries Commission (see below). The Code lays out the basic principles for museum governance, calling for each scheme to have a written constitution, or other document, setting out clearly its legal status and permanent non-profit nature. This is to be drawn up in accordance with appropriate national laws in relation to museums, the cultural heritage and non-profit institutions. Accompanying this should be a clear statement of the aims/objective/policies of the museum and of the role and composition of the governing body itself.

The proper care of their collections has resulted in the museum profession encompassing a wide range of specialisations, not only in subjects as diverse as butterflies, ballgowns, ballistics, beermats and bones, but in skills such as conservation, science, engineering, education, documentation, computing, marketing and security.

By its world definition, a museum is an institution in the service of society and of its development, and is generally open to the public. It should take every opportunity to develop its role as an educational resource to all sections of the population or specialised group that it serves, and where appropriate employ professional staff to do so. It has an important duty to attract new and wider audiences within all levels of the community, locality or group, and it should offer them the opportunity to be actively involved in the museum and to support its aims and objectives. Access to displays should be during reasonable hours and for regular periods. Likewise, access to staff and non-confidential information. Commercial support and sponsorship should always be in relation to the policy of the museum, and ethical considerations should ensure that the standards and objectives of the museum are not compromised (for example, by not allowing smoking during sponsors' private view parties). Similarly, museum shops or other commercial activities should be relevant to the collections and the basic educational purpose of the museum. All items offered for sale should represent good value for money and comply with all relevant national legislation.

Exercise
Produce a short report outlining the reasons for the rapid development of 'heritage centres' and note the concerns that have been voiced about them. Try to visit a heritage centre and report on your experience.

Registration

The registration of museums has two main objects: first, to establish minimum standards for a museum in terms of its constitution, collecting policy and curatorial care; and second, to enable a museum to demonstrate to the public, and to potential funding agencies and benefactors, that it is worthy of support.

Following the successful pilot scheme in the North of England in 1986, the Museums and Galleries Commission decided that registration should be undertaken throughout the UK over a four-year period and in 1988/89 made a start in the North-West and North of England and in London, through the agency of the Area Museum Councils (AMC) concerned. Some 500 copies of the Registration Guidelines were sent to museums in these areas, inviting them to apply. A high proportion had responded by the end of the year. Applications, returned through the AMC, were considered by a Registration Committee chaired by a Commissioner, Dr Frank Atkinson, with a changing membership of museum professionals drawn from a panel.

Many small independent museums were able to demonstrate that they were able to meet the minimum standards required. A number of museums found registration an opportunity to clarify their constitutional arrangements, and almost all devised new or improved collecting policies. Documentation backlogs proved common, and full registration was often made provisional on the preparation of a documentation plan. The Commission planned a major public awareness scheme to reinforce the importance of 'registered' museums, with the following phased timetable:

1989/90   West Midlands, East Midlands, South-West, South-East (East).
1990/91   Scotland (part), Yorkshire and Humberside, South-East (West).
1991/92   Scotland (part), Wales, Northern Ireland, South-East (South).

Premises and Facilities

Half of the total number of museums in the UK are housed in buildings erected before 1850, and of these, half were built before 1750. Well over half of all museums occupy, at least in part, a listed building. This varies considerably between differing museum sectors, with the highest level being local authorities at around 70 per cent. This, no doubt, is the result of the need for a local authority to find an apparently sympathetic and appropriate use for its own listed properties. It follows from this that museums, in addition to the historical material they hold, manage and maintain historically significant buildings with a variety of styles and origins. It also follows that these institutions will be spending a larger proportion of their budget on the maintenance of buildings, as well as facing inefficient use of space due to planning restrictions.

The total amounts of floor space available within each building is also very variable, 75 per cent having 1000 square metres or less, with only 1 per cent having 20,000 square metres or more. The majority of floor space in a museum is given over to exhibition, whether temporary or permanent, with storage occupying much of the remainder. In the private sector, the ratio of display to storage can be as high as 81 per cent: 5 per cent, with local authorities as low as 49 per cent: 16 per cent.

Administration and Finance

Administration

The majority of private-sector museums are individual institutions without branch museums or outstations. The opposite is true of local authority museums where nearly three-quarters are museum services consisting of a parent institution and branches. On average, each local authority parent museum has two branches, but the range is from one to over ten. Just under half of the national and government museums are stand-alone institutions, therefore local government and national museums operate a more complex internal administration through specialised departments than does the private sector.

In local authority's policy-decision-making committees, just over half are within committees covering the combined fields of recreation, leisure and amenities, only 3 per cent are solely museum committees, 6 per cent combine libraries and museums, and 21 per cent are arts or education-based committees.

Apart from any indications that this has on the status of the museum within the application of overall council policy, the committee assigned to oversee the museum service has a direct significance on the tier of local government officer that it employs to direct and manage its museum. A council placing museums and galleries under a non-museum based committee (particularly a recreation, leisure and amenities committee) appoints its senior museum professionals at a lower tier than those with specialist committees. Local authority museums also receive the greatest amount of formal contact between staff and elected or nominated representatives, both in terms of the number of meetings and the size of committee.

Staffing

Nationally, around 500 museums employ no full-time members of staff and nearly three-quarters of these are in the private sector, predominantly those founded and operated by voluntary associations. Overall, the private sector employs far fewer full-time paid staff than the public sector, employing half of all part-time staff and relying on government training schemes and volunteers. The national museums are operated predominantly by full-time paid staff and do not use government training schemes or volunteers to any great extent. Local authority museums fall midway between.

The defined activities of a museum: conservation, curatorship, education, exhibition, research, library work, and documentation employ one third of the full-time staff in the public sector and a quarter of those in the private. The remaining staff are employed in management, support and ancillary services, including security.

There is a remarkable consistency of employment practices between the three major sectors of museums, with around 80 per cent of director level and 86–88 per cent of all full-time paid staff being male. Half of the latter are aged forty-four or over.

Finance

It is appropriate for the purposes of financial comparisons to divide museums into four sectors, separating government department museums from those national museums with boards of trustees, and retaining local authority and private/non-public sectors as before.

The total amount of money spent on museums in 1987/88 was in excess of £140 million and around half of this money (at constant 1984/85 prices) is from the local authority sector (see Table 3.2). This rises to 80 per cent when centrally-funded museums (government department and national) are included. The remaining 20 per cent representing the private sector is often derived from public sources, especially institutions with a turnover in excess of £10,000 per annum.

The amount of money available to each institution is obviously variable but there are general operating bands. Figures for 1985/86 show national museums operate with budgets in excess of £0.5 million, indeed 50 per cent exceed £5 million a year. Government department museums operate mostly on less than £10,000 a year. The majority of local authorities operate between £50,000–£500,000, with a top 8 per cent spending £0.5–£5 million. Around 70 per cent of private-sector museums operate on less than £20,000, with over half of these spending less than £5000. Unstaffed, purely voluntary museums (15 per cent of the private sector) spend less than £500.

Table 3.2 Expenditure on museums and galleries in the UK, from public sources by country*, in £ millions and pence per head

	1984/85	1985/86	1986/87	1987/88	1988/89	Pence per head 1988/89
England						
Central government						
Office of Arts and Libraries	86.3	92.2	105.5	107.1	153.6	
Other departments	15.4	17.9	18.5	25.0	7.7	
Total England	101.7	110.1	124.0	132.1	161.3	342
At constant 1984/85 prices[a]	107.7	104.4	113.9	115.3	131.2	
At constant 1984/85 prices, adjusted for replacement funding	101.7	104.4	102.4	104.4	120.2	
Local government	82.9	89.7	81.3	89.0	–	187[b]
At constant 1984/85 prices[a]	82.9	85.0	74.7	77.7	–	
Scotland						
Central government	9.4	9.5	11.3	14.8	–	290[b]
At constant 1984/85 prices[a]	9.4	9.0	10.4	12.9	–	
Local government	–	–	13.4	14.2	–	278[b]
Wales						
Central government	6.9	7.8	7.9	9.4	12.0	414
At constant 1984/85 prices[a]	6.9	7.4	7.3	8.2	9.8	
Local government	2.5	2.9	3.0	4.2	–	145[b]
At constant 1984/85 prices[a]	2.5	2.7	2.8	3.7	–	
Northern Ireland						
Central government	4.0	4.3	4.8	5.1	5.6	350
At constant 1984/85 prices[a]	3.9	4.1	4.4	4.5	4.6	
Local government[c]	–	0.5	0.5	0.6	–	38[b]
Total UK						
Central government	122.0	131.7	148.0	161.4	–	283[b]
At constant 1984/85 prices[a]	122.0	124.8	135.9	140.8	–	
Net of replacement funding	122.0	124.8	123.9	129.9	–	
Local government	–	–	98.2	108.0	–	189[b]

Source: *Cultural Trends 1989*, Issue 4 (1989).

*Revenue and capital expenditure.
[a]Deflated by GDP deflator.
[b]Figures relate to 1987/88
[c]Excludes capital expenditure.

Exercise

Study Table 3.2 and produce a graph or bar chart for a selected range of data. Ensure you use correct axis-labels, legend-labels, and data-labels. Also, produce an accurate title for the graph or chart. If you have the skill, use appropriate computer software to produce the graphics. In a short statement, explain what the information means.

Economic Significance

Museums and art galleries formed part of a major study published by the Policy Studies Institute in 1988, entitled *The Economic Importance of the Arts in Britain*. People going to the theatre or visiting museums spend more on food, shopping, travel and accommodation (sometimes called the 'multiplier effect').

The study found that attendance numbered 122 million in 1984/85. Of these, 73 million were to museums and galleries. In addition, 59 million visits were made to historic houses, while 70 million people attended the cinema. Spending on these visits totalled £4 billion and gave rise, both directly and indirectly, to 190,000 jobs. Of this spending, £2.7 billion would not have taken place without the events and attractions concerned. Museums and galleries have a significant rate of input with 13–19 jobs created for every £100,000 of turnover.

An example of this impact on job creation and income generation is given with reference to a 'blockbuster' exhibition, held in London, attracting 500,000 visitors. This would bring £30 million spending, over and above what otherwise might be spent in the economy: £10 million on shops and restaurants, and £8 million on hotels. It is difficult to assess the job creation in London, but an equivalent volume of spending in Glasgow would sustain 1650 jobs outside those in the gallery and further jobs would be generated by direct gallery spending.

Tourism is important to the arts, and the arts are important to tourism. Tourism with an arts ingredient (museum, gallery, theatre and concert attendance) was worth £3.1 billion, or 25 per cent of total tourist earnings, in 1984/85. Tourists and day visitors are particularly significant in London museums (66 per cent). Arts tourism constitutes a new market segment with distinct characteristics and demands. The potential for development is considerable as the demand is relatively new, upmarket, rapidly expanding and fed by high levels of satisfaction and willingness to repeat the experience.

Policy and Planning

There are many agencies, both governmental and non-governmental, who are directly concerned through either funding or statutory requirements, in policy and planning for museums and galleries.

Central government, in addition to direct grants to national museums through its government department, acts as a source of funding to a large percentage of museums through its advisory and executive agencies, the principal one of which is the Museums and Galleries Commission.

Museums and Galleries Commission (MGC)

The MGC was originally created as a government advisory body on national museums and as a promoter of co-operation between them and provincial museums, a role it strove to carry out with no power, few staff and minimal funding over a period of fifty years. The blossoming museum industry needed something stronger to act as a statutory guiding agent, and in 1981 the MGC was given its present name and additional mandate, to advise on development and take action as necessary. The four members of staff and budget of £72,000 in 1981, rose to 28 full-time staff and £6.59 million in 1988/89 as it took control of various scattered functions. Over 84 per cent of its 1988/89 expenditure went directly to museums in the form of payment of grants, £2.75 million through the English Area Museum Councils (see below). Of its £6.59 million income, £6.48 million was derived from the Office of Arts and Libraries.

The Commission administers annual schemes for grants to English museums, as well as certain funds made available following the abolition of the Greater London Council (GLC) and metropolitan county councils. It provides a substantial proportion of the funding to the Museums Documentation Association. In 1985 it assumed overall responsibility for the two Local Museum Purchase Funds now managed on its behalf by the Victoria and Albert Museum and the Science Museum. In England, Scotland and Wales the Commission operates, on behalf of the government, the systems for accepting and allocating works of art and other items in lieu of Inheritance Tax, and the Government Indemnity Scheme for loans to non-national museums and galleries. It also offers general advice on arrangements for private treaty sales.

Through the National Museum Security Adviser the Commission advises the government, as well as the directors of governing bodies of national museums and galleries and other interested parties, on all aspects of the security of museums and exhibitions. In 1987, the Conservation Unit was set up, which acts as a forum for information and advice relating to conservation matters, as well as operating grant schemes for conservators.

A Travelling Exhibitions Unit was established in 1988 to channel information, and to promote and encourage travelling exhibitions. The Commission is currently implementing, with the assistance of the Area Museum Councils, a Registration Scheme for museums in the United Kingdom. Only registered museums will be eligible for grant aid from the Office of Arts and Libraries scheme.

From time to time the Commission publishes reports on its own work, on policies for the development of museums, and on professional topics of current concern.

Area Museum Councils (AMCs)

There is a network of AMCs throughout the United Kingdom, seven for England, one for Scotland, one for Wales and a three-year pilot project started in Northern Ireland in 1989. Most of the AMCs are incorporated as limited liability companies. The basic aim of the Area Councils is to help non-national (local) museums to improve the standards of care for their collections and service to the public. They do this by supplying technical services (such as conservation and design) at subsidised rates, offering grants towards improvement schemes, and providing advice and training. They do not support museums with their day-to-day running costs; in general, their aid is restricted to individual projects, although they may pump-prime the creation of new posts on a three-year reducing basis.

Although AMCs have a common aim, they have developed at different speeds and in response to differing local circumstances and priorities. Superficially they are very different. The Area Museum Service for South Eastern England (AMSSEE) covers an area from Norfolk to Hampshire, receives a base grant of £656,000 and has a staff of thirty-two. These include specialists doing conservation work, staff running a travelling exhibitions service, and four regionally-based Museum Development Officers. By contrast, the East Midlands receives a base grant of £180,000 and has had a staff of two; it has to rely on other agencies to provide specialist services.

AMC staff find that much of their time is devoted to advising people who want to start new museums (particularly in the independent sector) or who are planning other new developments. Some useful publications are now available to supplement this advice, and the Museum Registration Scheme sets a basic standard for grant eligiblity. Nevertheless, the provision of advice, both strategic and technical, is probably the fastest growing area of AMC activity. The enlarged role of the Museums and Galleries Commission has also put pressure on the Area Councils, with requests for information and demands to extend their work into areas such as registration and training. Most AMCs now experience some conflict of interest between their traditional role of providing services and subsidy in response to members' requests, their own 'strategic' assessment of a region's needs, and the MGC's demands. These pressures are particularly acute because the basic grant levels have shown little or no growth in real terms.

The Museums Association (MA)

The Museums Association, founded in 1889, is a membership organisation, incorporated as a company limited by guarantee, and a registered charity. Its purpose is to enhance the professionalism and standing of the museum community. In furtherance of this, it has four main objectives:

- To enhance the quality of collection care and public service by providing career-long professional development and related qualifications.
- To enable the museum community to seize the opportunities to meet people's needs provided by the rapid social, economic and demographic changes in society.
- To represent the views, needs and values of the museum community, and its users, to national and local government.
- To facilitate the exchange of information about new initiatives, best current practice and likely future trends in the museum community.

These objectives are put into practice through the medium of five programmes in the fields of training, publications, professional support, public affairs, research and information, together with the trading function which is undertaken by the Association's subsidiary company, Museum Enterprise Ltd. The latter covenants its profits to the Association.

Since the 1930s, the Museums Association has provided professional in-service training. The Museums Diploma is the recognised qualification for curatorial staff working in local government museums and is also recognised for promotion purposes in national and independent museums. However, the Association has helped to establish a new organisation, the Museum Training Institute, to undertake major new initiatives in the training field.

The MA has published a code of practice for museum authorities and a code of conduct for curators. It has also issued a series of policy statements on controversial issues such as admission charges (see the section below entitled Admission Charges: Case Studies).

Other Associations and Federations

In 1977, as a reflection of the growing members of private museums, the Association of Independent Museums (AIM) was founded. It represents the interests of museums outside the local authority and national structures. AIM produces a quarterly publication, a regular programme of seminars, and publishes a series of handbooks providing guidelines for independent museums.

There are a number of specialist groups that exist to provide a forum and represent their members' interests in specialised or related aspects of the museum function, for example the Art Galleries Association, the Group for Education in Museums, the Geological Curators Group, the Guild of Taxidermists, and the United Kingdom Institute for Conservation. There are also ten Federations in existence throughout the United Kingdom, formed to provide opportunities for museum and gallery staff in the regions to discuss matters of mutual interest. They are independent, and have differing constitutions. Most of the Federations are affiliated to the Museums Association with whom they have a consultative status.

Admission Charges: Case Studies

One of the most contentious areas of museum and gallery politics is the issue of charging for admission. It has exercised the minds of curators and trustees alike, especially with the 1980s increase in emphasis on value for money, earned income, and the resultant need for a more commercial approach by the public-sector museums. Admission charges have long been the mainstay of the private sector.

The introduction of admission charges in the national museums, as a means of securing extra income, was launched in a flurry of national publicity and even outrage. The National Maritime Museum introduced a charge in 1984, followed by the introduction of voluntary charges at the Victoria and Albert Museum in 1985, and the National Railway Museum and Natural History Museum followed suit in 1987.

The annual general meeting of the Museums Association in 1985 decided to undertake an attitude survey of its members towards the charge of admission to museums. The results were published in May 1986 and included the following findings.

Public-sector Museums

Of the respondents, 74.7 per cent believed that there should normally be free access to the core collections; 3.6 per cent thought there should be a fixed charge; 21.2 per cent felt that each museum case should be considered individually.

Non-public-sector Museums

Of the respondents, 8.9 per cent believed that there should normally be free access to the core collections; 10.8 per cent for a fixed charge; and 80.3 per cent that each case should be considered individually.

It was felt by 74.7 per cent of respondents that any charging museum should be free for at least one day a week. The majority thought that voluntary donations are an unacceptable way of raising money from the public. In August 1986 a conference was held in Edinburgh to launch the Free Access to Museums Campaign. This led to a national petition and lobbying to all political parties.

The President of the Museums Association announced a proposed new policy on admission charges in June 1987 to replace the 1970 policy, and this was subsequently accepted by the membership. In his introduction the President referred to the Free Access to Museums Campaign, and identified its avowed aim as political, warning against tying such an issue to the politics of a particular party, especially when there are sound arguments against charging which the profession ought to be able to make to, and have accepted by, politicians of all persuasions.

The Museums Association's policy specifically recognised the merits of the tradition of free access to publicly-funded museums and galleries. It considered that the tradition of free access is self-evidently of consider-able public benefit but not necessarily a natural right. It goes on to urge any admission fee income to be clearly identified in the accounts, to allow free access for at least part of each week, and to offer appropriate admission fee reductions to special groups of visitors. It also recognised, unlike the previous policy, the particular role which charging plays in the financial structure of most museums in the independent sector, although 21 per cent of independent museums do not charge admission.

Independent Museums

Even independent museums have to maintain a critical balance in their charging prices. Too high and no one will visit; too low and there is a danger of 'underselling the product'. As word of mouth is still the best way of generating visitors, the balance is crucial.

An interesting experiment was undertaken in the London Transport Museum, Covent Garden, from April to October 1987. The original visitor projections for the museum proved to be vastly optimistic at 400,000 a year and by 1986 they were around 175,000. This resulted in a shortfall in the projected income and an innovative scheme was set up aimed at increasing income through increasing visitor numbers. Previous research had established that 78 per cent of the existing visitors had decided to visit the museum before reaching Covent Garden and that relatively few passers-by paid to come in, indeed the total figure represented only 1 per cent of the available audience.

The scheme, therefore, was aimed at attracting passers-by, giving them a limited time to decide if they wanted to pay and stay longer. Research had demonstrated that over 80 per cent of the museum's visitors planned to stay longer than seventy minutes, so the free period was set at thirty minutes. The primary objective of the scheme failed, as visitor income was only 25 per cent of that taken the previous year. There was, however, a large increase in visitors (248,000 in the six-month period) and the retailing turnover more than doubled (in spite of the fact that there is no charge to use the shop).

This in itself caused problems. With staff under great pressure, extra casual staff had to be employed – thus increasing expenditure. Other problems also materialised: petty vandalism increased, clock-watching meant that the average length of stay for non-paying visitors was seventeen minutes, but even so, weekends and bank holidays were uncomfortably crowded.

On the plus side, the Museum received valuable national and inter-national publicity. The concept of pay and stay was sound and with adjustment for local situations could be applied elsewhere. But after six months the scheme was abandoned and the original charging scheme reintroduced.

Local Authority Museums

The experience of introducing charging when the admission had traditionally been free had a worse effect on two local authority examples.

Moyse's Hall Museum, in Bury St Edmunds, Suffolk, is a local museum in a Norman town house in the market square. In the five years prior to the introduction of charges in 1971, the average annual visitor figures were 25,410. Following the introduction of charges to deter vandalism and unruly behaviour, the figures dropped to 14,343 in 1972 and, in spite of national trends showing steady increases in museum visitors generally, never regained its former level (the yearly average was 15,158). Admission charges were suspended for an experimental period in 1986/87 and in the first full year of operation the figures rose to 46,923 and have averaged 45,505 subsequently. Income from donations and sales showed a substantial increase.

A similar story was unfolded at the Woodspring Museum in Weston-super-Mare. The museum had opened in 1975 and was located in a back street. Nevertheless the visitor figures had increased to 74,000 by 1979. A summer admissions scheme was introduced in an attempt to offset a financial cutback elsewhere in the museum service. The summer of 1979 (June–August) showed a total of 40,070 visitors with 50 per cent of annual shop takings being received during this period. During the summer of 1980, a charge of 30p was introduced for adults, with accompanied children and school parties free, and a 10p charge for other concessions. Admission figures fell to 10,744 paying customers (8,352 at 30p, and 2,392 at 10p), and an estimated 5000 free,

The financial result was said by the curator to be ludicrous. The total income without VAT was £2334, expenditure £784; the shop takings down 33 per cent and there was a £300 decrease in the donations box. The short-lived experiment was not only financially unproductive but resulted in a poor relationship with the local community.

National Museums

Research by the Policy Studies Institute, published in *Cultural Tends* 1989, Issue 4, found that visitors to national museums and galleries which charge for admission have dropped by more than a third in the last ten years, against a steady increase in visitors to institutions that have remained free (see Table 3.3 on page 94).

In noting these dramatic changes, the report cautioned that attendance figures in the free group were considerably augmented by the opening of two outstations, the National Museum of Photography, Film and Television (0.7 million visitors in 1989) and the Tate of the North (0.5 million visitors in 1988). Also that charging admission obliges the museum to collect accurate statistics on visitor numbers, while the attendance at free museums is estimated. It concludes that even with these facts taken into account, charging admission does have a significant effect on attendances and it is too early yet to tell whether the lost visitors will return.

The National Maritime Museum, which in 1984 became the first of the national museums to introduce admission charges, has had the longest time to assess the permanent effect. The head of marketing stated in a report in the Museum Association's Journal in September 1989 that in real terms the museum is now attracting more visitors than it did in the old free-entry days. Before charges, attendance was around 900,000 a year but counting was thought to be inefficient and that this was an over-

Table 3.3   English national museums and galleries: effect of admission charges on attendance, in millions

	1979	1984	1985	1986	1987	1988	1989[d]
Free Museums[a]	8.4	9.0	9.6	9.9	10.9	11.3	11.5
Museums and galleries charging admission[b]							
Imperial War Museum (1989)	1.4	1.4	1.3	1.2	1.2	1.1	1.2
National Maritime Museum (1984)	1.1	0.6	0.6	0.4	0.4	0.7	0.4
National Railway Museum (1987)	1.2	0.9	1.1	0.9	0.6	0.6	0.6
Natural History Museum (1987)	2.9	3.0	3.4	3.2	2.0	1.7	1.5
RAF Museum (1988)	0.6	0.4	0.4	0.3	0.3	0.3	0.2
Science Museum (1988)	3.9	3.2	3.0	3.2	3.4	2.5	1.1[e]
Victoria & Albert Museum (1985)[c]	2.0	2.1	2.1	1.4	1.4	1.4	1.4

Source: Cultural Trends 1989, Issue 4 (1989), with 1989 figures supplied from A. Feist and R. Hutchison (eds) *Cultural Trends in the Eighties* (PSI, 1989).

[a] British Museum; National Gallery; National Portrait Gallery; Tate Gallery; Wallace Collection; National Army Museum; National Museum of Photography, Film and Television (from 1984 – an outstation of the Science Museum).
[b] Date of introduction of charge or voluntary donation at main building in brackets. National Railway Museum is an outstation of the Science Museum.
[c] Voluntary donation.
[d] 1989 figures taken from A. Feist and R. Hutchison (eds) *Cultural Trends in the Eighties* (PSI, 1989).
[e] 1989 figure for South Kensington site only.

Exercise
Examine Table 3.3 concerning the effect of admission charges on attendance. What conclusions can you draw from the data? Can you see any problems regarding the accuracy of the data collected?

estimate. A National Maritime Museum 'guesstimate' was that it actually lost 15 per cent of visitors in the first year of charging. The popular Armada exhibition saw a visitor figure of 707,000 in 1988 and with the reopening of the Queen's House site in 1990 they now hope to reach the one million mark. Recent market research shows that no fewer that 93 per cent of visitors feel that the National Maritime Museum offers value for money. The Victoria and Albert Museum saw an increase of 10 per cent in attendances in 1988, and an almost identical attendance for 1989, the first increases since the introduction of the voluntary donation scheme in 1985. An estimated 52 per cent of visitors do not pay the voluntary £2.00.

Government Policy on Charging Admission

The Commons Select Committee on Education, Science and the Arts published a report in January 1990 called *Should Museums Charge?: Some Case Studies*, which divided the committee producing the report and caused the resignation of its Chairman. A minority report was also issued by the Labour members of the committee. The committee looked at three London museums, the National Gallery (which makes no charge), the Victoria and Albert Museum (which encourages a donation) and the National Maritime Museum (which charges). The majority report says:

> The national museums are facing a need to modernise their displays and methods against the background of a more competitive environment in the wider museum world. Real increases in public funding have not enabled museums and art galleries to meet all these pressures.

Museum charges were first introduced in 1974 following the Conservatives' Museum and Galleries Admissions Charges Act in 1972. Present government policy has been to allow institutions to decide whether or not to charge. The National Gallery's evidence was that the founding principles in 1824 were to provide access to paintings to as many people as possible. Admission charges might lead to a 40 per cent fall in visitors and lower profits from publications and restaurants. Sponsorship might also fall.

The Victoria and Albert Museum said its voluntary scheme was 'somewhat less cost-effective than a full compulsory charges scheme'. There had been a 40 per cent fall in attendance in the first year, but the figures were slowly recovering.

As with library provision, the future for museum services in a period of charge capping and general local authority cutbacks is uncertain. For some years local authorities have been spending more on museums than the Rate Support Grant allocated by central government, and the gap had grown to 33 per cent on the current account by 1985/86 (Boylan, 1988). The effect of the Community Charge on local authority spending is likely to squeeze funding even further in an already underfinanced and undervalued service.

Further Study

Visit both a charging and a non-charging museum and work through the following checklist of comparisons. Obviously, you will gain more from this if you are able to visit a wide range of types within each category (i.e., small and large versions of independent, local authority, national, and university museums; purpose-built or historic buildings, etc.).

If you are able to gain the extra information listed at the end of the checklist it will help you in any analysis of your findings.

Checklist

Charging

- charge for entry?
- voluntary donation for entry?
- donations box?
- temporary exhibition charge?

Ease of visit

- correct information on opening times and location?
- signposting and sign boarding?
- car parking?
- ease of access?
- local awareness of museum's existence and location?

First impressions

- welcoming?
- introduction to layout?
- clear internal signs?

Customer care/facilities

- cafe?
- shop/sales area?
- toilets?
- provision for people with disabilities?
- children's provision?
- study area?
- leaflets, guidebooks, etc.?

Displays

- clean, attractive and cared for?
- labels easy to read and understand?
- specimens available to touch?
- some displays at children's level?
- ease of viewing for those in wheelchairs?

Extra information: Try to find out the answers to the following:

- main source of funding?
- charging policy, and has it changed?
- number of visitors a year?
- average length of stay of visitors (by observation)?
- whether the museum is known for a particular object or collection or association (i.e., a famous person)?

Finally, ask yourself the following questions:

1. Was your visit value for money and/or the time invested in it?
2. How long was your visit?
3. Would you go again?
4. Would you recommend a visit to a friend?

Questions
1. Outline the differences between a museum and a heritage centre and say what conflicts, if any, occur as a result of the differences.
2. Give arguments for and against major 'blockbuster' temporary exhibitions.
3. Give arguments for and against the introduction of admission charges to existing public-sector, national and small (less than £10,000 annual expenditure) independent museums, and for the policy of charging in new public-sector museums.

References

P. Boylan (1988) 'The changing world of museums and art galleries', in
J. Benington and J. White, *The Future of Leisure Services*, Longman.

A. Feist and R. Hutchison (eds) (1989) *Cultural Trends 1989*, Issue 4, Policy
Studies Institute.

R. Hewison (1987) *The Heritage Industry*, Methuen.

HMSO (1990) *Should Museums Charge?: Some Case Studies*, HMSO.

Museums and Galleries Commission (1988) *The National Museum*, HMSO.

Policy Studies Institute (1988) *The Economic Importance of the Arts in Britain*,
PSI.

Further Reading

K. Hudson and A. Nicholls (1987) *The Cambridge Guide to the Museums of
Britain and Ireland*, University of Cambridge.

Museums and Galleries Commission, *Annual Reports*

J. Myerscough (1988) *The Economic Importance of the Arts in Britain*, Policy
Studies Institute.

S. Tait (1989) *Palaces of Discovery – The Changing World of Britain's Museums*,
Quiller Press.

Yorkshire Dales National Park: people walking in the woods at Bolton Abbey
(photograph by Charles Meecham, Countryside Commission)

4 Countryside Recreation

Dr Terry Stevens

Public interest in, and concern for, the countryside is greater now than at any time in our history. The 1980s witnessed an unprecedented focus of attention upon the quality of our environment and conservation in general, and upon the future of the countryside in particular. The 'greening of politics', with environmental issues becoming an increasingly important part of the rural debate, have been widely discussed. The future of the rural economy is a complex issue involving a range of economic strategies, notably the effects of the Common Agricultural Policy. It also embraces policies relating to the future of development, forestry, watershed management, and conservation of our natural resources.

The 1982 World Conservation Strategy identified the need for establishing programmes for sustained rural development balanced by the conservation of our natural resources. The late 1980s can be identified as the period in Britain when this premise was firmly accepted. Public concern about the future management of the countryside, and of the countryside's resources, may be directly related to our use of the countryside for leisure, tourism, and its general amenity value. The full extent of our interest in, and use of, the countryside has only recently been acknowledged. The research associated with the development of the Countryside Commission's review document *Recreation 2000* identified the scale of countryside recreational activity in Britain. The National *Survey of Countryside Recreation* 1984 established that in the course of a twelve-month period some 80 per cent of the population of England and Wales made a visit to the countryside for a recreational activity. The majority of these visits used resources in the countryside which were not specifically managed for recreation.

These figures confirm that the countryside is a major recreational resource. In addition, recent analysis of tourism research indicated that the fabric of the British countryside is considered by most overseas visitors to be the essence of the tourist product which characterises the British Isles. There is evidence to suggest that the countryside's recreational value is increasing.

In short, the countryside is important as the setting for a wide range of active and passive recreation uses. These may be of a formal or informal nature and are likely to involve an increasing number and diversity of users.

The countryside is under increasing pressure to provide the venue and the resources for recreation. A careful review of the daily newspapers will illustrate how often the use of the countryside for leisure and tourism is actually reported. The news item may be about a planning enquiry, it may be about proposals for a new long-distance footpath, or it may be a protest against restrictions on public rights of way. The reporting indicates the growing concern to secure access to, and enjoyment of, the countryside. This chapter examines the changing character of demand for countryside recreation, and the nature of facility provision to meet that demand.

The type and character of recreational activities which take place in the countryside is constantly changing. How is the countryside coping with these challenges? What are the thoughts of those responsible for the management and planning of the countryside? How can different demands satisfactorily be incorporated into a living countryside that provides homes and jobs for those who live there, and habitats for a rich variety of wildlife? The opportunity to create a multi-purpose countryside has a greater chance of succeeding now than at any stage in our history. Recreation and leisure are legitimate activities in this scenario. However, they must be successfully integrated with the growing range of other claimants for space and resources in the British countryside.

Provision and Facilities

Under these conditions, it is not surprising to find that today's visitors to the countryside are increasingly interested in and, becoming part of, the issues associated with the management of rural resources. This concern is expressed in the growing membership of conservation and amenity bodies. The National Trust; Royal Society for the Protection of Birds; Cadw: Welsh Historic Monuments; and the Councils for the Protection of Rural England and Wales, are all reporting increased levels of membership. In many instances, membership is directly related to the recreational experience afforded by membership giving access to historic properties or nature reserves. However, there is also a relationship between individuals' motivation to join a membership scheme and an explicit interest in the environment. Thus, many people who enjoy the countryside are also involved in bodies engaged in its conservation.

Until recently the countryside has had to meet the requirements of the traditional and primary land users: agriculture, water collection and watershed management, mineral extraction, and forestry. These land users clearly have a dominant function other than recreation or amenity. The secondary claimants for land use in the rural areas, including recreation, amenity and conservation, have had to compete for resource allocation and were often developed as a by-product of the primary land use. Under these circumstances, recreational activities in the countryside were tolerated. The needs and demands of those seeking recreation were generally treated as being inferior to the requirements of farmers, foresters, and others. Visitors to the countryside, even into the early years of the 1980s, were considered to be intruders and the cause of problems.

Until the mid-1960s the recreational use of the countryside in Britain was very limited in scale, and in the type of use, in many ways reflecting use patterns of the previous 100 years. Upper-class Victorians were the pioneers of modern countryside recreation: visiting country estates, and converting much of the upland areas for field sports (notably grouse shooting and deer stalking).

By the mid-1930s, increased leisure time and the need to escape the towns and cities, combined with increased mobility, prompted the working classes to discover the countryside for recreation. These first expressions of 'mass recreation' brought conflict with traditional land users and focused attention on the privileged use of the countryside by a minority.

During the early 1940s a series of government committees examined a range of rural problems: the loss of agricultural land, the protection of high-quality landscape areas, and the pressure to accommodate a rapidly expanding population. The Scott Report (1942) recognised the need to provide adequately for recreation and amenity in the countryside. The provision of a Footpaths Commission and the creation of National Parks were recommended – not for the first time, it must be noted.

As a result of further political lobbying, and a special review by John Dower (the Dower Report, published in 1945), the foundations for the Access to the Countryside and National Parks Act, 1949 were laid. The Act, the first piece of significant legislation to positively acknowledge the need for providing for countryside recreation demand, had the following aims:

- To make provisions for national parks and areas of outstanding natural beauty.
- To make provisions to create nature reserves.
- To improve public paths and to secure access to open country.
- To preserve and enhance natural landscape beauty.

The National Parks

Since 1949, eleven national parks have been designated in England and Wales (more than one tenth of the land area). The Countryside Commission is supporting the application of the New Forest Review Group for National Park status to be given to the New Forest, although the Government has already turned down one application in 1990. The 1949 Act did not include Scotland and Northern Ireland, but the Countryside Commission for Scotland has recently recommended the establishment of four National Parks in the Cairngorms; Ben Nevis/Glen Coe/Black Mount; Loch Lomond and the Trossachs; and Wester Ross. The National Parks have the twin objectives of conserving the landscape and facilitating public enjoyment. At the end of the war these were seen as compatible, rather than competing objectives. No one could be blamed for not predicting the enormous growth in leisure, and especially the demand for informal recreation in the countryside in the 1960s and 1970s.

Over the years there have been several reviews of National Park purposes, and of their organisation and function. In 1974 the Sandford Committee published its review. This important document confirmed the principle that where the twin objectives of conservation and recreational use were in conflict, there should be a decision in favour of conservation. The Secretary of State's ruling to refuse planning permission for a large-scale tourist attraction development at Clogau in the Snowdonia National Park, confirmed the government's adherence to this principle. Many leisure developers now particularly avoid locations in National Parks as a result of these policies.

The National Park authorities, which themselves came into being in 1974 following local government reorganisation, have used the Sandford recommendations as a template for their operations. Each park has produced a National Park Plan which details its objectives, policies and work programmes. These were first published in 1977, and are reviewed every five years.

A further aim of the park authorities is to ensure the socioeconomic well-being of the population which lives and works in the National Parks. Unlike other national park systems around the world, which tend to be based upon large areas of unpopulated wilderness, National Parks in England and Wales are home for more than 250,000 people, and the work-place for many.

Only small areas of land within the parks are actually owned by the park authorities. Almost three-quarters of the land area is privately owned. There are large areas of land in public, or semi-public, ownership held by organisations whose objectives or policies are not directly aligned with those of the National Parks, (for example, the Forestry Commission, the Regional Electricity Companies and the Generating Companies, the Ministry of Defence, and the Water companies). The extent of their ownership varies from park to park. In Dartmoor, the Lake District, and Northumberland over 40 per cent of the land in each park is in public ownership. In the Pembrokeshire Coast and in the Yorkshire Dales, less than 15 per cent of the total land area is owned by public bodies.

Is the actual ownership of land the most effective way of achieving the parks' objectives? Are there other methods which can be used to positively promote conservation and the development of appropriate forms of recreational use and access? There is a trend to dispose of the land owned by several of the public agencies as they are privatised. This will further reduce the amount of land owned by public bodies in National Parks, and increase the need to find alternative methods to achieve the purposes of the parks. These mechanisms will see further use of formal and informal agreements securing access and management, and a greater need to use financial incentives and alternative support systems. The parks would also benefit from a clear, unambiguous statement from the government as to their status so that planners and developers alike can establish appropriate long-term strategies. This reaffirmation and confirmation of park principles is embodied in the Ministerial Review of Parks of 1990/91 and the review *Fit for the Future* published in 1991.

Exercise
Many of our National Parks suffer from congestion – car users are a particular problem in the summer. Can you suggest any solutions?

Much is talked of in terms of the 'family' of National Parks in England and Wales. The eleven parks established in England and Wales have similar roots and operate within the same broad policy framework. Although the framework is different from that of parks in Europe and North America, the philosophy behind their establishment is similar. However, the parks envisaged for Scotland will be different to those in the rest of the UK, the idea being to establish a system of zoning to protect the mountainous core of the proposed parks. Consequently, the English and Welsh parks are part of a much wider family of National Parks.

In July 1989, the Secretary of State for the Environment, and the Secretary of State for Wales jointly announced the reorganisation of conservation bodies in Scotland and Wales in the Environment Protection Bill 1990. Their proposals, enacted in new legislation in the autumn of 1990, created two new conservation bodies in these two countries. The new organisations undertake the statutory work of the Countryside Commission and the Nature Conservancy Council, including responsibilities for National Parks. With the designation of four new National

Parks in Scotland in the course of the next ten years there is a considerable amount of debate taking place about the future of National Parks. It is a debate which will generate much public interest and receive a lot of attention in the media. Students should follow this discussion with interest as National Parks will be one important issue on the political environmental agenda.

Country Parks

In 1966, a White Paper produced by the government reflected the growing concern about the implications of increased leisure demand in the countryside. It proposed tackling the challenges created by increased affluence, mobility, and leisure time by:

- Extending government support, through grants and loans, for providing recreational facilities in the countryside.
- Encouraging and designating country parks and picnic sites.
- Widening the functions of the former National Parks Commission and renaming it the Countryside Commission.

The proposals were enacted in the Countryside Act and the Countryside (Scotland) Act, 1967. This legislation was a milestone, being a major step in the development of a national policy for countryside recreation provision. The Acts ensured government involvement and intervention in an attempt to create a system of countryside recreational sites throughout Britain.

The legislation was designed to stimulate the creation of new venues in the countryside for recreation, to be provided by the public, private and voluntary sectors. On first reading, the results would seem impressive, with over 200 designated country parks being established since 1968 in England and Wales alone. But upon closer inspection, a number of serious questions can be asked about the success of this scheme.

Firstly, country parks were not a mandatory provision: no one *had* to provide them. Consequently, although over 200 country parks exist, the response has been fragmentary. Park designation cannot be regarded as having a strategic approach. The geography of designated country parks show gaps in provision in areas where demand could be expected (see Figure 4.1).

Secondly, the country park system was designed to create new opportunities for recreation. However, it has been estimated that of those areas now designated as country parks, over 60 per cent already hosted some form of recreational use. In reality, there was little added to the recreation stock of the country.

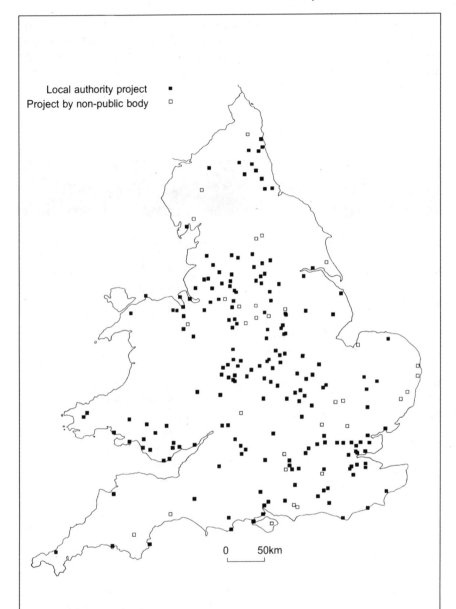

Local authority project   ■
Project by non-public body   □

Figure 4.1   Designated country parks in England and Wales

Source: Countryside Commission (1986).

Finally, country parks were conceived as facilities to be provided by the public, private and voluntary sectors. Approximately three-quarters of the total number of parks are provided by the public sector (county and district councils). The existence of grants and the promotion of the concept did little to interest the private sector, primarily because countryside recreation, especially that of an informal nature, was seen as having very little commercial potential.

Administration, Finance and Participation

The notion of 'free' access to the countryside for recreation is an on-going issue. Many argue that the countryside is part of our inheritance and that everyone should have an equal right to enjoy it, but increasing pressures upon the countryside inevitably lead to the temptation to make a charge in some form.

Whilst private sector organisations shied away from the idea of country parks, they did invest in creating ventures which could make an admission charge. Often the motive for entering the leisure business was forced upon them: for example, when the upkeep of a stately home required new sources of income. In other instances, public interest and demand prompted owners to open their houses, gardens, collections and museums, forests and reservoirs.

The public were not deterred by having to pay an admission charge for access to the properties. Indeed, evidence has emerged which shows that there is generally very little public resistance to pricing policies if the product is of a good standard and seen as value for money.

From such simple beginnings as opening the gates of stately homes and private parks to the public emerged the embryo of the British leisure and theme park. Many of today's major visitor attractions – Longleat in Wiltshire, Beaulieu in Hampshire, Woburn in Bedfordshire, Alton Towers in Staffordshire – grew out of this impetus. This phenomenon is discussed later.

Economics of supply and demand segregated and distinguished the type of provision by the different sectors. However, informal recreation in the countryside is still regarded as 'free', being difficult to charge for, and having a market which is often reluctant to pay.

Exercise
Do you think the public should be charged a fee to use the countryside? Give reasons for and against such a policy.

A number of public agencies have been encouraged to make formal and informal provision for countryside recreation over the past twenty years as a means of getting more use out of their land and increasing marginal income. Thus the Forestry Commission has opened its forests for walkers, picnickers, campers, pony trekkers and car rallies, so that over twenty-five million people annually use the forests for recreation. Similarly, the old Water authorities (now the Water companies), and other national utilities with large land holdings explored the idea of the multiple use of their land, that is, land for primary use (water catchment or forestry), and also for recreation. Privatisation of these resources has caused much concern about the future of recreational opportunities, especially if they are commercially based.

The change of emphasis in British agriculture in the late 1980s and early 1990s away from production, due to surpluses within the EEC, led many farmers to consider alternative uses for their land. Farmers were encouraged to diversify their sources of income and to 'set aside' productive land. Leisure and tourism in the countryside proved to be one of the most popular areas of diversification. Ventures range from pick-your-own-fruit to pony trekking and country sports. In these instances, most of the grants have come from agricultural sources. Consequently, increased leisure provision in the countryside is being developed by a new group of people (see Figure 4.2 on page 110).

New venues for countryside recreation, with managers of little experience in providing and hosting recreation, together with many new forms of recreational activities, has produced an exciting and dynamic situation.

In these circumstances, the need for adequate management is very important if potential conflicts between different land uses, different users, and different activities are to be avoided. The skills and techniques required to manage guests in the countryside are becoming increasingly sophisticated. Investment in facilities, including car parks, toilets, heritage centres, litter prevention and control, signposting, waymarking and adequate access, is vitally important if the management effort is to be successful at popular sites.

For many visitors to the countryside, their recreation experience is based purely upon the natural resources – the quality of the landscape, peace, solitude, and remoteness. Such experiences are increasingly hard to find, and to maintain. Wild places, relatively remote and undeveloped, are an important feature of countryside recreation provision.

More significant still are the thousands of miles of public rights of way, especially footpaths. The majority of the public's recreational use of the countryside takes place close to their homes. Local footpath networks and other local resources such as commons and woods are vital in facilitating the use of the countryside for recreation.

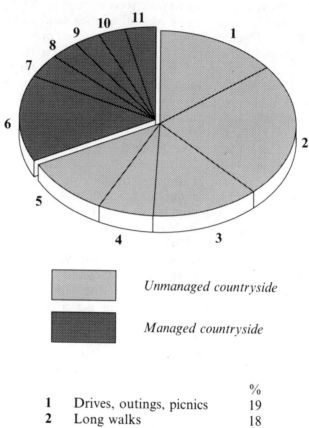

Unmanaged countryside

Managed countryside

		%
1	Drives, outings, picnics	19
2	Long walks	18
3	Visiting friends, relatives	14
4	Sea coast	8
5	Informal sport	12
6	Organised sport	7
7	Pick your own	4
8	Historic buildings	4
9	Country parks	4
10	Watched sports	3
11	Others	7

Figure 4.2 *Countryside recreation activities*

Source: *National Survey of Countryside Recreation*, 1984. Reproduced with permission of the Countryside Commission from *Recreation 2000* (May 1987).

Exercise

With the help of a 1:50,000 Ordnance Survey map, plan a walk in the countryside on the urban fringe utilising public footpaths. Walk the route and comment on signposting; ease of access; the maintenance of the path; stiles and gates; any aspect of potential conflict with landowners or other users.

Although traditional passive forms of recreation still account for the majority of countryside recreational trips, there is increasing evidence that people are searching for more active pastimes. This is attributable to new interests in health and fitness, increased leisure time and disposable incomes, and new technology becoming available and applied to leisure. For some of these the countryside is merely a convenient venue, for others it is an integral part of the recreation experience. Planners and managers of the countryside have to determine which of these activities are acceptable, which are detrimental, and how they can be managed in our multiple-use countryside.

After gardening, trips to the countryside are the most popular form of outdoor recreation. About thirty-seven million people make at least one countryside trip each year and twenty-five million make at least one trip to the countryside a month in the summer. More people take part in fishing, climbing, walking and riding than participate in organised sport. Surveys such as the General Household Survey (1983) and the *National Survey of Countryside Recreation* (1984) also show:

- Approximately one-third of trips to the countryside were made to specific points of interest such as stately houses and country parks.
- A further 20 per cent visited the coast and an additional 10 per cent targeted a particular village.
- Some 24 per cent head for the countryside in general without a specific facility in mind.

Once in the countryside the more popular activities are (in order of popularity):

1. Drives, outings, picnics
2. Long walks
3. Visiting friends, relations
4. Visiting sea coast
5. Informal sport
6. Organised sport
7. Visiting historic buildings
8. Visiting country parks
9. Watched sport
10. Pick your own

A slowing-down of demand in the market for overseas tourism, changing holiday tastes, and growth in overseas visitors will contribute to the growing demand for countryside recreation in Britain. The public are becoming more concerned about the quality of the countryside and this will lead to greater interest and awareness in the rural scene. This will reflect itself in the types of recreational activity which are likely to develop in the next ten years. Recreational use is likely to become more environmentally friendly.

There is likely to be a continued growth in demand for countryside sites for major recreational and leisure developments. Ironically, the reasons developers wish to locate in the countryside are the beauty, scenery and relative peace and quiet. But their very existence is likely to threaten and erode these qualities.

Policy and Planning

The various recreation policies since 1970 have emerged from the Countryside Act, 1968. As a result, the first response to the initial growth in demand for recreation in the countryside was defensive in character. Visitors were generally unwelcome. Their presence, particularly in the hitherto unforeseen numbers witnessed in the late 1960s and 1970s, brought specific erosion and overcrowding problems to individual sites. This reinforced the view (and confirmed the prejudices) held by planners, owners, and managers of the countryside, that recreational use by visitors created problems. Problems need solutions and those solutions were to control and restrict use. The emphasis is now changing. Recreation and tourism, the 'secondary' users, are now legitimate claimants for priority consideration.

Priority action has occurred as a result of the changing rural economy, referred to earlier. It is also reflective of the increasing number of people wishing to use our natural resources for recreation. There appears to be a growing relationship between the user and the resources used. For example, the emerging growth activities are reliant upon the quality of the natural resources to make them successful and enjoyable. Similarly, there is enhanced appreciation and concern for the countryside amongst visitors, which is leading to improved standards of behaviour. This later point is fostered and fed by the provision of interpretive facilities and services which positively, and actively, involve the public in understanding the rural scene.

The countryside continues to be an important venue for an ever-increasing range of leisure activities. Every indicator suggests that these demands will not only show an overall increase, but that more sophisticated forms of leisure will seek a countryside location.

Thus we have two basic leisure demands on the countryside. Firstly, the use of the natural resources of the countryside for recreation and amenity, and secondly, the selection of a countryside location for the development of a leisure facility. In the first instance, the leisure activity is determined primarily by the physical characteristics of the natural resource. In the second case, although the natural qualities may be important to a project's long-term success, we are essentially talking about artificially-created facilities for which the countryside is a convenient and attractive setting.

Irrespective of the inherent suitability of a countryside area for recreational use, intervention is necessary before the resources can be used. Resources can only be used for recreation if:

(i)   they are accessible;
(ii)   appropriate facilities are provided; and
(iii) people know of their existence.

As an example, a lake may have all the qualities of water depth, size of water area, and good wind conditions for dinghy sailing, but if there is no access to the foreshore for launching, the resource is worthless. An access road, a slipway and perhaps a boat park are needed to convert the natural resource into a valuable recreational facility.

Similarly, new recreational activities are constantly being designed. Some are purely modern developments of a traditional activity, for example mountain bike riding is simply an extension of cycling. Growth of these activities is the result of individuals constantly demanding ever more exciting and challenging experiences. It is also the result of technological advances and new materials being applied to leisure goods. Stronger, lightweight metals, linked to innovative design, brought about the sturdy mountain bike capable of tackling the most rugged terrain. Consequently, new recreational activities are capable of taking place in the countryside, and hitherto unused natural resources are utilised. This creates problems, challenges, and opportunities for those managing the countryside.

Exercise
Note recreational activities in the countryside that maybe in conflict with one another. What would your solution(s) be to resolving any conflicts?

Mention has already been made of the need for access, facilities, and awareness (by users or potential users) to exist before a natural resource can be used for recreation. Successful recreational use depends upon an essential fourth component – *management*. Planning and managing the resource for recreational use should ensure that potential conflicts

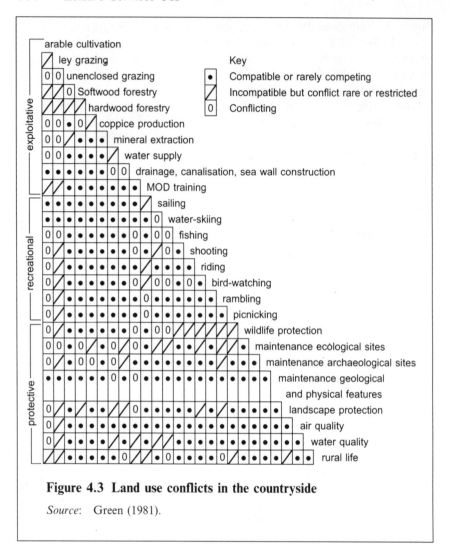

Figure 4.3 Land use conflicts in the countryside

Source: Green (1981).

between recreational activities and between recreation and the resource, are controlled (see Figure 4.3). Management should determine appropriate types and levels of recreational use; decide which natural resources to conserve and ensure that facilities are provided.

Management of the resource and of the recreational activity is of fundamental importance in today's countryside. This is especially true in those sites where multiple use is a feature. Multiple use entails several different land users, or recreational activities, coexisting at the same time in the same place.

Throughout this chapter, the term 'countryside recreation' has been used. Traditionally, resource-based activities have been linked to venues in the countryside, but the cosy separation between urban and country-side recreation is becoming increasingly blurred. The new forms of recreational activity, improved equipment, more varied open space provision in our cities, and pressure upon existing resources, has created a constant search for new venues for these new activities. For example, urban reservoirs are widely used for sailing and wind surfing, whilst urban forests are used for orienteering and rambling. In these instances, actual recreational demand exists because the resource offers the potential for use, and action has been taken to manage the resource for recreation.

Future Prospects

It is of no coincidence that the most successful recent major leisure developments in Britain have a countryside location. The developers of Alton Towers, Beaulieu, Woburn and Longleat Safari Park recognise the recreational importance of the journey into the countryside for the British public. Travel to the attraction is an essential component of the recreational day trip. For the majority the one-way journey is often less than thirty miles; none the less, it is an important element of the day visit. Despite the growth of city centre attractions and leisure-related retailing developments, it is clear that demand for sites for attractions in the countryside will continue to grow. Indeed, there is likely to be increased pressure for attractions in open countryside. In many instances, such attractions will probably be based upon a natural or heritage feature that is inextricably tied to its location – an historic garden or parkland, a castle or renovated mill, a waterfall or a cave. In these circumstances, the legitimacy of the siting is easily accepted. However, when the develop-ment of facilities and projections of large numbers of visitors exceeds an acceptable scale for the site, there is often an outcry. Protest comes from conservationists, local residents and others concerned that the very values which make the place attractive to visitors are likely to be eroded.

These protests are particularly strong when a new development is proposed in an area of notably attractive countryside, especially if the area is designated a National Park or an Area of Outstanding Natural Beauty. Cable cars at gold mines in Snowdonia, artificial ski slopes in the Peak District, marinas and timeshare developments in the Lake District, and holiday villages on the Pembrokeshire Coast, were all actual leisure proposals in National Parks in the last few years. These developments focused attention on the dilemmas facing leisure in the countryside. Should such facilities, which in theory could be located anywhere, be allowed to develop in our most valued areas of countryside? How can modern structures and their ancillary facilities be designed to integrate into the landscape if they were allowed? Are certain developments acceptable and others not? Is it simply a matter of scale?

Several innovative developments demonstrated that harmony could be achieved, even on a large scale, with quality design and management. The Sherwood Forest Centre Parc Holiday Village (near Nottingham), developed by the Dutch Company Sporthuis Centrum and now owned by Scottish and Newcastle plc, illustrates how an integrated 600-acre leisure/self-catering complex can not only be accommodated in the British countryside, but can actually enhance the natural history content of the site. In 1990, a second Centre Parc operation opened in the Thetford Forest in East Anglia within a Site of Special Scientific Interest, and four further complexes have subsequently been planned.

The National Motor Museum at Beaulieu attracts over 600,000 visitors each year. Since the early 1970s a continuous programme of developments, including a monorail, a museum complex and a catering centre were created. This, together with extensive car parking provision, is located in the southern sector of the New Forest, housed on a traditional English country estate. Considerable efforts have been made to add diversity to the amenities offered to visitors, for example, creating nature trails and other education and interpretive facilities.

Similar challenges and opportunities were successfully overcome by the Madame Tussaud's company in their developments at Wookey Hole in Somerset, and in the urban fringe of the Surrey countryside at Chessington World of Adventures.

Most observers agree that whilst there will continue to be a demand for land for these large-scale visitor facilities in the countryside, they will be limited in number – especially compared to the demand placed on the countryside for out-of-town shopping malls. Certain areas of the countryside will, inevitably, be under more intense pressure than others. Venues close to motorway intersections are likely to become prime targets, especially selected sites close to larger cities on orbital motorways, and close to the Channel Tunnel.

Are these large-scale developments really a threat to the values of the countryside as a whole? The economics of attraction development means that, in Britain, there will be relatively few mega-attraction developments in the foreseeable future. Perhaps too much attention and resources are focused upon these large-scale features? As we have seen, by far and away the greatest current use and likely future demand for countryside recreation will be from people who simply want to enjoy the pleasures of walking and viewing in pleasant surroundings. The greater challenge for recreation planners and managers is how to cope with and meet this demand.

The countryside is changing faster now than at any previous time in our history. The most profound effects upon the landscape and life of the countryside will emerge as a result of the increasing diversification in agriculture, changes in economic activity, shifts in the geographic distribution of population, improved access, and the most recent indication that the British planning policies are to be redefined. The Countryside Commission, in its discussion paper, *Planning for Change: Developments in a Green Countryside* (1988) suggests that the challenge is to use the changes imaginatively to protect and enhance the importance of the countryside in the life of the nation.

There are clear needs for the countryside. These are

- an attractive countryside;
- a diverse countryside;
- a living countryside;
- an accessible countryside; and
- a multi-purpose countryside.

The changing nature of recreational demand will add to the dilemmas facing those responsible for planning and managing the countryside. New forms of provision will be required to meet both the traditional and the emerging forms of recreation. New solutions will have to be found to improve access to the countryside for an ever-growing number of people. Developers wishing to locate in the countryside, or farmers looking to diversify into recreation and leisure, will be required to pay increasing attention to environmental design and the quality of their contribution to the landscape.

The next decade will see increasing demand for countryside recreation, and growth in demand for leisure with a countryside setting. However, these demands grow hand-in-hand with a public desire to see more effective conservation, increased concern for the environment, and awareness of the aesthetic qualities of the countryside. Hence, there is a superb opportunity for all of us to contribute to the planning of a new countryside in which those seeking recreation value respect the very qualities which give them their pleasure.

These new landscapes for recreation will be created in areas which have often been ignored by planners and the public alike. The new landscapes for recreation will be found in the urban fringe, giving purpose to the rehabilitation of industrial wastelands, and in the new Community Forests. Recreational use will give new direction to areas of Britain dominated by agricultural activities for the last two hundred years. Developers will increasingly incorporate countryside features in their projects to satisfy some elements of demand. Conservation will become a recreational activity in its own right, with growing numbers of people becoming directly involved in the conservation efforts of the Royal Society for the Protection of Birds, the National Trust, and others.

The role of environmental interpretation will rapidly increase in importance in the countryside as people demand to understand and know more about the landscape and heritage all around them. We can predict that there will be growth in the number of interpretive facilities and services in the countryside. There are already a network of visitor centres, self-guided trails, and guided walks which interpret to visitors. Provision of these, and other interpretive activities, will be a fundamental part of recreation supply, and an important management tool in the future.

Increasingly, these various changes and trends will bring people into the countryside for reasons which have rarely been encountered previously. They will need help and assistance to make the most of their visit. Interpretation is one method of providing this help. There will also be a much broader need to consider how the demands of these new visitors can be met. When they visit a tourist attraction someone should say, 'Welcome ... here's what you can do ... here's how you can enjoy yourself...'. In the countryside a small number of wardens or rangers are employed to undertake this work, but there are too few to cope at present. Clearly, the countryside should not be viewed in the same way as we manage any other visitor attraction ... or should it?

It is likely that over the next decade the public will become increasingly involved in decisions affecting the countryside. The way they use the countryside, and the manner in which they are welcomed and provided for will determine their reactions. Recreational use is, for many, their first encounter with the countryside. A high-quality recreational experience should be the key objective of planning and managing leisure in the countryside to lead us into the next century. The implications for wider environmental conservation gains are immense and should not be ignored.

Further Study

The countryside is an emotive subject, and when competing demands conflict in the countryside, people's feeling are very often heard. Our concern for the countryside is matched only by our desire to enjoy it. This, as we have seen, creates inherent conflicts and challenges. Consider how your immediate family uses the countryside for recreation and leisure. Keep a diary of day visits and other uses for set periods throughout the year for each member of the family and compare them. Compare them also to the national patterns highlighted in the *Recreation 2000* booklet from the Countryside Commission.

A useful exercise is to monitor for a week the main daily newspapers and make a note of the issues and stories concerning the countryside reported in their columns. How many of these relate to recreational uses and conflicts? What is the nature or bias of the newspaper reporting? And where are the stories geographically based?

Finally, as an example of the type of opportunities, conflicts and management solutions available to meet the challenges of recreation in the countryside, undertake the following exercise. Select any area of countryside or urban fringe near your home then:

(a)   List all the natural features that exist on site (woodland, rivers, ponds, rock outcrops etc.).

(b)   Describe the current provision of facilities and access artificially-created.

(c)   List all the existing forms of recreational activities, and describe the natural resources that they need in order to take place.

(d)   List all the potential types of recreational activites which could take place at this site without further provision of artificial facilities on-site.

(e)   Design a matrix, or grid, which will allow you to easily identify those activities which are mutually compatible and those which will require some form of management to allow them to take place using the same resources. What action can you take to make those non-compatible activities compatible with the others? Describe the management opportunities available to you.

Areas of countryside around our urban centres will increasingly be important venues for recreational and leisure activities. Why should this be the case, and how should provision be developed? There are a number of experiments and projects taking place around the country which are exploring these issues. Groundwork is at the forefront of these initiatives. Local Groundwork Trusts are working with communities to achieve environmental improvement and recreational opportunities. It is likely that a Groundwork Trust is in operation close to you. The Trusts are charged with developing new partnerships to achieve environmental and access improvements. How are they doing this, and how are they being funded?

A major feature in the planning and provision of recreation in the next ten years will be the development of 'countryside' opportunities in close proximity to urban centres. The importance of these areas cannot be overestimated. An experiment in monitoring local access in the Neath Valley in South Wales has shown that a vast proportion of the population regularly use the footpaths and open spaces in the urban fringe for the majority of their leisure time. Most of this activity is informal and consists of activities such as walking, strolling or jogging. Further use would be generated if simple provisions were made to encourage use, namely the waymarking and signposting of footpaths, and the availability of local access maps.

The Groundwork Trust is one example of putting this information into practice. Possibly the most exciting initiative of recent years is the joint proposal by the Forestry Commission and the Countryside Commission to create 'Community Forests' around our cities. These forests will embrace a rich variety of landscapes and wildlife. A key component is the development of new opportunities for a multitude of sports and leisure activities. These functions will combine with imaginative ways for encouraging economic development and environmental improvement. Community Forests are designed to provide imaginative ways to use the land between town and country, and to create new landscapes in which recreation and leisure demand can be satisfied. A number of locations have been selected for these forests, the priority sites chosen in 1989 were: Tyneside, the East Midlands, London and South Wales.

The Community Forest concept, and its development, is likely to produce a number of fresh ways of developing recreation in the countryside. These forests will rapidly become an integral part of recreation provision to complement the existing facilities in the system, such as country parks and private-sector provision. To this list will be added the network of Forest Parks which will be designated by the Forestry Commission during the next ten years, and the exciting developments being established by the private sector in association with new forms of tourist investment. For example, Centre Parcs and the proposed Lakewood Developments aspire to fully integrate conservation with a wide range of recreational activities and tourist accommodation on relatively large (400 acres plus) blocks of land. These are year-round, multiple-use developments. Their management methods and techniques could have wider application in the countryside as a whole. It is suggested that students review one of these developments to examine the intensity of recreational use and the manner in which conservation objectives have been fulfilled. How could these principles be applied to the urban fringe, and in particular the site you have chosen for your case study?

Questions

1. Why do developers of large scale theme parks and attractions seek countryside locations for their activities? Can you name five large attractions located in the countryside?

2. Give three reasons why farmers are increasingly adding recreation facilities to their agricultural operations? What is this development known as?

3. Choose an area of countryside close to your home and list all exisiting recreational uses taking place and all the potential use for which the land/water could be used.

References

Countryside Commission (1984) *The National Survey of Countryside Recreation*, Countryside Commission.

Countryside Commission (1987) *Recreation 2000 – Enjoying the Countryside...*, Countryside Commission.

Countryside Commission (1988) *Planning for Change, Developments in a Green Countryside*, Countryside Commission.

B. Green (1981) *Countryside Conservation*, Allen & Unwin.

Ministry of Town and Country Planning (1945) *National Parks of England and Wales* (Dower Report), HMSO, Cmnd. 6628.

Ministry of Works and Planning (1942) *Report of the Committee on Land Utilisation in Rural Areas* (Scott Report) HMSO, Cmnd. 6378.

National Parks Review Panel (1991) *Fit for the Future*, Countryside Commission.

Further Reading

J. Blunden and N. Curry (1985) *Countryside Handbook*, Croom Helm.

J. Blunden and N. Curry (1985) *The Changing Countryside*, Croom Helm.

J. Davidson and G. Wibberley (1977) *Planning and the Rural Environment*, Pergamon Press.

T. L. Goodall and P.F. Witt (1980) *Recreation and Leisure*, E. & F. N. Spon.

P. Lowe *et al.* (1985) *Countryside Conflicts*, Temple Smith.

J. Jernie and A.S. Pitkethey (1985) *Resources: Environment and Policy*, Harper and Row.

C. W. N. Miles and W. Seabrooke (1977) *Recreational Land Management*, E. & F. N. Spon.

C. Pye-Smith and R. Smith (1985) *Working the Land*, Temple Smith.

M. Shoard (1980) *The Theft of the Countryside*, Temple Smith.

Pagoda, Kew Gradens
(*reproduced courtesy of Barnaby's Picture Library*)

5 Parks and Amenities

Tony Gentil

The term 'parks' is generally understood to mean those areas of open space which are set aside for human leisure and pleasure. Parks draw heavily on landscape and horticultural features for their impact and these provide a framework or backcloth for the activities within. 'Amenities' is a much broader term, encompassing all those sites such as golf courses, playing fields, allotments and water features that are not parks in the strictest sense but have a common recreational bond with them. The two elements, parks and amenities, have been grouped together traditionally for the sake of convenience in identity and administration.

This chapter discusses a wide range of facilities in order to give an overview of the current situation. It explains how this sector of the leisure services industry interlinks with other areas of recreation such as tourism, countryside recreation, entertainment and the arts, and sport and physical recreation.

In order to understand the current situation in parks and amenities, and to grasp the enormity of the changes that are taking place, it is important to have some understanding of their recent origins.

Urban parks in public ownership are very much based on the garden fashion of Victorian England. They were designed to allow passive recreational activities such as strolling along pathways, admiring the floral displays and listening to a band. Many such urban parks still exist. Some have changed little in a hundred years except in the reduction of their horticultural complexity. This has been largely due to a reduction in available finance and an escalation of labour costs. They have become hollow shells of their former glory.

Compulsory Competitive Tendering (CCT) is creating a major upheaval in traditional park maintenance and administration. As a result of a need for greater accountability and cost effectiveness, radical changes are being introduced. Many parks are now being used as a framework within which a multiplicity of leisure events can be staged.

Today there is a vast range of facilities which come under the banner of amenities. Many of these facilities are relatively new and are developing their own technology of provision and maintenance. A prime example is the range of sports played on artificial pitches. In exchange for extended hours of use these artificial surfaces are demanding maintenance techniques vastly different from those used on traditional grass surfaces. This is generating a need for the retraining of workforces.

Environmental awareness is also having a major impact on parks and amenity provision. National Parks, country parks, nature reserves, wildlife and safari parks and, most recent of all, regional parks and garden festivals are all making exciting demands on those who provide for this sector of the leisure industry.

Concern for nature has generated a need for new facilities that are environmentally friendly. Pressure from environmental groups has initiated legislation, such as the Food and Environment Protection Act, which has tightened up the way in which chemicals are used for pesticide control. And this legislation has had an effect on the way that maintenance is carried out and supervised.

Today there is far less compartmentalisation of parks and amenities into discrete units with limited specified uses. The trend, increasingly, is to integrate recreational activities across the whole spectrum of facilities. As examples, it is just as common to have a nature trail around a disused urban cemetery as round a nature reserve; and flower beds, artificial ski slopes and performances of medieval plays could all be encountered within the same urban park.

This chapter looks at some of the major providers in both the public and private sectors. It also discusses the role of the voluntary sector and explains how this dovetails into the work of the other two.

For completeness, this chapter should be read in conjunction with the previous chapter on Countryside Recreation.

Provision and Facilities

There are many providers of facilites within the spectrum of parks and amenities. The principal ones, as listed for 1986 by the Institute of Leisure and Amenity Management (ILAM), are:

- Local authorities
- Regional and National Parks authorities
- Countryside Commission
- Nature Conservancy Council
- Water authorities
- The Historic Buildings and Monuments Commission
- Sports councils
- The National Trust
- The Forestry Commission

Some of these, such as local authorities and Regional and National Parks authorities, have recreation as one of their main raisons d'être. Others, such as the Forestry Commission and Water authorities (now the Water companies and the National Rivers Authority), provide facilities as a secondary, albeit important, aspect of their major work. As you will see from other chapters in this book, notably Countryside Recreation, and Sport and Physical Recreation, many of these organisations are active in those areas as well. These major providers are supplemented by a legion of smaller private organisations such as golf clubs, sports and social clubs, breweries, theme parks, and zoos.

The range of facilities that are provided is enormous and include:

Parks (urban and regional), gardens, botanical gardens, sports grounds, golf courses, artificial pitches, allotments, trimtracks, cycleways, zoos, bird gardens, festivals, shows and exhibitions, cemeteries and crematoria.

In order to help the reader understand something of this wide range of facilities there follows a brief summary of each of these elements.

Parks

Parks are an important feature of local government provision. They provide a focal point for a community and usually contain elements of both active and passive recreation. Urban parks have their roots in the mid-nineteenth century. Regional Parks are a much more recent innovation.

Urban Parks

These arose in response to a need, in urban areas, for the working population to have somewhere to relax from their labours. The Industrial Revolution had sucked huge numbers of people from the countryside into the towns. They lived close to their work and this meant that they now had little chance to rub shoulders with nature. Pressure for public parks came from two sources. Firstly, there was a demand from the working people themselves. Sometimes they formed pressure groups and lobbied MPs, wealthy landowners and industrialists. Secondly, many industrialists saw the need for the working population to relax and take part in constructive leisure activities. Many of the urban parks in existence today were given to the local community by public benefactors. But the idea of providing urban parks was not totally philanthropic. It was felt that the workforce would work more effectively if they could recharge their batteries locally. In the restfulness of a park, they could draw inspiration from nature and return to work refreshed.

The first public parks followed the landscape design ideals of mid-Victorian England. Typically, they had meandering walkways, large areas of shrubbery, and expanses of grass with collections of exotic trees. They had intricate bedding schemes using plants raised in heated greenhouses in the park. Conservatories, bandstands and ornamental lakes with waterfowl were also common features.

The first public park owned by a local authority was The Arboretum at Derby. This was designed by John Loudon, a well-known Victorian horticulturalist. It was presented to the local authority in 1840 by a local benefactor. Close on the heels of Derby came Birkenhead Park in the Wirral, designed by Joseph Paxton, who was head gardener to the Duke of Devonshire at Chatsworth in Derbyshire. Paxton later designed the Crystal Palace for the Great Exhibition of 1851. Birkenhead Park is said to have been the inspiration for Frederick Olmstead who laid out New York's famous Central Park.

Present-day Provision

Many urban parks constructed over a century ago still retain their original design features. Often they contain the highest levels of horticultural expertise within a local authority's recreation provision. Sadly, however, some urban parks have deteriorated to a depressing degree. The blame is laid at the door of reduced financial provision and reductions in labour. Bedding schemes have been replaced by grass, bandstands and conservatories demolished and protective boundary railings removed.

The recreational needs of the working population have changed radically since urban parks were first created. People are far more mobile. They do not have to take their recreation on their doorsteps. There has been a trend towards abandoning the urban park in favour of more diverse recreational opportunities elsewhere. Where local authorities have not responded to the challenging needs of their clients, urban parks are generally uninspiring. More progressive local authorities have totally revitalised their parks and have made them centres for local community activity and introduced new design features.

Exercise
Visit an urban park in your local town or city and list the facilities and activities available in it. Also comment on the quality of provision. How clean is it? Is the play provision for children stimulating and safe? Are benches and resting places in good repair? Is there access and provision for people with disabilities?

A good example of change in provision is in play equipment. This no longer needs to be a range of steel and cast-iron structures, set in a sea of concrete. New designs feature adventurous plastic and wooden constructions, with safety surfaces underneath them. The range of activities available to the community, in the more progressive urban parks, is shifting from passive to active recreation. A good example is the Crystal Palace Park, administered and organised by the London Borough of Bromley.

Maintenance

Maintenance of urban parks is generally in the hands of a workforce based in individual parks. It is quite common to find a local authority's glasshouse nursery based in one of its larger parks. Such a nursery will often produce all the bedding plants required for use throughout the local authority. Less common is the practice of producing hardy nursery stock in-house.

Staff within a large urban park will often be deployed on specialist duties. For example, the greenkeeper will maintain fine-turf areas only and nursery staff will concentrate on plant production. Less regular specialist activities, such as arboricultural work and the repair of playground equipment, are usually carried out by mobile teams ranging over the whole of the local authority. Due to increasing vandalism in urban parks, many local authorities employ mobile park wardens who operate out of normal working hours.

Regional Parks

Regional parks are an interesting development of recreational facilities. They have been created out of sites of industrial dereliction which have been linked together to create a multiplicity of recreational opportunities.

The Lee Valley Regional Park

This was the first Regional Park to be created. It was set up in 1967, under the Lee Valley Regional Park Act, 1966. It is administered by its own special body – the Lee Valley Regional Park Authority – and as such has more in keeping with the National Parks than with the traditional urban parks.

The Act of 1966 designated 10,000 acres (4046.8 hectares) as the Lee Valley Park. Currently the park authority controls or occupies 3000 acres (1214 hectares). The authority employs 232 full-time and 81 part-time staff. The Lee Valley Park is a vast undertaking. There are over forty different leisure activities provided, which between them attract over two million visitors each year.

The Lee Valley Park is continually changing and it will take many years before it reaches maturity. In March 1986, the Park Authority formally adopted a new plan of proposals to guide development and land-use up to the turn of the century. Proposals in the pipeline included a water sports centre, a golf-lovers paradise, a motorcycling centre and a youth adventure centre.

The Colne Valley Regional Park

This Regional Park was also conceived in the 1960s and the area designated stretches from Rickmansworth in the north to Staines in the south. It covers 40 square miles (103.63 sq.km) and is 14 miles (22.53 kilometers) long. As yet the park has not reached the level of development of the Lee Valley Park.

The facilities currently available are for walking, riding, sailing, fishing and other countryside pursuits. The intention is to develop these types of facilities further but *not* to introduce playing fields, covered sports areas and intensive recreational provision. It is felt that such activities would detract from the rural concept of the park.

The management objectives for the park are:

- the safeguarding of the area from further urbanisation so that it will remain an integral part of the Metropolitan Green Belt and thus continue to form a stretch of generally open countryside separating London from the towns and villages within and beyond it;
- the conservation and enhancement where necessary of the landscape, including the villages;
- the conservation of wildife, particularly in those parts of the area which have been identified by the Nature Conservancy Council or the Colne Valley Naturalists Liaison Committee as being of special importance;
- the encouragement of agriculture and forestry;
- in so far as is consistent with other objectives, the development of the potential for a variety of rural recreation facilities, particularly on selected worked-out gravel pits where local residents would largely be unaffected;
- the minimising of noise disturbance by planning control and any other available measures, having regard to practical and financial considerations;
- the minimising of pollution of the atmosphere, land and water by planning control and any other available measures, having regard to practical and financial considerations; and

- the termination, at the earliest opportunity, of tipping and other activities which are inconsistent with making the area attractive for local residents and visitors to the Regional Park.

Gardens

What is a Garden?

The term 'garden' is a broad, all-encompassing one. Here it will be used to mean all those land features which are purely horticultural in concept. There are a wide range of features that may constitute a garden or part of a garden, including: flower beds; herb, rock or water gardens, and vegetable plots.

The type of specialist features listed above would have been common in most large Victorian country gardens. Originally, urban parks were modelled on the concept of a large Victorian country garden and pleasure grounds, but few urban parks retain such a range of features today. Reductions in labour forces have led to the demise of many of these labour-intensive horticultural features within larger parks and gardens. As a result, many urban parks have become increasingly 'park-like', where this landscaping term means an area of grass and trees only.

Gardens are not only the preserve of local authorities. They are features of many of the homes in Britain. As such, they may appear as the most modest window box of high-rise flats, or the most prestigious gardens of lavish, privately owned properties.

The Importance of Gardens

Gardening is one of the most popular of all recreational activities in the UK. It involves all sections of the community at all levels of activity, from passive to very active recreation. A huge, economically-important industry has developed to satisfy the demand for plants and materials and, according to one source, the outdoor garden and gardening equipment market in the UK was worth £2.11 billion in 1988. It has been predicted that this will increase to £3.44 billion by 1993.

Visits to gardens account for an important part of the British tourist industry. There have always been local authorities that have associated themselves with tourism. Coastal resorts such as Brighton, Bournemouth and Torquay have always paid particular attention to the quality of their horticultural efforts. Now other local authorities are seeing the importance and relevance of gardening as a leisure pursuit and are taking steps to upgrade the quality of their existing gardens, and often providing new ones.

Nowadays, it is not the general practice for any provider, public or private, to try to include every horticultural permutation, because to do so would require not only enormous space but also a range of expertise which, however desirable, is almost impossible to employ. The trend therefore is to specialise. For example, the National Trust has reconstructed many of its gardens in the particular historical style appropriate to the property. One example is the Elizabethan Knot Garden at Little Moreton Hall in Cheshire. Local authorities such as Cardiff have provided rose gardens, while Manchester has developed model fruit and vegetable gardens. These have been designed to help the general public get an idea of the things they might grow in their own gardens or allotments. In recent years, under the auspices of such initiatives as The Year of the Disabled, there have been attempts by some local authorities to provide gardens specifically for use by disabled groups.

Organisations such as the National Trust help disabled visitors by providing access to existing facilities, rather than special facilities that lead to segregation from the rest of the community, and by identifying those properties under their control which would be the most worthwhile to visit.

Exercise

Find out from your local authority how much is spent on the maintenance and upkeep of gardens. Visit one or two gardens in your locality and try to discover what plants are included and how displays are organised and managed. Talk to gardeners who tend them and try to find out more about the work involved.

Botanic Gardens

Botanic gardens are one of the oldest types of horticultural institution. They developed from the herbal and medicinal gardens established in the Middle Ages in monasteries, and later with the universities. Many of the modern botanic gardens maintain these links today.

A modern botanic garden is, in essence, a collection of plants intended to assist scientific study, but most, while fulfilling this role, are also very attractive gardens in their own right. The best-known botanic garden is Kew, which has a world-wide reputation for scientific and horticultural excellence. Others of importance are at Edinburgh, Cambridge, Oxford, Leicester, Glasgow and Birmingham.

Botanic gardens are funded from a variety of sources. Those closely allied to universities, such as Ness Gardens on the Wirral, are funded by the university itself. Additional monies may be provided by registered charities acting as 'friends' of a botanic garden. Others, such as Kew Gardens, are owned by the nation and are government-funded. Local authorities own and maintain botanic gardens as well. Fletcher Moss Gardens in Manchester were once in private ownership but are now part of a wide range of recreational facilities operated by the city.

The development of the modern botanic garden began in the early nineteenth century. The Victorians were lovers of all things scientific, and the botanical collection had a special appeal for them. This enthusiasm was fuelled by an increasing tide of new plant introductions from all over the world. The arrival of new plant species continued at a relentless pace throughout the reign of Queen Victoria. The botanic garden was the ideal platform on which to display new-found collectors' items.

Developments in glasshouse technology allowed plants from even the hottest climates to be grown successfully in Britain. Both Joseph Paxton and John Loudon were important pioneers in developing this new technology.

The Role of Botanic Gardens Today

Most botanic gardens, by the very nature of their need for maintenance, have proved very valuable training grounds for horticulturists. The Royal Botanic Gardens of both Kew and Edinburgh run diploma courses which are regarded as amongst the finest available. Trainees work in the gardens during the day to gain practical experience and also attend lectures to develop their theoretical knowledge. Entrance into botanic garden training schemes is fiercely contested and each year both Kew and Edinburgh turn down many more applicants than they take on. Many of today's senior recreation staff embarked on their careers via a botanic garden.

As well as the living plant collection housed outdoors or under glass, botanic gardens provide other facilities. Lecture theatres and demonstration areas help the public understand and appreciate horticulture in all its diverse aspects. Most of the larger botanic gardens provide facilities for people with disabilities, such as toilets and ramps. Ness Gardens has some plant labels in braille.

The principal function of the botanic garden is the housing of plant collections for scientific study, with subsidiary functions of recreation and education. They act as banks of genetic material which could have a future value in plant-breeding programmes. Internationally important gardens, such as Kew, are actively involved in plant conservation. They have advanced micro-propogation facilities and are able to bulk up the number of species threatened with extinction in the wild. This role has become increasingly important in recent years because of the continuing threats to the environment.

Until 1984, the Royal Botanic Gardens at Kew were part of the Ministry of Agriculture, Fisheries and Food. Under the National Heritage Act, 1983, a Board of Trustees was set up to administer the gardens, which on 1 April 1984 became a QUANGO supported by grant-in-aid from the Ministry of Agriculture, Fisheries and Food. There has recently been a good deal of new development at Kew, in terms of building programmes to enhance the plant collections. Other botanic gardens have not fared so well. The City of Liverpool, under severe economic pressure, had to close down and dismantle their botanic gardens at Calderstones Park in 1984.

Sports Grounds

Sports grounds are provided and maintained by both the public and private sectors. The range of facilities available is very diverse and both sectors might provide for similar activities within the same geographical area. Although there are similarities in provision between the public and private sector, there are also important differences.

Local authorities aim to provide sports grounds for the entire population in their own area. The sports grounds may be sited in parks, playing fields or school grounds. Most local authority sports grounds are heavily subsidised and the fees for their use are often tailored to suit the financial resources of the user. For example, certain groups such as the unemployed or senior citizens may be granted reduced fees. This is an important aspect of local authority provision, without which many sections of the public might not be able to participate in their chosen sport.

On the other hand, sports grounds in private ownership tend to be exclusive to some degree. They may charge an economic fee for the use of the facility or restrict its use to certain groups only. Such is the case where a company provides sports facilities for the exclusive use of its employees. Privately owned sports grounds tend to cater for a single or a limited range of sports, whereas the local authority sports grounds usually provide for a cross-section of those sports most commonly in demand in a particular area.

Local authorities provide sports grounds in both schools and parks. Until recently it has been the usual practice for a school to have exclusive use of the on-campus facilities. This has led to complaints from the general public that school sports grounds were under utilised at certain times of the year. Therefore, it is now quite a common practice for school sports grounds to be made available for dual use – that is, by both the school and the public. New school sports grounds are often built using joint funding, where a proportion of the costs are met by both Education and Recreation Departments.

The Crownpoint Sports Park is a development which encompasses all these elements. It is owned by the City of Glasgow District Council and was built on a site of some 37.06 acres (15 hectares). The sports park consists of the following facilities:

- a floodlit athletics area with an eight-lane track;
- two floodlit artificial pitches for a wide variety of sports such as football, netball, hockey, volleyball and tennis;
- two grass pitches suitable for football and rugby;
- a synthetic pitch suitable for football and hockey; and
- an extensive sports centre and administrative block.

These facilities are supplemented by two additional pitches at two local primary schools. A covered corridor links the sports centre with the games wing of St Mungo's Academy which incorporates a large sports hall, two gymnasiums, a swimming pool and changing accommodation. A joint-use agreement has been reached between the education authority and the district council. This will allow use of the school's sports facilities out of normal school hours.

The Crownpoint Sports Park was jointly funded by the City of Glasgow District Council, the Scottish Development Agency, the Scottish Sports Council, the Scottish Development Department and Strathclyde Regional Council. It illustrates an excellent example of a local authority providing a wide range of facilities for the community and taking advantage of both dual use and joint funding.

Exercise
Identify and visit a dual-use or joint-funded facility in your region. What is the basis of the agreement? Who provided the capital? Who provides the management? What are the benefits to the partners? Find out if there are any problems with dual use and joint-funded provisions.

Golf Courses

Golf is by no means a new sport; it has been played for several centuries. However, its main growth and increase in popularity has been over the last fifty years. It has traditionally been a participative sport but recently, with increased television coverage, it has become very much a spectator sport as well. It attracts players of all ages, four out of five of whom are men.

The *General Household Survey* (1983) showed that approximately 1.2 million people played golf in 1983, half a million less than in 1977, placing it well below walking, swimming, snooker and darts in popularity as a participative sport. However, as can be seen from Table 5.1, the English Golf Union is the largest governing body of sport in Britain, having some 445,000 male members in 1325 clubs. At the begining of 1991 this had increased to 501,000 male members in 1372 clubs. Ladies' golf has also shown an increase in membership with over 240 new clubs affiliated in the UK since 1980, an increase of over 12 per cent.

Table 5.1   The ten largest governing bodies of sport, 1985

	Affiliations	
Governing body	Members (thousands)	Clubs
English Golf Union	445	1325
National Federation of Anglers	333	4310
Lawn Tennis Association	230	2443
Camping and Caravanning Club	174	–
Ladies Golf Union*	154	1866
English Bowls Association	120	2682
Badminton Association of England	104	5068
English Ladies Golfing Association*	91	1162
Scottish Bowls Association	88	874
British Association for Shooting and Conservation	75	358

Source: *Governing Bodies of Sport* (1985). Reproduced with acknowledgement to NALGO (correspondence course for ILAM/BTEC examinations).
* 1984 figures

As a sport, golf has several advantages, some of which, although by no means all, are shared with some other sports:

- It can be played all the year round – it is not seasonal like football and cricket.
- It can be played with the minimum of supervision – no referee or umpire is needed.
- It allows direct competition between participants with varying degrees of skill – through the handicapping system.

But it does have certain disadvantages when viewed in direct competition for resources with other sports:

- It makes large demands on land. For example, an 18-hole course will occupy a minimum of 98.84 acres (40 hectares).
- It is not compatible with other recreational pursuits. The golfer needs exclusive use of the entire facility. This is not the case, for example, with an athletics stadium, where several different activities can operate concurrently.

The majority of new golf courses are in private ownership. In the period 1968-82, 400 new golf courses were built. Of these, 243 were provided by the private sector. In 1985 there were a total of 181 local-authority-owned golf courses, compared to over 1200 privately owned clubs. A cost breakdown of local authority expenditure on golf is shown in Table 5.2.

Table 5.2   Expenditure on golf by local authorities in England and Wales

	1976/77	1984/85
Number of Courses	125	181
	(£s)	
Expenditure	4 559 000	13 227 000
Income	3 561 000	11 620 000
Net expenditure	997 000	1 607 000
Subsidy per course	7 976	8 878
Recovery Rate%	78%	88%

Source: CIPFA (1985).

The demand for new provision has outstripped supply and as a result most clubs have waiting lists to either join or to use the facilities. In 1976, the South Western Sports Council suggested that if only 10 per cent of the total number of children introduced to the sport by the Golf Development Council continued to play golf, they would need another fifty-five 18-hole courses to accommodate them.

The major difference between private clubs and those owned by local authorities is the way in which they obtain their funding. Private clubs usually charge a fee to join the club and then an annual subscription to use the course, whereas the local authorities usually charge for each round played. These different types of funding have resulted in polarisation of the types of people that use private and public courses. Private clubs in areas where demand is high can charge fees that tend to exclude any but the moderately wealthy. For example, the first year's golf at a private club can cost anything from £250 to £3000, whereas at a local authority course the year's play is likely to cost less than £100.

Artificial Pitches

Many sports, such as football and cricket, have long been played on natural surfaces, particularly grass. This works well if the grass can grow under good conditions and be well maintained. Unfortunately, this ideal situation occurs only too rarely. Football pitches with grass surfaces can rapidly deteriorate to the extent that the game becomes unplayable. It is against this background that providers in both public and private sectors have actively sought alternatives to grass.

The result has been that there are now a wide range of alternative materials for pitch surfaces. Although many of these materials are expensive to install, they can extend the use of a facility considerably. For example, it has been claimed that one synthetic grass soccer pitch can accommodate the amount of use equivalent to that of ten natural turf pitches.

Types of Surface

Types of artificial surface can be broadly grouped into four categories:

1. *Concrete or asphalt*
    These are hard wearing but abrasive and can cause injury in contact sports such as five-a-side soccer.

2. *Hard, porous water-bound*
    These are made from materials such as cinder and fine stone which are regularly watered to bind them together.

3. *Synthetic grass*
    This is material rather like carpet and is widely used as an alternative to grass for football and hockey pitches.

4. *Rubber and plastics*
    These can take the form of carpet like sheets or be poured as a liquid to set into a wearing surface. The latter technique is currently widely used for laying running tracks.

Current Provision

Many local authorities have installed artificial pitches. Although the initial cost can be high, for example, £500,000 for a full-size synthetic football pitch surface, there are many advantages. In urban areas where demand is high and recreational land unavailable, an artificial pitch can solve several problems. It allows maximum playing use of minimum space. Scotland's first synthetic grass pitch was installed at the municipally-owned Anfield Stadium. Here, the emphasis is on community use and it is estimated that this pitch is capable of handling at least ninety-one hours use each week. This amount of use is far in excess of anything a grass pitch could cope with. Local authority provision can range from massive Olympic-size provision, as in Manchester, to individual artificial cricket wickets in rural primary schools.

The Sports Council has actively encouraged the use of artificial pitches by initiating research and providing grant aid. For example, the Sports Council produced two reports on artificial surfaces in 1985 which set down desirable standards for playing surfaces (Sports Council 1985a & 1985b). They have also been active in working with the Rubber and Plastics Research Association in the production of the three-volume *Specifications for Artificial Sports Surfaces.*

Private organisations such as football clubs have also installed artificial pitches: Luton, Oldham and Preston being examples. Because these pitches are so durable, professional clubs are able to gain extra revenue by hiring them out to private organisations when not in professional use. Recently there have been strong objections in professional football to the use of artificial pitches, which are said to give an unfair advantage to the home team, as well as affecting the way the game is played, and they have been banned for Football League fixtures in the first and second divisions from the beginning of the 1991 season.

Artificial surfaces are now in use for a wide range of sports, including football, rugby, hockey, tennis, bowls, cricket and athletics, and increasingly as surfacing under children's play equipment. It is quite common to find a variety of sports played on the same pitch.

Exercise
Find out from your local authority or Regional Council for Sport and Recreation how many artificial grass surfaces there are in your region. Try to discover how many matches are played on them each week and compare the results with what would be possible on turf.

Allotments

Background and Definitions

The word 'allotment' literally means a share of land allotted, or allocated to an individual, as a result of an enclosure award. In the modern context of recreation provision, it is generally taken to mean a parcel of land allotted to an individual to raise crops. The emphasis is on vegetable growing, fruit and flowers usually occupying a very secondary position. Some allotment contracts in fact limit the amount of non-edible crops that may be grown. Allotments may occasionally be used for animal produce, but this is usually restricted to poultry- or bee-keeping.

There are basically three types of allotment sites:

1. *Statutory*
    These are sites provided by local authorities in response to their legal obligation to do so.
2. *Temporary*
    These are provided by the local authority, on a temporary basis, to fulfil a recognised short-term need.
3. *Private*
    There are two types of private allotment landlord:
    (i) Large national organisations such as British Rail, who have large parcels of land that are incidental to their main function and are let as allotments because they cannot be effectively used for other purposes.
    (ii) Smaller organisations or individuals who let parcels of land on an *ad hoc* basis.

Fluctuations in the popularity of allotment gardening have closely mirrored social events and changes over the same period. The two major peaks in the popularity and need for allotments in this century are associated with the two world wars. Allotment tenancies in England and Wales rose from 58,000 in 1909 to 1,330,000 in 1920 and fell off to about 500,000 in 1938. World War II caused difficulties in importing food, and the government organised the 'Dig for Victory' campaign. This brought about an increase in allotment tenancies to 1,750,000 in 1944. The figure has dropped off steadily to a current level of about 400,000.

The Thorpe Report

In 1965, the Government set up a Committee of Inquiry into allotments, chaired by Professor H. Thorpe. The committee's terms of reference were:

To review general policy on allotments in the light of present day conditions in England and Wales and to recommend what legislative and other changes, if any, are needed.

The Thorpe Report was published in October 1969. The Committee took a searching look at the state of allotments and suggested that landlords and tenants should be encouraged to upgrade their image – it was suggested that allotments should become 'leisure gardens'. Although there was general agreement with the findings of the report, few local authorities made a serious attempt to upgrade the quality of their allotment sites. There were a few notable exceptions, including Birmingham, Manchester and Stockport.

Over the years, allotments have tended to become the poor relation of local authority provision. Many local authorities have regarded allotment sites as a necessary evil and an embarrassing eyesore, laying the blame at the door of allotment tenants. The tenants in their turn have accused local authorities of ignoring the allotment movement and not providing adequate funding. There has been a significant improvement in allotment provision since local government reorganisation in 1974 and relations between tenants and local authorities are generally better.

Allotment Administration

Local authority allotment sites are usually administered by the Recreation Department or its equivalent. Some of the larger authorities employ a full-time Allotments Officer and administer their sites through an allotments subcommittee which includes co-opted members from the local allotment movement. Tenancies may be held through an individual agreement with the local authority or through an allotment society holding a number of sites on 'block agreement' with the authority. In recent years there has been a general trend towards the latter type of arrangement. There are certain advantages to both landlord and tenant of block agreements:

- For the local authority, a site under this system will have the rents collected and day-to-day administration carried out by the society, thus saving considerable administrative costs.
- In return, the society is usually given a percentage of the rents collected as a rebate. The society also has the advantage of clear control over its affairs.

This trend towards self-administration by allotment site societies has been one of the reasons for the easing of tension between tenants and the local authority.

Trimtracks

Trimtracks are a fairly recent development in recreation. They are a development of the mid-1970s craze of jogging, which came to Great Britain from America on the wave of a new awareness of the value of health and fitness. Jogging was, at first, a rather *ad hoc* activity – devotees simply donned a track suit and a pair of light shoes and ran around the neighbourhood. The activity grew into something more structured, with serious participants entering long-distance races and marathons. A National Jogging Association was formed.

Local authorities, which were sensitive to trends in recreation, responded to the new development by providing jogging trails through parks. From this it was an easy step to include other activities along a jogging route. Many of these took the form of a series of stations where users could perform different exercises.

The major advantages of trimtracks are that:

• they enable individuals to undertake exercise of an intensity and level of skill suitable to their own needs;
• they provide for more intensive and varied exercise than a simple jogging track;
• they enable individuals to progressively improve their fitness and skill at a measurable rate; and
• they are a fairly inexpensive facility to provide and maintain.

A good example is the trimtrack at Woolston Park in Cheshire, installed by Warrington New Town Development Corporation in association with the District Sports Council and a local college specialising in sport and recreation. It was constructed using labour employed under a Manpower Services Commission scheme. Trimtracks are now widely established throughout Britain. They are regarded as a recreational facility in their own right and as being distinct from the sport of jogging. The Irvine Development Corporation in Scotland opened a wheelchair trimtrack at the Irvine Beach Park in 1982 which was developed with the help of the Scottish Sports Council at a capital cost of £30,600.

Cycleways

Cycling has been a popular sport and a cost-effective means of transport for over a century. It has also spawned a series of specialist sports, some of which are Olympic events. But as a mode of transport it has become increasingly hazardous as the number of motor vehicles on the roads are increased. Over the ten years from 1975–85 there was a 23 per cent increase in the number of deaths and injuries to cyclists.

Despite the dangers, the popularity of cycling is increasing. In 1982, 1.7 million new bicycles were sold in the UK, a figure substantially in excess of the number of new cars sold. Many people have turned to cycling because it is cheap, healthy and a quick mode of transport.

It is felt that interest in cycling could increase even more if it were made safer. A National Opinion Poll survey undertaken in 1976 found that problems with traffic and fears about safety were the main reason why more people did not cycle.

Cycleways parallel in many ways the development of trimtracks and have risen in popularity on the upsurge of public interest in health and fitness. They are routes designed for cyclists that enable them to be segregated from motor traffic. They differ from the cycle routes designed alongside main roads in that their prime function is recreational use.

Cycleways are often constructed on existing transport routes where a change of use to allow cycling is possible. Redundant railway lines offer enormous scope for their creation. They have easy gradients, follow direct routes and often have a natural history value. In Bristol, the 'Cyclebag' group organised the conversion of the derelict Bristol to Bath railway line into a very well-used cycleway. Forest paths represent another opportunity to create cycleways. The Forestry Commission produced a document in 1983 entitled *A Policy for Cycling in the Forest* which suggested that trial cycle routes could be opened on the better forest paths. It is also possible to hire bicycles in some forests.

Canal towpaths are another under-exploited resource, particularly when they pass from the countryside into the heart of the town as with the Cromford Canal. Derbyshire County Council improved the towpath which now provides a route into the Peak District. The Peak District National Park actively encourages the use of bicycles and operates a very successful cycle hire scheme.

Country Parks and Regional Parks are an ideal location for safe cycling. Tatton Park, jointly administered by Cheshire County Council and the National Trust, has a cycle hire facility for visitors. The Lee Valley Regional Park also operates cycleways. Organisations such as the Cyclists Touring Club and Friends of the Earth Trust have campaigned actively and successfully for improved facilities for cycling.

Generally, cycleways are not the exclusive preserve of cyclists and may allow passage for pedestrians and horse riders. Cycling may also be allowed along existing footpaths or bridleways which are not specially constructed as cycleways. Waymarking for cycleways, to help users find their way, is becoming common practice. The Cumbria Cycleway has adopted a distinctive motif along its routes and many local authorities, such as Cheshire, East Sussex, Wiltshire and Lancashire, have produced cycle trail guides to promote cycling routes.

To summarise, the main advantages of cycleways are that:

- they provide for healthy, safe exercise in an interesting environment without causing noise or atmospheric pollution;
- they allow users to cover distances more quickly than they would on foot;
- they provide a relatively cheap recreational facility for a wide range of ages and levels of proficiency; and
- they are relatively easy to establish and maintain.

Zoos and Bird Gardens

Historical Development

The word 'zoo' is an abbreviation of 'zoological garden', which gives us a clue to its origin. There are obvious parallels between zoological gardens and botanical gardens – both are collections of living organisms intended for human entertainment, education and study. Zoos in Britain began as private menageries or collections of wild animals in cages. These were often displayed in garden settings and some still continue today as a combination of both zoological and botanical gardens.

The original concept of a zoo was to have a living museum of animal species. The emphasis was on the collection rather than on the realism of the display or the quality of life of the captives.

Attitudes have changed radically in the last thirty years; cages have been replaced by enclosures which give the animals much greater freedom of movement and room to exercise.

Modern Zoos

Chester Zoo not only illustrates the range of facilities available in a modern zoo, but also the large, field-like enclosures where the various groups of animals are kept. Modern enclosures are designed to resemble, as closely as possible, the natural habitat of each animal. The change in attitude to the housing of animals in zoos has been due to two main factors:

1. A greater scientific understanding of what animals need for healthy survival in captivity.
2. Changes in public attitude to the keeping of animals in captivity.

Much of this change is due to the stimulation, by the media and particularly by television, of an increased public awareness of the natural history of animals in the wild.

Today, zoological societies' concerns are with animal behaviour, ecology, and conservation, and many zoos are actively involved in conservation projects on an international scale. There is a growing list of animals whose survival in the wild is seriously threatened by man, and zoos co-operate to assist with breeding programmes using both animal exchanges or artificial insemination techniques. It is usual for them to specialise in certain species or genera in which they have a particular interest or expertise. The idea is that threatened species can be bred in captivity to increase population levels. The animals are returned to their native habitat, where this still exists, to ensure their continued survival in the wild.

Zoos and the Public

Zoos represent an important recreational facility and continue to be popular attractions, having appeal for visitors of all ages. Often zoos have facilities other than collections of animals to attract the visitor. Chester Zoo prides itself on the quality of its gardens and floral displays, and many people visit the zoo as much to see the roses, bedding displays and tropical plants as to view the animals. Dudley Zoo in the West Midlands has a chair lift and miniature railway as well as the ruins of the historic Dudley Castle.

The larger zoos have education units which assist schools by supplying teachers' packs. Chester Zoo has established a group called the Friends of the Education Department Service (FEDS). About forty volunteers conduct guided tours and run a brass rubbing centre where brass-rubbings can be made of a wide range of endangered species. They also look after a Tropical House Touch Cart where members of the public can touch objects such as feathers, skins, and bones and discuss them with the attending volunteers.

Financing Zoos

A major source of income for zoos is the entrance fees charged to visitors, so in order to ensure their continued survival for scientific and conservationist purposes, they must still recognise the importance of providing a worthwhile recreational experience for the public.

Another means of generating income from the public is the idea of animal adoption schemes. Chester Zoo operates such a scheme, which is very popular. Sponsorship is based on units of £25 which buy 'shares' in the cost of the upkeep of a particular animal for one year and go towards the zoo's total annual food bill of around £140,000. Sponsors receive a certificate, two free entrance tickets and regular progress reports on their adopted species. Private companies may also be encouraged to sponsor enclosures or individual animals in return for having their company logo placed in a position of prominence.

Chessington World of Adventures is an excellent example of how a modern zoo has diversified to offer a more attractive, varied recreational experience and at the same time secured sponsorship from a range of private companies. As well as the zoo, a range of imaginative adventures are provided, each sponsored by a separate company or companies (including Coca-Cola and Schweppes, Hitachi, the AA, the Singapore Tourist Promotion Board and Singapore Airlines, and Kodak) who are acknowledged in the World of Adventures brochure and display their logos on the facility they sponsor.

Bird Gardens

There is a long tradition in Britain of the keeping of exotic birds in captivity. Generally this has taken two forms. The smaller birds, such as song birds and brightly coloured finches and parrots, were confined in cages or aviaries. The large birds such as ornamental game birds and wildfowl, were given much greater freedom of movement, being free to roam but being limited by the trimming of their flight feathers and by being provided with regular food.

Like zoological gardens, bird gardens have always had a recreational and educational value. However, their aesthetic and ornamental value has often been of prime importance. More recently, conservation has assumed a more important role and many bird garden establishments are actively involved in breeding and research programmes that aim to ensure the survival of endangered species.

One of the most significant events in changing traditional attitudes to the keeping of birds was Sir Peter Scott's initiative in establishing the Severn Wildfowl Trust at Slimbridge in Gloucestershire. Here, totally wild populations of migratory wildfowl are encouraged to visit, while exotic species that are under threat in their native habitat are studied and bred in captivity.

The first area of marshland purchased by Sir Peter at Slimbridge was an important stop-over point on the migratory route of geese. Over the years this developed into a combination of research station and tourist attraction that became the model for several others. The Wildfowl Trust property at Martin Mere in Lancashire is listed by the North West Tourist Board as one of its top ten attractions.

Exercise
Some people have objected to the concept of zoos and bird gardens. List the possible objections, and counter these with aspects of good

practice. Find out how much it costs to operate your local zoo or bird garden, and identify the major areas of income and expenditure.

Festivals

Festivals have a very long history pre-dating that of the Ancient Greeks and Romans. They were often celebrations associated with events of a religious nature and were characterised by merrymaking, music and a variety of other entertainments, as well as the feasting from which the name derives. Modern festivals have not changed much in character but are less often of a religious nature. Their themes vary greatly but they all provide a platform for recreation on a grand scale and often include whole communities. Visiting crowds and contributors to the festival can spend considerable sums of money, which is a further benefit to the community.

Festivals have their critics as well as their supporters. Criticism usually relates to the problems associated with a massive influx of visitors to the area, as can be the case with certain rock and pop festivals, where participants have been accused of causing vandalism and encouraging drug abuse.

Typical examples of festival themes include:

- arts and music festivals, such as the Edinburgh Festival;
- jazz, rock and pop festivals, such as the Hayfield International Jazz Festivals and the Glastonbury Rock Festivals;
- flower festivals, such as that held in the bulb-growing areas of East Anglia in the spring;
- garden festivals; and
- community festivals, such as the Notting Hill Carnival.

Garden festivals have proved outstandingly popular and serve as a good example of how festivals can play a leading role in providing recreational activity.

Britain adopted the idea of garden festivals from Europe, where they had been used for many years to revitalise derelict land and generate enthusiasm, finance, and civic pride in communities. The first festival of this nature held in Britain was the Liverpool International Garden Festival in 1984. It was felt by the Conservative Government, after the Toxteth riots of 1982, that a Festival would help to revitalise the Liverpool area by increasing employment prospects and bringing in an influx of visitors.

The site chosen for the International Garden Festival was an area of 50 hectares of derelict land alongside the River Mersey. The work was overseen by the Merseyside Development Corporation, with funding of over £20 million from central government and the private sector. The festival aimed to attract five million visitors paying a standard entrance fee of £3.50 which amounted to only a fraction of the associated spending generated directly and indirectly by the Festival. The International Garden Festival at Liverpool was followed by the National Garden Festival at Stoke-on-Trent in 1986, Glasgow in 1988, Gateshead in 1990, and plans are in process for a site in South Wales in 1992. Both the Liverpool and Stoke festivals were intended for a single summer life, but due to public demand they opened in subsequent years, albeit on a smaller scale. Both sites have now largely been used for housing development.

The garden festivals have featured horticultural displays of the highest order and have provided a framework for a variety of activities, both outdoor and under cover, designed to provide recreation and entertainment. Among its attractions, the Stoke Garden Festival featured a shopping mall, a pottery museum, sculpture, and overhead cable cars.

Garden festivals on large derelict land sites require several years of intensive pre-planning and development. This activity is intended to generate work for local labour and boost the local economy. There was some criticism, at Liverpool in particular, that this theory does not necessarily work in practice. A large percentage of the labour force used at Liverpool was contract labour brought in from outside.

Shows and Exhibitions

Shows and exhibitions are another of the oldest organised recreational activities. They are documented as occuring in Ancient Rome and probably pre-date this by many thousands of years. Modern shows are regarded as displays with a competitive element and 'exhibitions' as displays with a commercial or educational bias.

The modern local-authority-sponsored shows, with classes for flowers, vegetables, pets and handicrafts, are little different from the village shows of past centuries. Local authorities play an important part in presenting shows, having taken them over from the agricultural societies of the nineteenth century; in co-ordinating them; and often providing financial backing. An example of co-operation between a local authority and show society is the Tameside and Northern Counties' 'Spring Show'. The local authority also provides free use of its hall, a floral decoration and some of the judges.

Shows can provide a valuable vehicle for local authorities to promote their activities and it is traditional, especially in the larger authorities, for them to stage impressive floral displays. Some even travel beyond their own boundaries to exhibit in national events such as the Chelsea Flower Show.

Shows, in common with many other forms of entertainment, are currently suffering a difficult financial period as a result of the universal economic dilemma; if organisers raise fees to try to cover costs and/or make a profit, attendance figures drop and the show is still not viable. An interesting example of this dilemma is the case of the world-famous Southport Flower Show, first staged in 1924. After local government reorganisation in 1974, the new authority, Sefton MBC, decided that the show should break even. In 1978, it made a record profit of £20,880, but from this peak it suffered a series of setbacks. The main causes were the general recession and high levels of unemployment in the North West, which adversely affected local spending power. In 1977, the show cost £186,000 to stage and by 1986 this had risen to £319,000. Income generated by the show was unable to keep pace with the rising costs and Sefton MBC decided that the show must be wound up. However, a show society was formed with members from the local business community, amateur exhibitors, a landscape architect and an accountant. Sponsorship was raised from local firms, and the show continues. Not all shows have been so fortunate. Some, such as the Manchester Show, have been discontinued, partly for financial and partly for political reasons.

Cemeteries and Crematoria

The disposal of the dead must be one of the oldest of organised human activities and most cultures have treated it as a matter of great religious significance. In Britain, until the middle of the last century, disposal of the dead took the form of burial and was a matter for the Church. By the mid-nineteenth century, Church burial grounds were unable to keep up with the requirements of an expanding population. As a result, provision was made by Acts of Parliament for additional facilities to be provided.

In broad terms, these Acts established which organisations, outside the Church, had the authority to carry out burials. Legislation concerning cremation was introduced in 1902, when the first Cremation Act was passed. Currently the most important Act is the Local Government Act of 1972 and the regulations following from it. There is a general trend towards an increase in cremations as a method of disposing of the dead. At the present time, 70 per cent of all funerals take the form of cremation.

Within local authorities it is usually the Recreation and Amenities Department, or its equivalent, that administer burial and cremation.

Cemetery Administration and Maintenance

It is absolutely essential that all matters relating to burial are handled with the utmost professionalism. The systems for recording burials and checking graves prior to reopening must be absolutely foolproof.

In modern cemetery layout, there is a trend towards the 'lawn system'. This is a method of burial which keeps the internal obstructions of kerbs and headstones to a minimum so that maintenance can be as effective as possible. Many existing traditional cemeteries which have become unsightly through neglected maintenance have been converted to the lawn system.

In recent years, new technologies have been introduced for the excavation of new or existing graves. These include mechanised diggers for the excavation of spoil, and hydraulic rams to provide safety shuttering for the grave-diggers. Local authorities work in close liaison with private funeral directors who organise disposal of the dead on behalf of the relatives of the deceased.

Crematoria

The same need for rigid adherence to professionalism that applies to cemeteries also applies to crematoria. The recommended procedures are contained in a series of Cremation Regulations and the Cremation Act of 1952. Crematoria are usually sited within landscaped grounds that have provision for the scattering of ashes. In place of the headstones of a cemetery, crematoria may record tributes to the dead in the form of wall plaques or entries in a book of remembrance.

Cemeteries and crematoria are not usually associated with thoughts of recreation but many of them are havens for wildlife. Some disused cemeteries, particuarly in urban areas, have been treated as nature reserves with nature trails. There are several such sites in London. Some local authorities have organised open days at their crematoria to help allay public fears about the mystique surrounding the subject of cremation. These have generally proved to be very well received. For example, Bolton and Stockport have operated annual open days for several years.

Principal Organisations

There are many organisations involved in the provision of parks and amenity recreation. Some of these organisations, such as Sports Councils, have recreation provision as one of their primary objectives. With others, like the Forestry Commission, it is a secondary but none the less significant objective.

This section looks at two of the major providers that are not dealt with elsewhere in this book. It examines their organisational structures and how they have developed to their present positions. It explains their roles today and how they fit into the framework of recreation provision.

The Forestry Commission

Historical Background

Some 5000 years ago Britain was well wooded. Clearance over the centuries and particularly during the Industrial Revolution and the Napoleonic Wars, meant that by 1918 only 5 per cent of the land remained wooded and we were almost totally dependent on imported timber.

The Forestry Commission was established by an Act of Parliament in 1919 and was given the general duty of promoting the interests of forestry, the development and expansion of Britain's forests and supply of timber. The Wildlife and Countryside (Amendment) Act of 1985 has most recently had an impact on the Forestry Commission's policy, which must now try to achieve a reasonable balance between the interests of forestry and the environment.

Structure

The Forestry Commission has both the status of a government department and a state-run industry. It reports directly to three Forestry Ministers:

1. The Secretary of State for Scotland.
2. The Minister for Agriculture, Fisheries and Food in England.
3. The Secretary of State for Wales.

The Forestry Commission is headed by eleven commissioners, of whom seven, including the Chairman, are part-time. The remaining four are full-time and are also senior officers in the Commission.

For the purposes of administration, Britain is divided into seven conservancies, each under the control of a Conservator. Currently there are also approximately 8000 other officers and manual staff, including contractors, working for the Forestry Commission.

The structure looks like that in Figure 5.1.

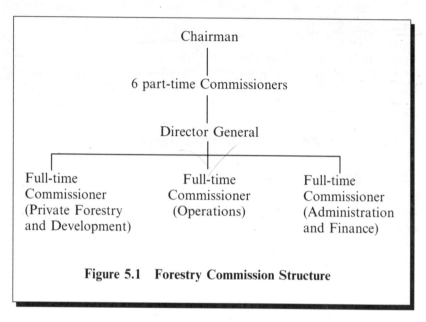

Figure 5.1   Forestry Commission Structure

Table 5.3   Activities on Forestry Commission Land

Archery	Nature study
Backpacking	Orienteering
Camping	Picnicking
Caravanning & touring	Pony-trekking
Canoeing	Potholing
Caving	Rambling
Clay pigeon shooting	Rock-climbing
Coarse fishing	Rough shooting
Deer stalking	Rowing
Field studies	Sailing
Forest drives	Skiing
Game fishing	Swimming
Horse-riding	Walking
Motor rallying	Wildfowling

Source: Forestry Commission 'Recreation in Forests', in *The Forestry Commission and Recreation Commission Paper No. 2* (Forestry Commission, 1988).

The Forestry Commission and Recreation

The commission is responsible for managing over 1.1 million hectares, which provides ample scope for recreation. There are seven Forest Parks within the estates, and many other areas are also open to the public. There is also a division responsible for Conservation and Recreation which administers the following:

Camping and caravan sites	33
Picnic places	615
Forest walks and nature trails	611
Visitor centres	20
Arboreta	20
Forest drives	8
Forest cabins and holiday homes	192

In addition there are facilities provided on lands leased to other organisations for recreation purposes. The range of activities on Forestry Commission land is shown in Table 5.3.

The National Trust

The National Trust as a charitable organisation was founded by private individuals in 1895. Its first purchase was 4.45 acres (1.8 hectares) of land in North Wales, overlooking the Barmouth estuary. In 1907, the Trust was incorporated by Act of Parliament, which gave it certain important benefits. Its mandate is 'to promote the permanent preservation for the benefit of the nation, of land and buildings of beauty or historic interest'. The Trust has been granted the power to declare its property inalienable which means that it can resist compulsory purchase orders. Trust property cannot be sold or mortgaged.

The Trust's Country House Scheme followed the 1937 Act of Parliament, which allows a country house, with or without its contents, to be presented to the Trust with an adequate endowment fund to maintain it in perpetuity. In return the donors and their descendants may continue to live there rent-free, subject to there being reasonable public access, and that the original character and fabric of the property be preserved.

In 1965 Enterprise Neptune was launched, which is a scheme to acquire as much unspoilt coastline as possible in the British Isles. Over 500 miles (804.5 kilometres) of coastline is now owned by the Trust. The Trust is the third largest landowner in the United Kingdom and owns 1 per cent of all land in England and Wales including 230 historic houses and a number of entire villages. It also owns 7.5 per cent of the National Park land.

The National Trust and The National Trust for Scotland are not government bodies, but have received government finance. There are well over one million members of the Trusts and the annual subscriptions make a substantial contribution to their income.

There are about 170 administrative staff who work in the head office in London and in the sixteen regional offices. The head office for the National Trust for Scotland is in Edinburgh. Trust policy is decided by a Council which consists of fifty-two members. Half are elected by trust members and half nominated by national institutions such as the Royal Horticultural Society, the British Museum and the Ramblers' Association. The twenty-eight strong Executive Committee appointed by the Council in turn appoints a number of voluntary regional committees, the members of which have expert knowledge of subjects concerned with the Trust's work, such as horticulture, forestry, fine arts, and architecture.

The primary objective of the National Trust is that of preservation, and it believes that this should always take precedence over public access. This conflict between preservation and access is resolved by the policy of the Trust to limit access in order to preserve. Annually over 6.5 million people visit the Trust's houses and gardens and such a pressure of visitors could easily spoil the amenity that visitors have travelled to enjoy. The gardens were originally laid out for the pleasure of the owner and were never intended to accommodate thousands of visitors. Damage becomes inevitable. Foot traffic can cause serious damage in houses, and erosion on sand-dunes and moorland. Some tenanted farms, and young plantation and nature reserves, are kept out of bounds to visitors, especially when breeding birds may be put at risk by disturbance.

The National Trust undoubtedly plays an important part in recreation provision in Britain. The tourist industry draws heavily on its resources and the number of foreign visitors adds a welcome boost to the nation's economy. The Trust provides an important service to the nation by preserving and maintaining much of what is considered to be the best of the British countryside. Few other organisations could claim to attract anything like the same number of visitors on a regular basis.

Exercise

Visit a National Trust facility and find out as much as you can about it, for example who owns it, how it is maintained, what it costs to run, the income, how many visitors it has, and so on.

Future Prospects

It is difficult with any subject area to predict the future, but a combination of past records and current trends gives valuable pointers to the way ahead.

As far as local government is concerned, one of the future issues of concern is that of contracting out parks management to the private sector. This is the result of a government belief that local authorities should compete in the market place for services that they have traditionally provided without competition. Many people in local government are concerned that competitive tendering inevitably means that work will be lost to the private sector. They are also worried that standards will fall, particularly in the case of the maintenence of amenity facilities. It will be several years before the true picture emerges.

To overcome the continual financial problems inherent in an organisation that is largely funded externally, closer links are being forged with the private sector. There is also a trend to encourage the public in self-help schemes and to extend the use of volunteers to make the available resources stretch further.

Dr Terry Stevens, in his chapter on Countryside Recreation, has explained some of the major issues facing parks and countryside landscape over the next few years. With reference to our National Parks, the threats can be summarised as follows:

- Quarrying and mining.
- Water and power schemes.
- Trunk road building.
- Military training.
- Pressure for development.
- Changes in agricultural practice.
- Inadequate funding.
- Increasing numbers of visitors.
- Rural depopulation.
- Insensitive forestry planning.

The National Parks need public interest and involvement to maintain their current status. In a democracy, large numbers of people banded together can form pressure groups to influence public decisions. The National Parks themselves were born out of such public commitment.

The Council for National Parks aims to promote the National Park objectives and to represent the interests of all who care for their future. The member organisations represent voluntary wildlife, recreation and conservation interests. Critics comment that the membership of the

National Parks Authorities has become biased towards the farming community. The numbers of members with a farming background has increased by 50 per cent since 1979. Proposals for new National Parks, such as in the South Downs and a Cambrian National Park in mid-Wales, have been unsuccessful. In the latter case, the concept was opposed by local farming interests. Regional Parks have a bright future in that they enable huge numbers of the population to have access to an extensive range of facilities at relatively close quarters. The Regional Parks perhaps provide a solution to the potential threat to green belt land by housing and industry, and they also give a structured framework for the redevelopment of land damaged by neglect or industrial abuse. They have the flexibility to respond to recreational needs as trends change, because they provide a venue for such a wide range of activities. It is highly likely that many more will be created in the near future, probably using money obtained from both the public and private sectors.

It seems likely that the Forestry Commission's role will continue to change in the future. Greater emphasis may be placed on providing for recreation and protecting the environment, and less on commercial timber production. If current trends do continue, the Forestry Commission could possibly become the most important provider of recreation, and guardian of the environment in Britain.

For other agencies, such as the Countryside Commission, the Sports Council, and the new Water companies, future prospects are particularly uncertain. The major issues have been dealt with elsewhere in this book, but there can be little doubt that the 1990s will prove a watershed for the future health and vitality of our parks, amenities and open spaces.

Further Study

Each week, obtain a copy of a local newspaper. Read through it carefully and thoroughly. Cut out and save any articles relating to parks and amenity matters. Collate the information in chronological order.

After a period of six months, go through the articles that you have saved and write short notes on the following:

(a)   Which single topic received the greatest press coverage? Explain why you think this topic was considered so important.
(b)   Calculate the percentage of articles containing references to financial matters. Of these, what percentage referred to financial cutbacks?

(c) Give three examples of articles containing references to proposed developments. What are your views on these developments?

(d) Calculate the percentage of articles criticising the quality of service provided to the community. Give one example from the public sector and one from the private sector.

Questions
1. Briefly outline the differences between Urban Parks and Regional Parks.
2. What role can botanic gardens play in conservation?
3. Describe the main advantages of cycleways.

References

CIPFA (1985) *Leisure and Recreation Statistics Estimates*, CIPFA, February 1985.

Countryside Commission, *Cycle Hire*, advisory leaflet No. 6, Countryside Commission.

Forestry Commission (1983) *A Policy for Cycling in the Forest*, Forestry Commission.

Forestry Commission (1980) *Recreation in Forests*, Forestry Commission.

Lee Valley Regional Authority, *Annual Report*, Lee Valley.

London Borough of Hillingdon (1985) *Colne Valley Park* – proposals for the Regional Park, London Borough of Hillingdon.

Office of Population, Censuses and Surveys (1985) *General Household Survey 1983*, HMSO.

Scottish Tourist Board, *Economic Impact of the Edinburgh Festival*, Scottish Tourist Board.

Sports Council, *Trim Trails – their design and use*, Sports Council.

Sports Council (1984) *Specifications for Artificial Sports Surfaces*, 3 vols, Sports Council.

Sports Council (1985a) *Artificial Grass Surfaces – for Soccer, Hockey and Multi-Games Areas*, State of the Art Report, Sports Council.

Sports Council (1985b) *Artificial Grass Surfaces for Association Football*, Sports Council/Football Association.

H. Thorpe (1969) *Committee of Inquiry into Allotments* (the Thorpe Report), HMSO.

Garden Festivals – individual guides from the festival office as published.

Further Reading

F. W. Hawtree (1983) *The Golf Course*, E. & F. N. Spon.
The Institute of Recreation Management (1981) *The Recreation Management Handbook: A handbook for organisations*, E. & F. N. Spon.
R. King (1985) *Royal Kew*, Constable.
A. J. Patmore (1983) *Recreation and Resources*, Basil Blackwell.
G. Plumtree (1985) *Collins Book of British Gardens*, Collins.
G. S. Thomas (1979) *Gardens of the National Trust*, National Trust.
T. Wright (1982) *Large Gardens and Parks*, Granada.
M. Young (1987) *Guide to the Botanical Gardens of Britain*, Collins.

158

Keith Goodwin (left) obviously has great faith in his daredevil son Darius (8) as he kicks off his father's hat from his stunt bike while standing on the saddle (*reproduced courtesy of Camera Press; photograph © John D. Drysdale*)

6 Play and Playwork

Stephen Rennie

All children play. Play is a universal process, most evident in the young. Like the processes of eating, sleeping and procreation, play is easily recognised, but not well understood. Every major reference to children since the dawn of recorded time has acknowledged their play, though few have recognised its crucial role in childhood. Without play there are no arts, no sports, no games. It is argued that it is the most powerful tool of all in developing understanding of the social and physical environment.

There are a variety of definitions of this process, ranging from the simple to the highly technical. For the purposes of this chapter, play is taken to be the enjoyment of social, physical, imaginative, intellectual and emotional activity for its own sake. This is a practical definition aimed at the needs of adults working with children at play or providing facilities to meet the needs of children at play. It works well for that purpose, but does not go into the depth a student of play would need.

Play is not something limited to humans. The young of all higher animals play. The more complex their adult social behaviours and decisions, the more complex their play. It is a learning process developing physical, social, emotional and intellectual skills, and reinforces behaviour which benefits the player.

Like the other biological processes, play carries its own reward. There is a pleasurable feeling to be gained from engaging in play, just as there is in eating something you like. The pleasure comes from the engagement, not necessarily from any achievement. We do not really understand the biological role of play. We know that animals will play even when they are hungry or tired and that they will expose themselves to risk in pursuit of their play. The fact that play has not been bred out of animal behaviour shows it must have very high survival value.

Given that basic understanding, it is hardly surprising that almost every historical account of childhood contains reference to their play. It is perhaps surprising that play has been held in such little respect by adult society. As far back as the Ancient Greeks, a philosopher was publicly criticised for playing dice with children. The Roman Emperor Augustus was rebuked in the Senate for spending too much time playing knuckle bones with children. Adulthood came to be equated with seriousness, childhood and play with frivolity. Yet, in the words of the philosopher J. Huizinga, 'Play is a thing by itself. The play concept as such is of a higher order than is seriousness. For seriousness seeks to exclude play, whereas play can very well include seriousness.'

Despite the development of this general attitude, there have always been some attempts by adults to understand the nature of play, as distinct from its effects. Theories such as 'burning excess energy' have gained general credibility in the past, despite their illogical nature. The Duke of Wellington's view that the battle of Waterloo was won on the playing fields of Eton has been seen as a commendation for the activities of sport and physical exercise, rather than an insight into the growth of understanding inherent in the play process.

Once child psychology was established as a serious field of study, it became possible for adults to examine the role of play without looking frivolous. Its nature as a fundamental learning process is becoming more and more clearly recognised and, as that recognition gains wider public acceptance, its role in our leisure services will assume greater and greater significance. An increasing number of researchers and serious writers now believe that play is fundamental to all cultural development.

Table 6.1. Breakdown of play staff in England and Wales according to type of work

Type of work	Number	Percentage
Organiser	229	4
Supervisor	754	14
Face-to-face worker A	3076	57
Face-to-face worker B	1305	24
Face-to-face worker C	38	1
All face-to-face workers	4419	82
Total classified	5402	100

Source: Play Board (1986a) D. Clarke, J. Coffin and C. Parkinson, Survey of Play Staff Working in 11 local authority areas.

Notes: Face-to-face worker A: staff with face-to-face contact with children, supervising or facilitating their activities, who may be left in sole charge of children.

Face-to-face worker B: staff with face-to-face contact with children, but who may not be left in sole charge of children.

When the returns were received, it was apparent that a fifth category was needed –'face-to-face worker C who the authorities had been unable to classify as A or B. Only 38 members of staff came into this category.

Commercial providers of recreation facilities have always given play a high profile, for adults as well as children, the fairground with its vivid new experiences being the best example. By the late nineteenth century, some local authorities were providing play areas and running summer playschemes as their contribution to children's play. Platt Fields in Manchester had a holiday playscheme in 1880 and some London boroughs started even earlier. In Denmark, in 1944, came the first facility to express modern understanding of the nature of play with the creation of the 'Junk' playground at Emsdrupp, soon after followed by the first of Britain's adventure playgrounds. Since then, supervised play facilities have flourished in the statutory and voluntary sectors in Britain.

Playwork – adult involvement in play provision – is here to stay. It is an essential factor in leisure management wherever and whenever children are involved. Most local authorities and voluntary agencies recognise this relatively new field of work as one which has a great deal to offer them in their provision of leisure services. The commercial sector has been slow to catch on, but now started, may catch up quickly. An analysis of the number and different types of playworkers in the public sector is given in Table 6.1.

Provision and Facilities

Toys

Toys are by far the commonest form of play provision. There can be very few households in Britain that have children in residence but no toys for them. They represent a significant factor in family expenditure. Yet play with toys is only a small proportion of the totality of a child's play (see Table 6.2 on page 162).

At their best, toys enhance and enable play. They can increase the span of attention of a child to a particular activity, encourage the development of complex skills, improve communication between children playing together, and give depth to fantasy play. Some have been around, essentially unchanged, for generations. The best tend to be simple and flexible to respond to children's varying needs.

Not all toys are helpful in this way. Some are downright dangerous. Others are boring and unimaginative. A few are so complex, fragile and expensive that their use is work, rather than play. The tale of the child who would rather play with the box or wrapping paper than the expensive gift is based on real observation, and is far from uncommon even in this designer age. Cost does not appear to be a major factor. Some of the least played-with toys are the most expensive. Some of the cheapest and most crassly commercial are effective and well-used.

Table 6.2   Children's preferences for after-school activities

Activity	Percentage of children who mentioned activity	
	Summer	Winter
Outdoor	57	36
Indoor (not at home)	9	15
Indoor (at home)	31	42
Particular activities mentioned		
Non-specific play	20	19
– outdoor	12	9
– indoor	8	10
Swimming	14	8
Watching TV	12	16
Cycling or BMX	11	5
Organised sport		
(apart from others listed)	9	9
– outdoor	7	3
– indoor	2	6
Football	5	3
Horse-riding	4	5
Read/write/draw/paint	4	9
Total organised activities	25	26
Total non-organised activities	75	74

Source: 'Makeway for Children's Play', Play Board (1985).

Toy figures and models have always been popular. They are to be found buried with their owners in graves thousands of years old. Whether in the form of dolls, soldiers, Action Man, Star Wars, He-Man, or My Little Pony, they can be a focus for emotional soothing through fantasy, as well as for more exploratory role play. They are popular with children of all ages, and some adults as well.

Construction kits build on the desire to create real things, to express those imagined, or to enhance imaginative stories. The best of them are truly wonderful tools, combining the development of physical dexterity with imaginative expression that can be shared. If well designed, they are able to be used very flexibly. They do not impose limits on the child, but tend to stretch the imagination.

Computer games are a straightforward extension of books. They add an interactive dimension which has a magnetic attraction for many children. Curiously, they were not originally designed for children at all, but were devised by computer programmers for each other. The whole Dungeons and Dragons phenomenon is adult fantasy, which just goes to show how much play features in adult lives if allowed to flourish. Despite the fears occasionally expressed about the addictive nature of computer games, there is little indication that the activity itself has any harm to it, any more than compulsive reading.

Table games are another type of toy that has its roots in adult activity. They are often used more by the adults in a family than the children. Partly this can be due to their length of playing time, often well beyond the likely span of attention of the age of children at whom they are marketed. In addition, they can be very inflexible in use, which children find hard to take when at play. A common use of table games is to set up an activity that can be shared by adults and children. As with sports, this is a key role for play in a society that largely excludes children from sharing work with adults.

There is only a thin divide between toys and sports equipment, but it is a real divide. Children are as capable as adults of taking a sport seriously and they are not playing when doing so. It would be a great mistake for a playworker to treat a competitive game of football in the same way as a casual knockabout with a ball. In much the same way, bicycles, carts and other similar devices can be both toys and serious modes of transport. Children are very aware of the difference, as adults are, in those countries where they do not have ready access to vehicles.

British Standard 5665 governs the design and manufacture of toys. From January 1990 it is illegal to sell toys in the UK which do not reach this standard or an equivalent European Community Standard.

Play Areas

Play areas are the most obvious public provision for children's activities. Frequently located in parks, they have changed little from the time the Victorians first created them in quantity, to almost the present day. A great many still remain rather barren tarmac areas dotted with swings, slides, a climbing frame and perhaps a roundabout. Despite huge efforts by many parents, a great many designers, almost all playworkers, several manufacturers and not a few politicians, far too many are boring and dangerous.

The contribution to children's play made by equipped play areas is frequently exaggerated by local authorities, who lack the imagination to make more diverse provision. They are often used to excuse inadequate attention to the creation of safe residential streets, or to divert attention from unsatisfactorily high density developments. Yet there are documents readily available which clearly define this aspect of children's play need.

As far back as 1972, the Department of the Environment recognised some of the problems involved and noted that some other countries, notably Denmark, had made great progress in this field. Circular 79/72 *Children's Playspace*, gave local authorities both the power and the resources to increase provision for children's play in new housing. This was followed in 1973 by *Children at Play: Design Bulletin 27*, which expanded on the theme. Sadly, in 1981, the new Minister at the Department of the Environment, Neil McFarlane, reduced *Circular 79/72* to advisory status, despite the fact that he was this country's first ever Minister for Play.

British Standard 5696 sets out guidance for the construction, installation and maintenance of large-scale play equipment intended for permanent installation out of doors. Its provisions include test procedures for checking the suitability of equipment and it is paralleled by standards in other European countries. All will soon be overtaken by unified European Community standards, which are likely to be rather more far reaching than the British Standard.

Exercise

Question about twenty children aged 9–12 years in your locality. Where do they play after school and on Saturdays and Sundays? What do they do there? Assess how much of that play involves toys, play equipment, play areas. How much is informal activity 'on the street'? How much television do they watch?

Provision – the Public and Voluntary Sectors

Despite showing concern over toy safety and play-area provision, central government has never expressed any great level of interest in supervised play provision, development of which has largely come about through the efforts of voluntary organisations and community groups. Where central government *has* become involved, it has normally influenced development away from issues of good quality play provision towards issues of child-care. Local government has always had a more positive attitude towards *supervised* play provision, but distribution of its resources is strongly influenced by central government priorities.

Provision for children under five reflects this situation fairly vividly. Playgroups and Mother and Toddler Clubs receive no statutory blessing.

Despite their evident popularity with parents and children alike, they do not even receive specific mention in legislation. Other than checking the suitability of their premises and supervisors, few authorities give them much in the way of support. Yet the high level of demand is demonstrated by the Pre-School Playgroups Association, one of the largest and best-managed voluntary organisations in the country.

On the other hand, day nurseries and nursery classes have a high profile in central and local government. They are specifically approved of in legislation and all county and metropolitan authorities have officers with responsibilities for their development.

At first glance, the operation of a day nursery, nursery class or playgroup may appear to be very similar. An attentive person is likely to be with a group of children who are painting, playing with sand or water, listening to stories, or wheeling about on tricycles. The differences are more organisational than philosophical.

Most playgroups are child-centred. Not only is the child and its play the most important aspect of its operation, it is the prime reason for the operation of the project. The play needs of the children are the foundation of forward planning. Most will be managed by a committee of parents of children attending the sessions. Funding is likely to come from sessional charges, often supplemented by fund-raising through jumble sales, and other activities. A few may benefit from limited grants from the more enlightened local authorties.

Day nurseries are usually run by Social Services (within family centres), or the commercial sector. A few, usually called 'workplace nurseries' are run by companies for the children of their employees. Their principal rationale is to care for the children in the absence of their parents. The best are as good as playgroups in meeting children's needs; many, however, do not meet those standards. The hours of operation of day nurseries tend to reflect parent's needs, rather than those of the children, so they are normally much longer than those of playgroups.

Nursery classes may be grouped into a nursery school, or run within primary schools, the latter being more common. Their hours of operation are usually similar to those of playgroups, but their philosophy is closer to that of the day nursery. Many see themselves as countering an educational and social disadvantage of children, prior to entering school. As with the day nurseries, the best are as good as playgroups, though many fall short of that standard in terms of play provision.

In addition to these types of provision there is some recreational provision for very young children through sports. From the age of three, for example, they may undertake gymnastic courses with national awards. Commercial organisations such as Tumble Tots offer a similar type of activity.

Exercise
Find out, from your local authority and/or library, about play provision for children under five in your district. Who runs the sessions? How are they funded?

Supervised play provision for older children is more diverse and is less common than for the under-fives, though where it does exist, it is often better funded. In contrast, opportunities for more directed activity increase as children get older. Sports training and coaching, cadet forces, Scouts, Guides, Boys Brigade, and most other uniformed organisations, fall into this area.

The main types of supervised play provision are:

Full-time
- Adventure playgrounds
- Play centres
- Activity centres
- Children's houses

Part-time or part-year
- Holiday play schemes
- After-school clubs
- Junior youth clubs
- Play sessions in youth, community or leisure centres or in village or church halls.

None of these are well-defined or separated types of provision, but each is likely to show particular characteristics.

The *adventure playground* is likely to be open all year round, five to seven days a week. It will have at least two full-time members of staff, plus part-time staffing which may vary seasonally. There will be an area of land, securely fenced, where children and staff build play structures and dens. Some of these may be very large and complex. Children may well be allowed to have cooking fires and small bonfires on the site. A building with toilets, office, stores and play room is likely to be available. Activities within the building usually include table tennis, pool, arts and crafts of all kinds, refreshments and records or other sources of music.

Play centres normally only have a building, though they may have limited outdoor space as well. In the building they tend to offer a similar range of play opportunities to those available on an adventure play-ground, but they may be rather more structured and organised in their delivery. The age range of children using play centres is often a year or two younger than that of adventure playgrounds.

Where the title *activity centre* is used, this tends to reflect a slightly more structured approach than that of a play centre, though facilities are usually the same. This is not a hard and fast rule, but an observation of current practice. In the same way, an activity centre is likely to have more sophisticated activities on offer such as photography or pottery.

The term *children's house* really refers to a very specific type of play project promoted by the Children's House Society. These are complex projects with clear objectives in social education. Occasionally the title is used by projects more closely resembling play centres in their operation.

Holiday play schemes are an almost universal type of part-time supervised play provision in Britain. Most operate in the long summer holiday, but an increasing number run at Christmas and at Easter. The title covers a range of provision from a few volunteers in a church hall, to sophisticated staffed sessions planned into the programme of a play centre or adventure playground. The great majority of local authorities in England and Wales support holiday play scheme provision to some degree. Many provide their own programme of schemes. Some provide grant aid to voluntary organisations and community groups. Holiday play schemes vary widely in the type of play opportunities they offer. They are greatly influenced by the resources and the nature of the venue available to them and by the interests of the staff and volunteers they attract. Some are almost wholly arts and crafts based, whilst others are totally sports and games orientated. Voluntary schemes of this kind are often the starting point for community involvement in other types of supervised play provision.

The title *after-school club* usually implies an element of child care in the provision. Many of these clubs are established with a view to offering a service to working parents immediately after school. Some offer an escort service to the club from local schools and may even be able to provide transport. Where clubs are provided with this kind of service in mind, they will usually offer a snack meal to children attending. Activities tend to be very similar to those of a play centre, though they may be limited by their part-time nature or by the premises they are able to use. This is very much a growth area in the field of playwork and has its own national organisation, *Kids' Clubs Network*.

Junior youth clubs usually provides a similar service for the nine (or eleven) to fourteen-year-olds, to that which ordinary youth clubs provide for older children. Many are run in youth centres, though with earlier start and finish times than their regular sessions. They may be seen by their staff as introductory sessions to youth clubs, or as provision that has worth in its own right. More of these sessions appear to be run by voluntary youth groups than by statutory groups, particularly in areas where the Youth Service feels that there is severe pressure on resources.

Play sessions are run by many organisations in almost every type of community facility. Generally aimed at children of primary school age, they may be found in youth centres, community centres, village halls, sports centres, leisure centres, church halls and libraries. These sessions are usually run by volunteers, often supported by staff of the venue. An increasing number of local authority Leisure Services and Recreation Departments are providing staffing for this type of provision through part-timers. The timing, organisation and activities of these sessions are very variable. Some have a strong club structure and a name, others are far more casual. The majority make a small charge for attendance.

Country parks and heritage projects often provide a variation on play sessions based around environmental or heritage themes. Some of these are quite extensive and include links with local schools. An increasing number of libraries are also developing play sessions, mostly but by no means exclusively centred on reading and stories.

Virtually all local authority Leisure Service Departments worthy of the name will offer at least holiday play schemes and play sessions as part of their planned provision of a comprehensve service to the community. In addition to the service these sessions provide for children, they also enable a greater take-up of leisure opportunities by parents. It is very apparent that children who use major leisure facilities in this way are more likely to continue to use them as they grow older, than those denied the opportunity.

Exercise
Create a 'play map' of supervised play provision for older children in a designated area. Distinguish between adventure playgrounds, play centres, activity centres, holiday play schemes, junior youth clubs, uniformed organisations and leisure centres. Try and find out how the different kinds of provision are financed and managed.

Provision – the Commercial Sector

The commercial sector in Britain has been slow to develop supervised play provision for children of school age. In sharp contrast to the United States and to Europe, where children's residential and day camps are very common, we have only a few. Most of these are targeted at the children of upper income families, both by the nature of the activities they offer and by their cost. Holiday camps have their Redcoats, but few British campsites or caravan sites have an equivalent of the 'animateurs' who are almost universal on continental sites.

Over recent years there has been a steady growth in commercial supervised provision in holiday resorts. In the main, this provision is based on a development of the equipped play area found in most parks. The equipment is usually of larger size and is likely to be supplemented by an inflatable and a ball pond, but the nature of the provision is essentially the same. Supervision on these sites rarely extends beyond imposition of safety rules on behaviour.

Provision for children's play is a major component of most day-visitor attractions. Almost all market research in this field shows that children's wishes (or their parents' view of those wishes), are the main influence on choice of places to visit. The success and growth of theme parks is the most vivid example of this. Most theme parks are just greatly exaggerated children's playgrounds. Unlike the fairgrounds which they superficially resemble, with their giant roller coasters and other rides, theme parks have none of the subtle fringe-of-society feel of the fairground.

The Child in the Built Environment

The majority of children's play takes place in or very near their homes. Next to play in the home itself, the largest proportion of their play happens on the doorstep or within 25 yards (22.86 meters) of the house. In the majority of urban environments, including most estates, that means a large proportion of children's outdoor play takes place on the pavement or in the road. Small wonder then, that motor vehicles are the single biggest killer of children in Britain.

The National Playing Fields Association was formed in 1925 on the premise that urban children needed space in which to play. David Lloyd George welcomed its formation with one of the first recognitions of play by a ranking politician and statesman. His letter to the Inaugural General meeting said:

The right to play is a child's first claim upon the community. Play is nature's training for life. No community can infringe that right without doing deep and enduring harm to the minds and bodies of its citizens.

More recently, another major politician, Neil Kinnock, Leader of the Labour Party, wrote to the 1986 Annual General Meeting of the *Fair Play for Children Association*:

There is nothing more important in the world of the child than the right to play. Irrespective of cultural or social conditions, play is one of the most effective and universal methods of making relationships, of exploring the natural world, of beginning and extending the process of learning. As a route to citizenship its importance cannot be overestimated ... As the urban environment has become more depressing, as more and more families are condemned to unemployment and poverty, and to the despair and misery that this brings, the rights of children can sometimes be overlooked.

This must not happen. The privilege of power is the opportunity it gives to help the most vulnerable in our society – and among those who need the most vigilant care in the protection of their rights are the children. If we deny these rights, we prejudice and deform the future of our society ... This is something to which we, in the Labour Party, are deeply committed. That is why you have my personal support and my very best wishes for the future.

Given this kind of commitment, it might be expected that provision for children's play in and around the home would form a major component of planning legislation. It does not. With the exception of Circular 72/79, there is precious little mention of play in any legislation governing the way we design or build urban environments. And, as we saw earlier, even that Circular, which once gave firm guidance to local authorities and to developers of houses, has been downgraded to advisory status. Worse, the additional cash resources it once provided to enable local authorities to provide for play in housing developments, are no longer there.

Many of our planners and architects regard the problem of providing for play in an urban environment as being a very difficult one, to be resolved only by segregating children to play areas for their activities. The provision of these is often seen as discharging the responsibility of the developer to provide an adequate environment in which children might live and grow. Yet we have known for many years that such provision is inadequate of itself and, in recent years, further and better design solutions have become available. It is possible nowadays to provide adequate social amenities even in quite dense housing developments. Problems that resisted earlier attempts at resolution, such as the threat of the motor car, can be greatly diminished. Though they are usually more complex than their predecessors, these solutions are not necessarily more expensive for the developer. Their use in many of our new towns (Milton Keynes, Peterborough, and Warrington/Runcorn), has proved their worth.

Support Services for Supervised Play Provision

The ideas and abilities of any one playworker are soon exhausted by the demands of imaginative children. In addition, they may face, especially in the voluntary sector, demands for resources beyond the means of their project. Also, many playworkers feel they should recycle materials through the activities they provide.

The result has been the emergence of *play resource centres*, often with titles such as 'Children's Scrap Store'. These projects, built on the earlier work of adventure playgrounds, aim to persuade industry to part with waste materials that could be useful to children at play. The nature of these materials has changed over the years as industry has become more efficient at using the last scraps of raw materials. But offcuts of paper and card are still available from printers, a few newspaper publishers still pass out ends of newsprint rolls, and these projects have become ever more ingenious at finding raw materials and original ways of using them.

The larger projects of this kind offer bulk-buying arrangements for local play projects. By putting together the large number of small projects in a district, they can sell materials to them at greatly reduced cost. The range of materials is not usually very extensive, as individual projects vary greatly in the activities they offer, but paint, paper, clay and more basic art and craft materials can be purchased at prices well below those of local shops. Large items of equipment are likely to be available on hire. Camping equipment may be included in this, along with an inflatable and a generator for schemes running out of doors.

In addition, play resource centres may offer support services such as basic training for new playworkers. One or two of the larger ones also offer more advanced training. There is a national body set up by and for these projects, the Federation of Resource Centres. It is a voluntary body and has had a somewhat ambivalent attitude to statutory sector projects of this type over the years, but it enables most of these projects to exchange information and resources to make them more available to local groups. The power of this kind of exchange was demonstrated many years ago by the Resources Officer of the National Playing Fields Association, who obtained a large supply of gun nails from a firm in Wales. Within weeks, there was hardly an adventure playground in the UK which did not have a supply. Small stocks are still around today. Toy libraries offer a similar kind of service, but geared far more to the needs of parents and of the younger child. Through these projects, families whose income would not allow them to obtain a reasonable range of toys for their children, can borrow good quality toys for a period, often without charge. Many toy libraries have a service for children with disabilities, either obtaining adapted toys, or even running a workshop to adapt toys themselves. As with play resource centres, there is a national organisation for toy libraries, and in addition to other support services it produces an excellent periodical.

Other support services for playworkers include district Play Councils or Play Associations, a few regional Play Associations and a variety of national bodies. The national bodies, as listed below, tend to be specialist in nature.

National Playing Fields Association (NPFA) – the longest established of all, this body offers a wider range of services than its name implies. For many years it was the leading agency in the development of supervised play provision in Britain, encouraging, supporting and grant aiding the development of adventure playgrounds and play centres. Since the early 1980s it has pulled back more into the role its name suggests, but it still offers grants to a wide variety of play projects. Hundreds of playing fields around the country are owned by the NPFA or administered by them under trust arrangements.

Fair Play for Children – established as a campaigning organisation to promote more public play provision, Fair Play no longer gets the government funding which enabled it to employ staff and have an office base in its early days. It still produces publications addressing current issues in management of play areas, and remains often the only support available to small unfunded voluntary organisations.

The National Institute of Playwork was formed in the 1960s and is a membership organisation for playworkers. It concentrates on training and other issues that underpin the development of playwork as a profession and is the only body in this field of work that offers an endorsement service for playwork training. The Institute has never received grant support from local or national government.

Joint National Committee on Training in Playwork – playworkers as a group have always had a strong interest in training, as the durability of this body has demonstrated. From its early days, the organisation has struggled to establish the need for playwork training of a high quality as distinct from other professional training. Its vision is that playwork training should be closely tied to good practice, and that prior practice should be credited towards qualification. In addition, the organisation is commited to the principles of self-managed learning.

National Playbus Association (NPA) is a specialist organisation dealing with mobile projects. NPA has had remarkable success over the years in promoting the provision of playbuses in both rural and urban areas. The playbus rallies organised by NPA are spectacular events.

Pre-School Playgroups Association (PPA) – one of the largest and most effective voluntary organisations in Britain, PPA supports and encourages the provision of supervised play opportunities particularly aimed to meet the needs of three to five-year-olds. As the name suggests, playgroups are their main interest, though they influence and assist a much wider range of provision for very young children. The Association is a comprehensive organisation, employing training and development staff nationwide. The 'Doorstep' and 'Foundation' courses offered by PPA led the way in accessible high quality playwork training.

Kids' Clubs Network (formerly the *National Out of School Alliance*). With the growth in provision of organised facilities for after-school care, this group was formed to promote the special interests of this type of play project. A regular newsletter keeps members in touch with one another and the organisation has carried out some excellent research in this field.

Association for Children's Play and Recreation (Play Board) – this, the government's first attempt to create a link between its departments and the field of play was not an unqualified success. Play Board struggled along for three years with lukewarm support from the field of play, and even less support from the Department of the Environment, until its grant was withdrawn in 1987 and given to the Sports Council to operate directly. The organisation is of historical interest in that it was the first government body of its type ever to go into involuntary liquidation. Similar bodies such as the Countryside Commission, English Heritage, the Sports Council and the Arts Council have taken note of its fate.

National Children's Play and Recreation Unit. As a semi-independent body within the Sports Council, the unit inherited the mantle of Play Board, or at least as much as was covered by its grant funding. Unlike Play Board, it gives grants. Equally unlike Play Board, it is based only in London, with no regional offices. It is not possible to summarise the work of the Unit, as no comprehensive report of its operations has yet been published. It is evident though, that the Unit is involved in the promotion of examples of good practice around the country, both through grant aid in support of specific projects and the establishment of a small number of demonstration projects around the country. It is evident too, that the Unit is taking a serious interest in the endorsement of playwork training.

Administration and Finance

Unlike youth work, child care, sport, or social work, children's play has no 'home' in any one government department. Equally there is no uniform pattern of responsibility through any one local authority service. As a consequence, the administration of provision and its funding is wildly inconsistent from district to district around the country (see Figure 6.1 on page 174).

At central government level, the Department of the Environment (DoE) had a nominal lead role, though it took few steps in pursuit of this role other than to fund the National Children's Play and Recreation Unit through the Sports Council. The junior minister at the DoE traditionally had some responsibility for children's play but this has been subsumed under the general title of Minister for Sport. The same individual has had other responsibilities within the DoE, which have appeared more highly rated than children's play in the allocation of time to responsibilities. Following the transfer of the Minister for Sport from the DOE to the Department of Education and Science in the Autumn of

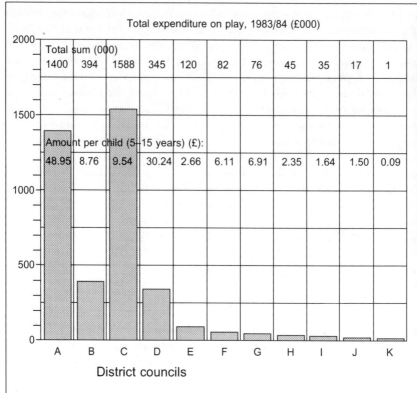

Total sum (000)										
1400	394	1588	345	120	82	76	45	35	17	1

Amount per child (5–15 years) (£):

48.95	8.76	9.54	30.24	2.66	6.11	6.91	2.35	1.64	1.50	0.09

Total expenditure on play, 1983/84 (£000)

District councils

Figure 6.1 Play provision in eleven district authorities

Source: Play Board (1985a); J. Coffin and C. Parkinson (1985a) *Play Provision in Eleven District Authority Areas: a feasablity study*, Play Board Research Project No. 1, January 1985.

1990, we will have to wait to see whether a closer alignment with school sport and education will benefit children's play.

Historically, central government has mostly funded play through short-term grant aid, rather than consistent targeted support of local government. For many years, the *Urban Programme* (originally called Urban Aid) was a major source of support for the development of play projects, especially supervised facilities. Initially under the Home Office, then under the DoE, the Programme saw the greatest expansion of this type of provision from around 1968 to 1984. Play projects maintained a high profile as the Programme grew more sophisticated. However, the development of projects suffered as Urban Programme resources were firmly redirected towards economic sector spending.

Other government departments have also supported the development of play provision, notably the Home Office through grants to national bodies, and the former Department of Health and Social Security in support of play provision for the under-fives. None of these grants have proved to be long-term in nature. The exception to this type of support was the funding established under Circular 79/72, which enabled local authorities to provide three square metres of playspace per child bedspace in new housing developments. To this was added £50 per child bedspace on the housing cost yardstick, a mechanism through which the government calculates grant aid and borrowing approval to local government for house building. But this was withdrawn in 1981, when the circular was reduced to advisory status. However, *Design Bulletin 27*, produced in support of this circular, remains the clearest advice from central government on play provision in new housing developments. It is now somewhat out of date, and it never did match up to the better standards produced in countries such as Denmark. Nevertheless, it is still an important document for architects and planners.

Exercise
Visit a high-density housing development locally or in your nearest town or city. Find out what provision there is for children's play in the immediate locality. Visit a village in a rural area and find out what is provided for children's play in that community. How does play provision differ between rural and urban areas, and why?

The effects of reliance on short-term grant aid was to further confuse the management of supervised play projects resourced by local government. A great many were initially run by voluntary management projects, particularly where the funding had come via the Urban Programme. However, there was always some level of supervision from a local authority department, as the local authority had to put up at least 25 per cent of the funding from its own resources.

Projects tended to be managed by the department which had supported the case for grant aid, or by the department responsible for general administration of grant aid. So play projects found themselves in Town Clerk's Departments, in Planning Departments, in Social Services, in Education, as well as in Engineer's, Park's, Recreation and Leisure. One or two even found their way into Housing Departments. New playworkers were given poor terms and conditions of employment, with the result that playworkers as a group had little chance of developing as a profession.

Over the years, many of the projects initially funded through short-term grant aid have been taken into main programme funding by local government. Indeed, this was one of the objectives of the Urban Programme, to enable new responses to growing urban problems. Sadly, however, a great many simply ceased to be funded, and closed. As a result, supervised play provision has gained a rather unfortunate reputation of being temporary in nature. It has also gained a similar reputation for being contentious, as few of the projects closed without a struggle, especially those funded through grants to voluntary sector groups.

Where supervised play has become established, even where it had a hesitant start, it forms an increasingly valued service today. It is no longer so isolated amongst colleague services, as its lessons are seen to have relevance to all those leisure services who number children amongst their customers, or whose customers tend to bring children with them. The recent growth of projects like the Bristol Exploratory has shown just how powerful play can be in regenerating other traditional services, such as museums.

Stereotypes and Relationships between Sectors of Provision

The origins of play provision in the statutory, voluntary and commercial sectors were quite separate and have largely remained so until quite recently. Each of these sectors has clearly established stereotypes of the others, and there has been enough truth in these to make the notions hard to change.

The statutory sector has been characterised by its parks, play areas, play leadership schemes and sports coaching. Both the other sectors have seen it to be unimaginatively represented by park keepers and men and women in track suits. The voluntary sector has been characterised by wild and woolly adventure playgrounds, largely staffed by the last of the 1960s dropouts or middle-class visionaries. Alternatively it is seen as village hall playschemes, provided by country ladies. The commercial sector has been characterised by 'Redcoats', at best poorly-trained, understaffed and working with a false enthusiasm. At worst it has been seen to be gross exploitation of parent and child alike in shoddy, unsafe seaside sites.

As a consequence of the strengths of these stereotypes, the relationship between each sector has rarely been strong. They tend not to share training, information, ideas or resources. Projects in partnership have been unusual. For example, the Federation of Resource Centres mentioned earlier, refused for several years to let statutory projects into membership, even though its voluntary sector members were heavily grant-aided by local government, and the resources they distributed came largely by gift from the commercial sector.

To everyone's gain, that situation is rapidly changing. There are a number of identifiable reasons for this. The voluntary sector is becoming less precious about its status and ideas, partly through increased confidence in its own strength and partly through partnership with enlightened local government in difficult economic times. The statutory sector has realised more and more the contribution that the voluntary sector has made over the years, and simultaneously, has been 'encouraged' to charge economic prices for leisure services. The commercial sector has become more aware of sophisticated consumer demand, requiring a far more professional approach to its provision and management of leisure services.

Legislation and Standards of Provision

Over the years, legislators have fought shy of mentioning children's play. As a term of its own, it has never been defined or specified in statute. Where is does occur, it is either found as 'play and recreation' or to be inferred from mention of activities such as sport, music, dancing or the arts in general. In relatively recent years it is inferred from the term 'children's welfare'.

The only directive legislation on levels of provision for children's play occurs in the 1944 Education Act. Section 53 of the Act lays a duty on Education Authorities to provide for children's recreation in places of education. It does not simply require the kind of hard-surfaced yards which schools traditionally provide, nor is it limited to the school day, but refers to a wide range of supervised and unsupervised opportunities for play, including off-site activities. Very few local authorities have implemented this legislation in the manner in which it was intended. Notable exceptions are Liverpool City Council, Manchester City Council, and the Inner London Education Authority, though none of these implements the section in full. A number of other county councils and metropolitan districts have some level of provision under this Act, but at a lower level. Lancashire County Council, for example, has significant provision in only one of its ten districts. Nottinghamshire County Council provides good support services right across the county, but little in the way of direct services.

In general, provision for play by local government is made under enabling legislation in the 1972 Local Government Act, but type, quality and quantity of provision is not defined by this legislation, which goes a long way to explain why local authorities vary so much in their provision. The Act applies to all levels of local government, from counties to parishes. It allocates no division of responsibilities in providing for play, with the result that there may be multiple levels of provision of a high quality in one area, while its neighbours have little or no provision at all.

In the following paragraphs, some of the enabling legislation more commonly referred to is summarised. They are well worth reading in their original form, as they are very general in their effect and more inferences can be drawn from them than is possible in this short section.

Directive and Enabling Legislation for Play Provision

Education Act, 1944 (repeated in 1981 Act)

Section 53 of this Act lays a duty on Education Authorities to provide within primary and secondary schools and centres of further education, adequate facilities for recreation. It goes on to enable these authorities to provide camps, holiday classes, playing fields and play centres. The Act defines an Education Authority as being the council as a whole, not just its Education Committee or Education Department, so provision can be made by any part of a county council or metropolitan district, to discharge its responsibilities under this section.

The phrasing of this section makes it reasonable to assume the intention of a general requirement to provide for children's needs within a district, rather than just a service to children attending a particular school. It is also apparent that the intention is that provision should be made outside of the school day and year.

Local Government Act, 1972

Section 137 of this Act is the one most often quoted to justify any expenditure by local government outside of mainstream services, as it gives them the power to spend money on anything which they think will be good for people in the area. It has a problem, however, in that the expenditure is very tightly limited. Where local authorities justify grants to voluntary sector groups under this section, there have been problems when other demands, such as economic development projects, have put pressure on the total amount available. In fact, local authorities should not pay for play provision under this section at all, unless it is in some very esoteric form, as all usual forms of play provision and grants in aid of this purpose to voluntary groups, are enabled by other legislation.

Section 144 empowers local authorities to provide facilities for recreation generally and allows them to encourage other people or agencies to do the same.

Section 145 specifically allows local authorities to provide for children's entertainments and to fund anything which contributes to their involvement in the arts. Sub-section (e) specifies a range of support costs which can be paid, including refreshments. This could be interpreted as allowing District Councils to provide meals at after-school clubs or other facilities, for play which has a child-care role.

Local Government (Miscellaneous Provisions) Act, 1976

Far and away the most general piece of enabling legislation for play. Section 19 of this Act, adds to the Local Government Act, 1972. This gives local government at all levels wide enabling power to provide any kind of facility for recreation, including equipment, supplies and staff. It also allows a local authority to fund facilities which are outside its own area, and to fund voluntary groups to carry out this work on its behalf. The section carries a definition of voluntary groups as being 'any person carrying on or proposing to carry on an undertaking other than for profit'.

Local Government (Miscellaneous Provisions) Act, 1983

Section 39 of this Act enables local authorities to offer personal accident insurance to volunteers providing services to local people. This includes services such as playwork, and can include work such as being on the management committee of a local play association.

Section 144 adds commercial and industrial activities to the general range of abilities of local authorities under Section 137 of the Local Government Act. This could be interpreted as meaning that grants or loans could be made to voluntary organisations to underwrite major fund-raising ventures of a trading or commercial type.

Children and Young Persons Act, 1963

Under Section 1, sub-section (1), metropolitan districts and county councils are required to give advice and assistance which will help to reduce the chance of children coming into the care of the authority. Most authorities of these kinds have special budgets for this purpose. Grants and other forms of assistance have been made from this source to many play projects offering a service to the children of familes under high levels of stress. This Act will be repealed and replaced by the Children Act as of October 1991.

Road Traffic Regulations Act, 1967

Section 26 of this Act allows a local authority to close a road so that children may use it for play. They can do this permanently or for limited periods.

Guidance and Direction on Standards of Play Provision

There is not much guidance available to playworkers or managers on play provision from government sources. Circular 79/72 from the Department of the Environment offers some guidance in the building of new housing. It originally gave local authorities power to spend a significant amount of money on provision for play associated with their own developments. It also lets them use Section 52 of the Town and Country Planning Act to require private developers to provide for children's play when building houses. *Design Bulletin 27* gives fairly detailed guidance on ways of meeting the directions of this circular. A new letter of guidance is in preparation by the DoE and is due for release early in 1991. It seems likely, at the time of writing, that this will concentrate on issues of child safety for equipped playgrounds. Unless local authorities specify play provision in their Local District Plans when identifying areas for future housing development, developers will always win on appeal against planning refusal, if the grounds are failure to provide for children's play.

It must be said though, that many local authorities still manage to persuade developers to provide for play, and to put up sums for later maintenance of play areas they provide. There is an agreed process for this, called the Leeds Formula, which most good planners are familiar with if pressed. Bolton Metropolitan Borough Council has a particularly good record in this respect. It has even managed to persuade a developer to put up a sum towards the revenue cost of a playworker in a local play centre, where that was a more effective way to meet children's play needs on a new housing development.

Nurseries and Child-minders Act, 1948

The provisions of this Act have generally been taken to apply to children under five, though the Act seems to refer to all children. Powers are given to metropolitan districts and county councils to set standards for the qualifications and number of staff who should be in charge. These vary from area to area and are available from the local Social Services department. Schools and other education authority premises and staff are exempt from the provisions of the legislation. The Act is due to be superseded by the Children Act in October 1991. This Act sets standards to include children up to eight years of age and broadens the powers of the Social Services departments in a number of ways, as they relate to supervised play provision.

Health and Safety at Work (etc.) Act, 1974

Heavy responsibilities are given to managers of supervised and unsupervised play provision by this Act, which covers both safe working practices and the provision of safe environments. Guidance notes are available from the Health and Safety Executive to explain the steps which must be taken, including the reporting and investigating of any accidents which occur. Serious breaches of this Act have led to criminal prosecutions. In addition to routine visits, Factory Inspectors can investigate complaints on safety matters from any source. They can close down facilities immediately, or issue instructions for remedial work to be carried out if they are dissatisfied with what they find on a visit.

Unfair Contract Terms Act, 1977

This Act limits the effect of disclaimer notices. It makes ineffectual those which say things like 'people entering these premises do so at their own risk'.

Occupiers' Liability Act, 1984

Under the terms of this Act, managers of playgrounds and play areas are required to show a higher level of care towards children than towards adults. In particular, Section 2(3)(a) states clearly that an occupier must be prepared for children to be less careful than adults. This section should be taken in conjunction with the duties conveyed by the Health and Safety at Work Act 1974.

General Duty of Care

In addition to statute, playworkers, whether in the statutory, voluntary or commercial sectors, are subject to a general duty to be careful of the well-being of children. This may be tested, if it comes to a court case, through the 'caring parent test', usually interpreted as meaning 'would a caring parent have done that in those circumstances?'.

It should also be borne in mind that although the British Standard on play equipment does not have the force of law, failure to provide equipment at least to that standard can be used as evidence against a manager in the event of an accident. The same will be true, possibly to an even greater extent, of the new European Standards (the SEN Standards), when they come into effect.

Local authorities and other statutory agencies are required to submit the names of people they intend to employ as playworkers, or use as volunteers, through a vetting process to check on previous criminal convictions. No convictions are regarded as 'spent' for this purpose, which primarily checks for offences related to children or use of violence. Job applicants or volunteers offering their services should always be asked for their permission before their names are submitted for this check.

Outside of the statutory sector, both the National Playing Fields Association and Fair Play for Children publish guidelines on standards of provision, covering quantity and quality. In addition, they offer advice on the provision of supervised facilities for chidren's play. The Out of School association will advise on provision which includes child care, and the National Playbus Association can help with information on mobile play provision.

Exercise
Review the various pieces of legislation referred to in the last few pages. Why is it advisable for leisure managers, playworkers, or others working with children to fully understand these aspects of legislation? Write a short report on what a 'general duty of care' means for people working in a specific area of children's play.

Training and Staff Development

The wide range of types of playwork has been referred to earlier in this chapter. It is reflected in provision for playwork training and in arrangements for staff development by their employers. Unlike the extensive and well co-ordinated network of training offered to youth workers, arrangements for playworkers are patchy and often poorly suited to their needs. Pre-school playgroup workers are the exception to this rule.

A very few local authorities, such as the London Borough of Islington, offer thorough and well-designed training for their staff. The great majority offer little or nothing in this field. The same holds true for the voluntary sector, though the proportion of their employees given some form of appropriate training is rather higher. There is almost no training for playworkers in the commercial sector.

Most training in playwork is little more than 'sitting by Nellie'. An individual with a skill is asked to pass it on to others in a fairly informal setting. The individual may have had no previous experience of training, or may not have had playwork experience, having brought the skill from another type of work entirely. The results are often deeply unsatisfying for all concerned.

Some of the college-based playwork training can also fall short of reasonable expectations. Several have been run by staff with good teaching abilities, but from another professional background. Without support from thoroughly experienced playworkers, their teaching has become distanced from the reality of working practices in the field. It is apparent too, that few of these courses communicate with one another, so many have had to go through their development processes without having the experience of their predecessors to inform them.

Bearing this in mind, about half of the local authorities who employ playworkers claim to offer some form of training, and seventeen colleges offer some level of play training on their premises, or support training for playwork staff elsewhere. Most play resource centres and similar projects offer some level of playwork training, and there are several specialist play training agencies, some in the voluntary sector and some in the commercial sector. The differences in these last two are often blurred, as many voluntary agencies are set up as trading companies, while several seemingly commercial companies in this field have little profit direction.

Though there is, as yet, no nationally agreed body to endorse play and playwork training, there are moves afoot in that direction and some effective benchmarks do exist. The Local Government Training Board has set the standard for training in respect of the management and maintenance of play areas. The National Institute of Playwork has been gradually increasing its endorsement of training courses for playworkers. Several BTEC courses in Leisure Studies have modules in playwork validated. CNAA have validated the Diploma in Higher Education in Playwork course at Leeds Polytechnic. From a somewhat dim past, playwork training may be about to creep into the light of day.

Exercise
List the various skills that you think a qualified playworker should have. Debate with colleagues whether such skills can be prioritised and outline what you think should be the key syllabus areas for a national training award.

Policy and Planning

One of the problems that has faced playworkers over the years has been the absence of any form of integrated policy on play provision at a local level. Though increasingly rare amongst metropolitan districts and the larger shire districts, this remains a problem in many counties and amongst smaller or relatively ineffective districts. There are still instances where the strategies of county and district not only fail to complement one another, but are firmly in conflict. Even in authorities with a strong commitment to play, it is not uncommon for there to be separate policies in a variety of departments, without any mechanism to co-ordinate effort.

The root of the problem would appear to be that provision for children's play is seen as an add-on service. Because it lacks directive legislation, and in other ways is not given fundamental priority, it is often planned into a council's services, and into the built environment, at a very late stage. The results can be chaotic. Take, for example, the desire of a local authority to persuade residential property developers to provide for children's play in new housing. Section 52 of the Town and Country Planning Act allows the authority not only to ask for the provision to be made, but to ask for a sum of money to be set aside for its maintenance for years to come. It is a very effective way of making provision. On many occasions, though, it fails, because the authority did not put a requirement for play provision in its Local District Plan, allowing the developer to appeal against refusal of planning permission on those grounds.

In similar vein, almost everyone recognises that a large proportion of shopping is done by women with children and that shopping centres are warm, bright and attractive places for young people to meet and socialise in a town centre. Yet few shopping developments provide for play, or are asked to by planning departments. Instead, after completion, the centre managers employ uniformed guards to keep children and young people out, to avoid the problems they can cause by blocking walkways and behaving boisterously around the shops.

There are many other examples of this type of problem, all with the same root cause. The answer is quite straightforward. We know that children play wherever they are. It is part of their very nature as children. As a society, we must provide for that play or live with the consequences. There is no point in complaining about vandalism and lack of respect by children towards adults, when we ignore their needs and show them no respect ourselves. Provision for play should be made wherever we know that children will be present. That includes housing, residential streets, schools and parks. It also includes shopping areas and leisure centres.

Every local authority needs a play policy which starts at the planning stage. That is the foundation on which its later provision can best be built. The example of those authorities with policies along these lines proves the point. Leicester City Council has a Play Council to oversee the implementation of its policy. That council includes representation from the voluntary sector and from the county council as well as its own departments. It suffers far less confusion in providing for play than most authorities, even though just as many different departments are involved in provision. Other authorities such as Rochdale MBC have equally successful arrangements. It is worth noting that not only do authorities such as these get more effective provision through good planning, they also get better value from their expenditure.

Developing a play policy is not just a matter of getting a few officers around a table, however skilled they may be. To be fully effective, it requires a consultation process with the community it is being designed to serve, including the children who will be its prime beneficiaries. The process of developing the policy can become a method of involving people in meeting children's play needs.

There can be considerable side benefits. Facilities in decline can discover a new lease of life through new user groups. New sources of support and funding can emerge. It can prove to be a major boost for local leisure services, make a major contribution to a district's visitor strategy, and even give a boost to flagging local economic development.

Exercise
Find out if your local authority has a policy for children's play. Which department(s) in the authority is/are responsible for implementing the policy? If there is a policy, try to find out what it is.

Future Prospects

As we gain a better understanding of play, so we realise more and more its crucial role in any form of provision aimed at families. Community workers have long recognised that one of the sure ways of catching and holding people's attention in communities under stress, is not to address their general needs directly, but to involve them first in providing for others. Holiday play schemes have been, and remain, a very common way of achieving this. After-school clubs are being used for this purpose more and more.

Provision made in this way can be very valuable in helping meet both the community work objectives and playwork objectives, but only if both are given due priority. Problems can arise if either is given precedence at the expense of the other. If community work priorities dominate those of playwork, the result can be unsatisfactory, even unsafe, provision for the children involved. If playwork priorities are given too high a level of importance, the result can be a loss of effort in tackling other community needs, or the local people involved can be made to feel inadequate in the face of demands for excellence in the service they provide.

Similar balances need to be struck wherever play opportunities are provided alongside other services. Since this is an increasingly common form of provision, the need to develop skills in making these balances is urgent. Managers of Leisure Centres do not need to be skilled play-workers, but if they are seeking to attract children, or offer services to children as part of developing a family leisure strategy, they need to have access to playwork skills at the planning stage as well as in the day-to-day operation of their centres.

Health services for children, especially hospitals, need to pay more attention to children's play needs. Most hospitals do provide some level of playwork support to the nursing of sick children, but too often it is very much an add-on service and given a very low priority. Since we know from extensive research that play is a crucial process in enabling a child to come to terms with sickness and disability and with grief, this is a serious omission in our provision for their health and well-being. Playwork has a major contribution to make to children's health services at many levels: in promoting healing; in coping with stress; and in coming to terms with new circumstances.

The therapeutic aspect of play also needs more attention in all fields of work where children's behaviour cause concern, including those dealing with seriously challenging behaviour. Children communicate very effectively through play, often more clearly than through language. The adult needs to try to understand the child's communication through its play at least as much as to attempt to give the child skills in communicating through use of spoken or written language. Many of our health care and similar services have come to this realisation. Others are beginning to turn more towards it.

In planning the built environment, there is clear evidence of a transformation in understanding the role of play provision. The growth of Woonervan (see B. Eubank-Ahrens, 1985) and similar treatments of residential streets, particularly in the New Towns, is a very hopeful sign. One day the playworker will rank in status with the traffic engineer, at consultations on the development of residential areas. Despite the advertisers, the car is slowly losing its shiny importance in our lives.

In general, the outlook for playwork is relatively rosy. Only sixty-five years after former Prime Minster Lloyd George sent his message about the importance of play to the development of a healthy society to the NPFA, its content is being taken seriously.

Further Study

The most effective way to develop an understanding of good practice in play provision is to experience it at first hand. Fortunately there are a number of local authorities and voluntary groups around the country which offer some aspect of this. The list of organisations at the end of this book is by no means exhaustive, but all have proved helpful to students in the past. Try to become involved in a practical aspect of children's play.

Another way of developing an understanding of play is to examine other cultures from a playwork point of view. Almost any film record of other cultures that includes children will show their play behaviours. Take, for example, the excellent film the BBC made of the Baka people in Africa, commonly referred to by us, but not by the Baka themselves, as pygmies. The film tells the story of one family in the main, following their daily lives over an extended period. Children feature strongly in the unfolding story. At one point the children of the group are shown in a play village they have created. The similarity between their activities and those of children on almost any adventure playground in this country is striking. They have built 'dens' out of leaves and branches. They have lit a small fire and are telling each other jokes and stories around it. They are cooking and eating treats around the fire. A great gulf may yawn between Western society and the lives of those pygmy villagers, but the difference between their children roasting bats over a fire in a hut made of leaves, and the British youngsters cooking sausages next to the adventure playground den is only a matter of materials. The process is identical.

Questions
1. Explain why it is important for the public sector to have a coordinated approach to planning for children's play.
2. Explain four aspects of legislation that a playworker should be aware of.
3. What do you think the skills of a playworker should be?

References

A. Bengtsson (1976) *The Child's Right to Play*, IPA.
Department of the Environment (1972) *Children's Playspace*, Circular 79/72, HMSO.
Department of the Environment (1973) *Children at Play : Design Bulletin 27*, HMSO.
B. Eubank-Ahrens (1985) 'The impact of Woonervan on children's behaviour', *Children's Environments Quarterly*, vol. 1, no. 4.
R. Fagen (1981) *Animal Play Behaviour*, Oxford University Press.
J. Huizinga (1949) *Homo Ludens*, RKP.
C. C. Marcus (1986) *Housing as if People Mattered : Site Design Guidelines for Medium Density Housing*, University of California Press.
Play Board (1985) *Makeway for Children's Play*, Play Board.
Play Board (1985a) *Play Provision in Eleven District Authority Areas: a feasability study*, by J. Coffin and C. Parkinson, Play Board Research Report No.1.
Play Board (1986a) *Survey of play staff working in 11 local authority areas*, Play Board.
Play Board (1986b) *Where Children Play*, Play Board.
Play Board (1987) *Children's Range Behaviour*, Play Board.
S. Rennie and W. Major (n.d.) *Environmental Design for Children's Play*, Peterborough City Council.
H. B. Schwartzman (ed.) (1978) *Play and Culture – Proceedings of the Association for the Anthropological Study of Play*, Leisure Press.

Further Reading

British Standards (1986) BS 5696, *Play Equipment Intended for Permanent Installation Outdoors*.
Canada Mortgage & Housing Corporation (1980) *Play Spaces for Preschoolers: Design, Guidelines for the Development of Preschool Play Spaces in Residential Environments*, Advisory Documents Revised 1980 (available from IPA/UK Resources).
E. Chace and G. Ishmael (1980) 'Outdoor Play in Housing Areas', in P. F. Wilkinson (ed.) *Innovation in Play Environments*, Croom Helm.
City of Birmingham (1984) *New Residential Development Design Guidelines*, City of Birmingham.
City of Newcastle upon Tyne (1985) *Play Provision in Residential Areas: Guidelines for Housebuilders*, City of Newcastle upon Tyne.
A. Clarke (1986) 'Safe Routes to School', *BEE* 178.
N. Coulson (1980) 'Space around the home', *Architects Journal*, December 1980.
Countryside Commission for Scotland/Forestry Commission (1984) *Providing for Children's Play in the Countryside*, Countryside Commission.
Department of the Environment (1985) *The use of conditions in planning permissions*, Circular 1/85, HMSO.

M. Francis (1984) 'Children's use of open space in Village Homes', in *Children's Environments Quarterly*, vol. 1, no. 4, 1984.

R. Hart (1979) *Children's Experience of Place*, Irvington.

R. Hart (1983) 'Wildlands for Children', *BEE* 141.

P. Heseltine (ed.) (1983) *Playground Management for Local Councils*, NPFA.

P. Heseltine (1985) *A Review of Playground Surveys*, Play Board.

P. Heseltine and J. Holborn, (1987) *Playgrounds: the Planning, Design and Construction of Play Environments*, Batsford.

R. Higman (1988) 'Traffic Calming', *Bulletin of Environmental Education*: BEE 199/200.

W. V. Hole and A. Miller (1966) *Children's Play on Housing Estates: a summary of two B.R.S. studies*, Ministry of Technology Design Series 46.

C. C. Marcus (1974) 'Children's Play Behaviour in a Low Rise. Inner-City Housing Development', in D. H. Carson, *Man–Environment Interactions*.

C. C. Marcus (1974) *Children in Residential Areas: Guidelines for Designers*, Landscape Architecture.

G. T. Moore (1983) 'State of the Art in Play Environment', in J. L. Frost and S. Sunderlin (eds) *When Children Play*, Conference Report.

R. C. Moore (1986) *Childhoods Domain*, Croom Helm.

National Playing Fields Association (1987) *Outdoor Playing Space Requirements 1986 review*, NPFA.

H. Naylor (1985) 'Outdoor play and play equipment', *Early Child Development and Care*, vol. 19.

M. Parker (1961) Report, *Homes for Today and Tomorrow*, HMSO.

Play Board (1985) *Make Way for Children's Play*, Play Board.

S. Plowden and M. Hillman (1984) *Danger on the Roads: the needless scourge*, Policy Studies Institute.

TEST (1988) *Quality Streets: How traditional urban centres benefit from traffic-calming*, TEST.

J. van Andel (1987) *Bibliography on Play and Play Environments*, Tilburg.

D. Verwer (1985) *Planning and Designing Residential Environments with Children in Mind: A Dutch Approach*, in P. F. Wilkinson.

P. F. Wilkinson (1985) *The Golden Fleece: in Search for Standards*, Leisure Studies, volume 4, No. 2, pp. 189–204, E. & F. N. Spon.

Hang-gliding in the Peak District
(*reproduced courtesy of Kay Simpson*)

7 Sport and Physical Recreation

Norman Borrett

Sport has been termed 'the opiate of the people'. Society is saturated with sporting events, sporting imagery, and sporting practice. We take part in it, discuss it, watch it, and consume it in increasing quantities. It has been suggested that sport takes up more time, for millions of people, than any other activity apart from eating, sleeping or working (Brohm, 1978). Sport has many forms, *The Oxford Companion to Sport and Games*, edited by John Arlott, lists over 200 activities ranging from animal-baiting to yachting, and many attempts have been made to define what sport is. In this introduction, the nature of sport and physical recreation will be discussed and then the popularity of different sport forms considered.

What is Sport?

The majority of activities are indulged in for their own sake, for the pure joy of participation. For many of us, sport is fun and provides an arena for being with friends and meeting new people, yet sport can also be a solitary experience that enables us to escape from others and the pressure of work and family life. Sport can provide physical thrills and 'peak experiences' that can stay with us a lifetime, and sport can be an entertainment, enabling millions of people to enjoy top-class performances from across the world. Sport can be relatively gentle, such as rambling and angling, or be very energetic, such as judo or squash. Some activities are highly competitive, whilst others have little formal competitive structure.

A useful model for examining the contrasting aspects of various *forms* of sport and physical recreation is that used by Haywood *et al.* (1989). The authors contrast forms of sport and physical recreation that are *active* and where the participants are involved in the *production* of skills or performances (association football and ice-dance are examples) with forms that are *passive* and involved in the *consumption* of experiences or performances produced by others (gambling on sporting events and spectating, for example).

Many writers have attempted to identify characteristics that are necessary and essential features for a satisfactory definition of sport. According to Haywood *et al.*, these features include:

- a symbolic test of physical or psychomotor skills;
- a competitive framework; which requires
- specific codified rules which constitute the activity; and
- continuity over time – a tradition of past practices. (pp. 52–3)

Together these characteristics are sufficient for an activity to be called a sport rather than any other aspect of physical recreation simply by applying a 'necessary' and 'sufficient' clause to the activity in question and noting the degree of match or mis-match in each case. Thus, a swimming race in the Olympic Games would satisfy all conditions at a high level in defining this activity as a sport, but a swim in the sea whilst on holiday would not satisfy conditions 2 and 3 and would thus define the activity as a form of physical recreation. Understanding the differences in sport forms is necessary for those who service sport if they are to identify the needs of participants and provide for different groups in society. Torkildsen (1986) argues that the more managers can understand about the form and nature of activities then the easier it will be to understand requirements, problems and solutions. A knowledge of sport forms will also assist managers in planning for and programming facilities and activities according to a range of criteria such as space, image, age, gender, numbers, skill, degree of competition, technical equipment, social and cultural factors. An analysis of sport forms will also guide managers on anticipated income and expenditure levels. Thus squash and keep fit generate high income but minority sports or those requiring a high degree of training or coaching are often costly.

What is Popular?

Table 7.1 demonstrates some of the most popular participation activities and demonstrate increased participation rates in a range of activities including walking, swimming (indoor), snooker and billiards, golf, and keep fit. There has also been a significant increase in the *frequency* of participation in a number of activities, as Table 7.2 demonstrates.

The increase in swimming participation does, however, need tempering as it is highly seasonal and the majority of the increase may be accountable to the increase in domestic and overseas tourism (Sports Council, 1988a). There is further evidence from the British Market Research Bureau (March 1990) that between 1985 and 1989 there were significant increases in participation rates in golf (+22.4%), hiking and rambling (+40.2%), and skiing (+40.0%). Another significant trend in

Table 7.1   Trends in participation rates in individual activities, all adults as percentage of persons aged 16 and over participating in 4 weeks prior to interview, Great Britain

	1977	1986
Outdoor		
Walking – 2 miles or more (including rambling/hiking)	17	19
Swimming (excl. public pools)	2	2*
Football	3	3
Golf	2	3
Athletics – track & field (incl. jogging)	1	3
Fishing	2	2
Cycling	1	2
At least one outdoor activity		
excluding walking	15	18
including walking	28	32
Indoor		
Snooker/billiards/pool	6	9
Swimming	5	9
Darts	9	6
Keep fit/yoga	1	3
Squash	2	2
Badminton	2	2
Bowls/tenpin	1	2
Gymnastics/athletics	–	2
Table tennis	2	1
At least one indoor activity	21	28

Source: Adapted from the Sports Council (1988a).

* See note 3.

Notes for Tables 7.1 and 7.2.

1. Only those activities undertaken by at least 2 per cent of respondents in either 1977 or 1986 in the 4 weeks prior to interview in the most popular quarter of the year are separately itemised in Table 7.1.
2. All Figures are rounded to the nearest whole number in Table 7.1 and to one decimal point in Table 7.2.
3. 1986 data groups together the two categories of 'outdoor swimming – excluding public pools' and 'outdoor swimming – public pools', previously shown separately, and is not therefore directly comparable with earlier data.

the popularity of activities is the rise of individual and solo pursuits and the stability, and in some cases decline, of traditional sports and team games.

Table 7.2 Trends in Frequency of Participation in Individual Activities (average number of occasions of participation by all persons aged 16 and over per year, Great Britain)

	1977	*1986*
Outdoor		
Walking – 2 miles or more (including rambling/hiking)	16.7	20.0
Swimming (excl. public pools)	1.4	2.2*
Football	1.7	1.9
Golf	1.4	1.6
Athletics – track and field (incl. jogging)	0.6	2.9
Fishing	0.9	0.9
Cycling	0.7	2.3
Tennis	0.7	0.8
Bowls	0.6	0.8
Camping/caravanning	0.8	0.6
Horse Riding	0.5	0.6
Swimming (public pools)	0.1	*
Cricket	0.4	0.4
Field Sports	0.3	0.2
Sailing (excl. windsurfing)	0.2	0.2
Rugby	0.2	0.3
Field Studies	0.6	0.4
Climbing/potholing	0.2	0.1
At least one outdoor activity		
Excluding walking	12.1	17.7
Including walking	28.8	37.8
Indoor		
Snooker/billiards/pool	5.0	7.9
Swimming	1.6	4.1
Darts	7.7	4.3
Keep fit/yoga	0.7	2.7
Squash	1.1	1.3
Badminton	1.0	0.9
Table tennis	1.7	0.7
Bowls/tenpin	0.5	0.7
Gymnastics/athletics	0.3	2.1
At least one indoor activity	20.2	26.1

Sources and notes as Figure 7.1.
* See Note 3.

What are the Benefits?

As well as the individual, social and aesthetic experiences that lead to general feelings of well-being and accomplishment referred to earlier, there are a number of other benefits that have been documented (in many cases to support funding requests from central government).

The Scottish Sports Council (1989a) refers to benefits under three broad headings: community benefits; international benefits; and economic benefits.

Community Benefits

There are three benefits that accrue to the community as a whole. Firstly, sport and physical recreation assist in the reduction of heart disease and thus lessen the use of the health services (Fentem, Bassey and Turnbull, 1988). Participation in sport has also been shown to contribute to a reduction in days lost through illness at work (Shephard, 1986). Secondly, participation in sport and physical recreation may contribute to the improvement in the health and well-being of the economically and socially disadvantaged (Whitehead, 1987). Finally, participation in sport and physical recreation can support community spirit and confidence. This may be particularly helpful in areas of social deprivation.

International Benefits

Success in sport at national and international level can contribute to national prestige and morale. Sport can also be used as a political catalyst to support certain policy initiatives (for example, sport in South Africa, and sport in the German Democratic Republic during the 1970s and 1980s). Success by nations in the international arena can also reflect on the spirit and attitudes of individuals in those nations.

Economic Benefits

Sport and physical recreation are major contributors to the national economy, generating an estimated £6.9 billion of total expenditure and generating over 370,000 jobs (Sports Council 1988a). It is estimated that central government receives a net gain each year of some £156 million from sport (The Henley Centre, 1986).

Provision and Facilities

The Public Sector

Until the early 1970s the majority of sports provision was supplied through the voluntary sector and via educational and military establishments. The reorganisation of local government in England, Scotland and Wales in the early 1970s served to release capital that outgoing local councils wished to invest, and this resulted in the building of many new sports and leisure complexes. Furthermore, stronger and more powerful authorities were established and many newly-formed authorities took advantage of reorganisation to bring together fragmented aspects of leisure provision such as baths, parks, sport, the arts, and tourism to form powerful and comprehensive leisure service departments. These two factors were partly responsible for the boom in sports provision during the 1970s. Within a decade of reorganisation, participation in indoor sport doubled, and participation in outdoor sport increased by 50 per cent (Sports Council, 1982).

Provision and facilities in the public sector derive from a range of agencies and organisations and can be summarised under the following headings:

1. *Central Government*
    - Royal parks
    - Defence establishments
    - Prisons

2. *Local Authorities*
    - Playing fields
    - Golf courses
    - Bowling rinks
    - Stadia
    - Marinas
    - Ski slopes
    - Swimming pools
    - Gymnasia
    - Sports halls
    - Ice rinks
    - Leisure centres
    - Urban, country and National Parks
    - Amenity open spaces
    - Beaches, lakes, rivers, reservoirs
    - Camp sites

3. *Local Education*   — School gymnasiums and playing fields
    Authorities   — Joint use sports centres
                          — Adult education centres
                          — Youth clubs
                          — Community centres
                          — College, polytechnic and
                            university sports facilities

There are a number of other agencies such as the Countryside Commission, the National Rivers Authority, the Forestry Commission, and the Nature Conservancy Council, amongst others, that influence and control provision and facilities for sport (see Figure 7.1). The key co-ordinating body for bringing together these different elements of provision in the public sector, *and* harnessing support from the commercial and voluntary sectors, are the Sports Councils of England, Scotland, Wales and Northern Ireland. The Sports Councils receive grant-in-aid from government on an annual basis to assist in the running of their affairs and to improve provision and facilities in line with stated policy objectives. More will be said about the administration, funding, and policy objectives of the public sector later.

The Commercial Sector

In direct contrast to the traditional social and welfare aims of the public sector, the commercial sector is mainly concerned with profit. A profit-dominated approach raises questions of whether the 'needs' of the population are being met, although the commercial sector often supplies similar goods and services (eg. weight training, aerobics and sauna). It is argued that the commercial sector often stimulates or creates demand by shrewd and effective marketing (although it is the customer who has the final word on whether he/she pays or not). It is also recognised that clients are prepared to pay considerable sums for leisure goods and experiences, provided the quality is high. The commercial sector will often attempt to extract the highest possible premium from clients, and this raises questions about provision for disadvantaged groups, as well as provision for minority sporting activities. However, many commercial operators have similar price structures to the public sector and are major providers of facilities and sporting experiences for the mass of the population.

In providing for the mass market, the most notable impact has been in the provision of facilities for health and fitness; the provision of sports clothing and footwear, the development of theme parks; investment in specific sports such as ten-pin bowling, indoor cricket, squash and golf;

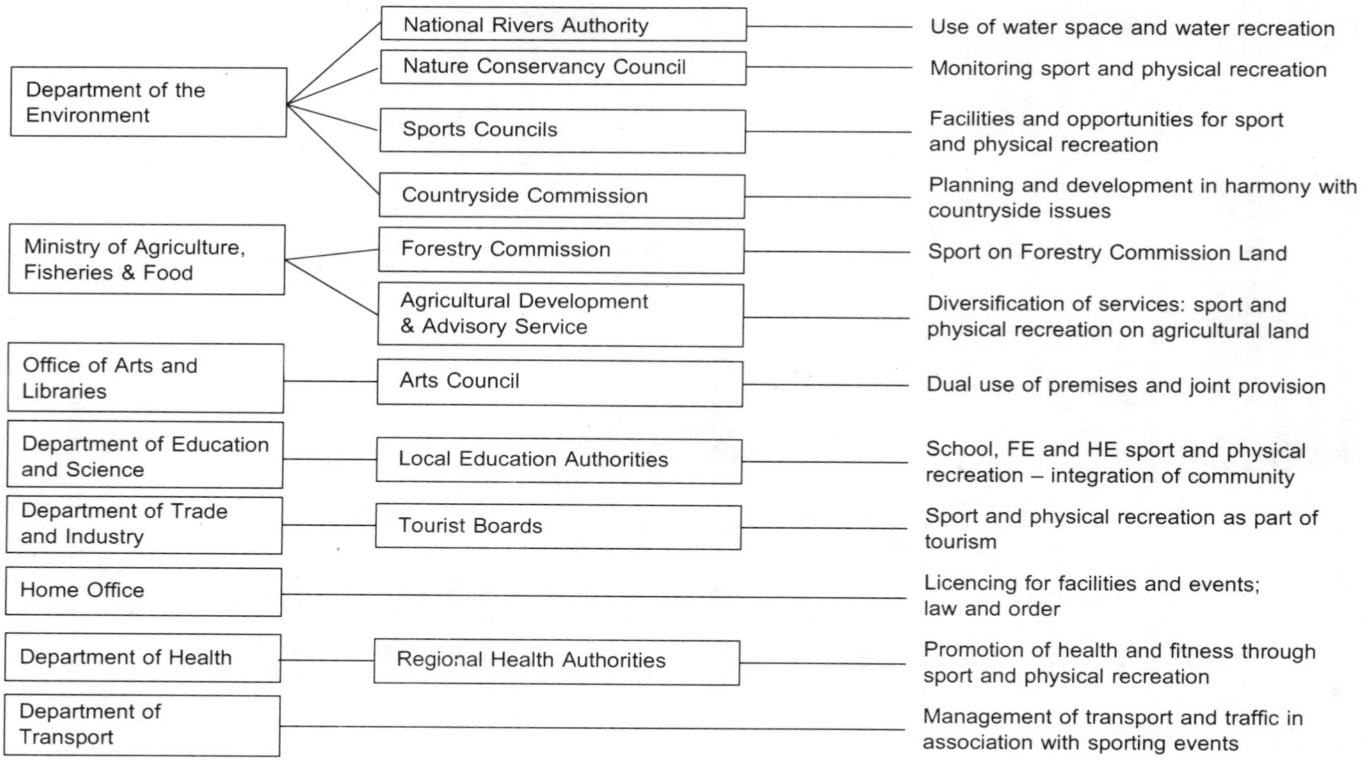

Figure 7.1 Government departments concerned with sport and physical recreation (England and Wales)

Department of the Environment
- National Rivers Authority — Use of water space and water recreation
- Nature Conservancy Council — Monitoring sport and physical recreation
- Sports Councils — Facilities and opportunities for sport and physical recreation
- Countryside Commission — Planning and development in harmony with countryside issues
- Forestry Commission — Sport on Forestry Commission Land

Ministry of Agriculture, Fisheries & Food
- Agricultural Development & Advisory Service — Diversification of services: sport and physical recreation on agricultural land

Office of Arts and Libraries
- Arts Council — Dual use of premises and joint provision

Department of Education and Science
- Local Education Authorities — School, FE and HE sport and physical recreation – integration of community

Department of Trade and Industry
- Tourist Boards — Sport and physical recreation as part of tourism

Home Office — Licencing for facilities and events; law and order

Department of Health
- Regional Health Authorities — Promotion of health and fitness through sport and physical recreation

Department of Transport — Management of transport and traffic in association with sporting events and in Scotland, curling rinks. Another major development in recent years has been the incorporation of sport, health and fitness within the concept of a leisure and retail mix. It is difficult to separate out retail investment from sports investment and general leisure investment, and any comment on provision is likely to include a proportion of mixed development. Total expenditure via the commercial sector in the UK on sports goods and services in 1990 was estimated at £3582 million, of which over 40 per cent comprised the manufacturing and retailing of equipment, clothing and footwear (Leisure Consultants, 1988). Commercial investment in large-scale sports provision has always been considered risky by financial institutions (Battersea Power Station in London and the World Student Games in Sheffield are two painful examples), and the current trend is to forge partnerships with other sectors.

In addition to providing for the mass market, the commercial sector has put considerable resources into developing luxury facilities. Examples include exclusive health and fitness clubs, golf and country clubs, marinas and water-based centres.

The Voluntary Sector

It is estimated that there are in excess of 500,000 voluntary officials working in sporting clubs and societies across the UK. These officials have been valued at £81 million at 1985 prices and control 150,000 sports clubs representing in excess of 6.5 million members.

The voluntary sector has been called the backbone of sport and physical recreation in the UK. Voluntary organisations are mainly concerned with serving the interests of like-minded members. In contrast with the commercial sector, voluntary clubs are seldom concerned with generating profit for shareholders or owners but aim for 'the maximisation of the net benefit of the typical member' (Buchanan, 1965). The more far-sighted clubs, particularly those fortunate enough to own their own grounds, invest in the future and manage their affairs on a commercial basis. They generate a surplus of income over expenditure so that funds are available for repairs, refurbishments and new developments.

Problems of Definition

There is a problem in defining what the voluntary sector comprises, and sometimes there is an overlap with the public and commercial sectors. Some industrial sports clubs and private member clubs can be viewed as hybrid organisations displaying some of the traditional characteristics of both voluntary and commercial organisations. Within this chapter a definition adapted from Butson (1983) is favoured:

> The voluntary sports sector is defined as inclusive and exclusive clubs that operate as non-profit making organisations and which are essentially managed by, and provided for, amateur sportsmen and sportswomen.

Within this definition non-profit making organisations excludes those clubs that set out to make a profit or a dividend for shareholders or owners, but includes clubs that make a surplus of income over expenditure for the sole purpose of the club's affairs. Thus, along with Torkildsen (1986), the following discussion of the voluntary sector will include recreational trusts, private and institutional clubs, charities, and industrial sports clubs.

Exercise
Make arrangements to visit a voluntary sports club. Arrange an interview with a club official and find out how the club is structured, how it is financed, who belongs, and what its immediate concerns and future plans are. Write your findings up in the form of a report to discuss with colleagues and compare the similarities and differences.

A further contrast with the commercial sector is the relationship voluntary sector clubs have with the mass market. The capacity of many voluntary clubs to take an active role in increasing mass participation is limited by the facilities available. The facilities of many voluntary sports clubs are stretched to their limits and for many grass-based sports a major problem in accommodating wider use has been the repair and preparation of grounds. This problem has been partly resolved with the development of many synthetic grass pitches.

The four Sports Councils, in their strategy documents, recognise the problems of facility and provision faced by many voluntary clubs but call for them to review seriously how they may meet community needs. There is little doubt that in an increasingly restricted economic climate, many clubs will have to decide whether to ignore involvement in increasing mass participation, and therefore risk reduced public sector support, or to examine ways they can contribute more fully to meeting Sports Council objectives. However, it needs to be recognised that many governing bodies of sport are voluntary organisations and wield considerable power. There are many examples of these organisations demonstrating their independence from central government, for example, the role of the Football Association and the Football League in fighting the Identity Card Scheme; the British Olympic Association and participation in the Moscow Olympics in 1980; and the Home Rugby Unions' support of the British Lions' tour of South Africa.

Partnerships – Provision and Service in an Era of Change

Although the underlying objectives of the three sectors of provision remain largely intact, there are now a wide range of partnership agreements in operation (see Figure 7.2 on page 202). The underlying principle is that partnerships between two or more sectors lead to developments that would be difficult to achieve by one sector alone. The best way of demonstrating the nature and extent of co-operation between sectors is by giving examples of good practice.

Example 1

In the late 1970s Denis Howell, then Minister for Sport, announced a £1.7 million grant to assist football league and rugby league clubs develop their grounds for community use. This not only improved amenities for the commercial and voluntary clubs in receipt of grants, but also provided new opportunities for the local community. In some cases full-time motivators were employed to assist with training and coaching, and in other cases indoor and outdoor training facilities were improved to enable wider use. The Sports Council has been particularly successful in encouraging voluntary-sector sports clubs to open their doors to the community by giving priority to those clubs seeking financial aid from the Council which best achieve the aims of the Council, that is 'increasing participation, improving performance, or helping to alleviate social or recreational deprivation in areas of social need' (Sports Council, 1987).

Example 2

The Indoor Tennis Initiative (ITI) is a partnership agreement between the Lawn Tennis Association, The Sports Council, and the All England Lawn Tennis Club, each of which has committed £500,000 per year over a five-year period. The intention is to pump-prime initiatives so that investment is stimulated in partnership with the commercial sector. As an example, the Delta Tennis Centre in Swindon was opened in 1989 as a result of co-operation between the ITI, the Borough of Thamesdown, and the developers Taylor Woodrow. The land for the centre was provided by the Borough, and construction costs were split between

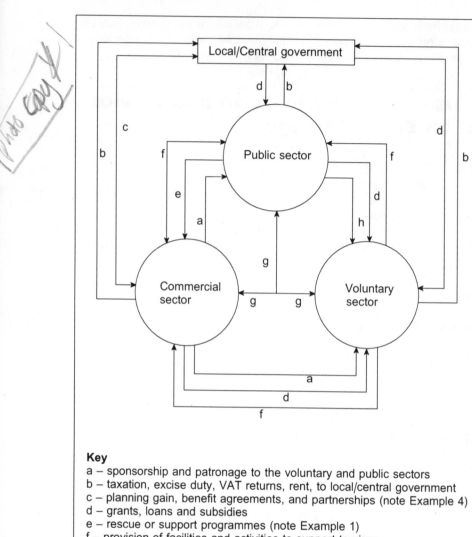

Key
a – sponsorship and patronage to the voluntary and public sectors
b – taxation, excise duty, VAT returns, rent, to local/central government
c – planning gain, benefit agreements, and partnerships (note Example 4)
d – grants, loans and subsidies
e – rescue or support programmes (note Example 1)
f – provision of facilities and activities to support tourism
g – mutual aid partnership agreements (note Examples 2 and 3)
h – administrative support, research, publications, and training

Figure 7.2 Sectors of provision for sport and physical recreation and interrelationships between sectors

the ITI and Taylor Woodrow. The Borough and the ITI have provided funds for a Tennis Development Officer, and Taylor Woodrow will be providing an annual £20,000 contribution to the running costs. A further example is the partnership between the Scottish Sports Council, the ITI, Stirling University and the private sector. The Scottish Sports Council has agreed to provide £170,000 of the £1.1 million development, and the remainder of the finance will be met by the other partners. The new centre, comprising four indoor and four outdoor courts, will be used by the Scottish Lawn Tennis Association for training squad players; host competitions for students; and be available to the general public.

Example 3

The new artificial grass surface at Reading Hockey Club has been made possible by a Sports Council grant, support from Wokingham District Council and a £100,000 sponsorship agreement with the brewers Heineken. The surface is known as 'Heineken Astro' and provides improved opportunities for the hockey club as well as for schools and other clubs in the area.

Example 4

Perhaps the most well-known of partnership agreements has been that of 'planning gain'. A commercial developer is permitted to build offices, hotels, shops or private residences provided that recreation facilities for the public form part of the provision. An example is the partnership between Broadlands District Council and IHS, a Swiss-based leisure developer, to produce Norwich Sports Village. The scheme incorporates indoor tennis, squash, health and fitness, and a large multi-purpose sports hall alongside a 150-bed hotel. The Council provided £1.05 million and no contribution to running costs. The land is leased to IHS over 150 years with a fixed annual base rent alongside a profit-sharing agreement which operates after IHS have received an agreed return on their equity investment. The sports facilities are open to the public on a 'pay and play' basis with no membership fees (Terry, 1989).

Example 5

A different type of partnership is that between agencies *within* one of the major sectors of provision. The co-operation between district councils and local education authorities (LEAs) is an example. The Sports Council has been successful in promoting the development of dual-use facilities including district-wide strategies in local authorities such as Birmingham, Tameside and Gravesham. Another good example is the Crownpoint Sports Park in Glasgow mentioned in the Parks and Amenity Chapter (pp. 133). Furthermore, around 43 per cent of new indoor sports halls provided between 1982 and 1988 were under the aegis of dual use (Sports Council 1988a). Partnership between LEAs and the

Sports Council include ventures such as Coventry's Active Life Styles Project and the teacher training Demonstration Project in Cheltenham (Sports Council, 1985 and Buswell and Escott, 1987). There are, however, problems for the development of partnerships within the public sector as a result of changes in the capital control system (see page 239).

The above examples demonstrate the strengths of partnership agreements. Each sector alone seldom has the ingredients for a successful new initiative but by working together exciting new schemes become a reality.

Administration and Finance

The administration and financing of sport and physical recreation takes place in a bewildering variety of organisations and agencies. As the previous section on provision and facilities demonstrated, three broad areas service sport and physical recreation. Although the trend is for closer partnerships between them, there are still distinct characteristics that distinguish the way they carry out their affairs and how they raise funds. However, the reader will note that there are many ways the sectors interrelate. Indeed, in many instances, new provision depends upon joint funding arrangements and co-operation in the administration of events and activities. The four Sports Councils, for example, consider new partnerships with the voluntary and commercial sectors to be a cornerstone in improving mass participation and excellence.

The public sector will be examined first, followed by the commercial and, finally, the voluntary sector.

The Public Sector

The public sector is administered and financed through funds made available by central government as well as funds generated from its own activities. A number of government departments have an interest in sport and physical recreation and we have seen (see Figure 7.1 on page 198) the complexity of current administration. The four Sports Councils have a pivotal role within this structure and often act as 'brokers' between government departments and agencies. However, there are occasions when the Sports Councils have to take a secondary rather than a leading role in the conduct of sporting affairs. The Home Office, for example, has a particular interest in the law and order problems surrounding football hooliganism. The Foreign Office is involved in issues that have international consequences, and the Department of Education and

Science (DES) has a leading role in school sport and the physical education curriculum. It is instructive that the current Minister for Sport, Robert Atkins, was moved from the DoE to the DES in the Autumn of 1990. This should enable the Minister to play a more central role in addressing concerns surrounding the place of physical education and sport within the National Curriculum as well as other policy issues, such as the selling of school playing fields for commercial development.

The role of the public sector in the administration and finance of sport and physical recreation will be considered by reference to the four Sports Councils, the Central Council of Physical Recreation, the local authorities (and district and islands councils in Scotland), Local Education Authorities, and the British Olympic Association.

Sports Councils

The (GB) Executive Sports Council (ESC), from now on referred to simply as the Sports Council, was established by Royal Charter in 1972 and replaced the Advisory Sports Council (ASC) as well as absorbing many of the staff and assets of the Central Council of Physical Recreation (CCPR). Although the Sports Council has overall responsibility for British sport, there are separate councils for Wales, Scotland and Northern Ireland. The Sports Council for Wales (SCW) and the Scottish Sports Council (SSC) were both established by Royal Charter in 1972. The SCW is financed by an annual grant-in-aid from the Environment Services Section of the Welsh Office, and the SSC receives annual grant-in-aid from the Scottish Education Department. The Sports Council for Northern Ireland (SCNI) was established under the Recreation and Youth Services Order 1973 and the Recreation (Northern Ireland) Order, 1975, and with effect from 1974 took over the work of the CCPR in Northern Ireland as well as other functions formally carried out by the Youth and Sports Council and the Ministry of Education. The SCNI receives grant-in-aid from the Department of Education (Northern Ireland). All four Sports Councils supplement their grant-in-aid with income generated from their own activities. Total grant-in-aid for the four councils for 1988/89 is given in Table 7.3 on page 206.

Under the influence of a strong monetarist policy, the 1980s witnessed a much leaner and business-orientated administration with financial planning more closely tied to entrepreneurship and commercialism. The growing congruence between the policies emanating from central government and those of the Sports Council has been noted by many commentators (Coalter *et al.*, 1986; Hargreaves, 1984; Carrington and Leaman, 1982). Furthermore, the establishment of a state-financed council has meant that the centre of gravity of sports administration

Table 7.3 Grant-in-aid and additional income generated for the Sports Council (SC), the Sports Council for Wales (SCW), the Scottish Sports Council (SSC) and the Sports Council for Northern Ireland (SCNI). Year ending 31 March 1989

Council	Recurrent grant-in-aid	Additional income	Total income
SC	38,412,000	7,260,120	45,672,120
SCW	4,199,000	1,679,774	5,878,774
SSC	4,813,020	1,304,371	6,117,391
SCNI	1,258,889	211,261	1,470,150

Source: 1988/89 *Annual Reports* of the four Sports Councils.

has shifted from the governing bodies and voluntary sports clubs firmly to the public sector (Coalter 1986, p. 54). Denis Howell has gone so far as to suggest that instead of putting forward the voice of sport in an independent manner, the Sports Council is now a 'wholly owned government subsidiary... doing the job the government wishes to be done and that is not necessarily the job sport needs to be done' (Coalter 1986, p. 65).

Two current issues have been identified for further consideration. Firstly, the radical reorganisation and streamlining of Sports Council membership, and secondly the move towards greater funding from the commercial sector.

Sports Council Reorganisation

Colin Moynihan inherited an unwieldy 32-member Council which contained representatives absorbed through the asset-stripping of the CCPR. In 1989 the Minister announced a new Council of fourteen members that, in his own words, was 'young, decisive, experienced and small'. The new Council was heavily weighted towards competitors and businessmen, and reflected the need for an administration that was dynamic and prepared to implement policies in tune with that of central government. At the beginning of 1991 the Council was sixteen strong, of which two were women. As one of the major objectives of the Sports Council over the next few years is to increase women's participation, it is unfortunate that, of the sixteen members, women are so poorly represented.

Funding

In his address to the CCPR conference in 1988, Colin Moynihan painted a picture of sport in the future existing more off membership fees and commercial sponsors. In line with central government policy of reduced public sector expenditure, sport is being encouraged to be less dependent on government hand-outs, and to exploit more effectively the money available in the world of commerce and business. Sponsorship does not just benefit top level performers, but through 'packaged' arrangements significant sums can be gained for training, coaching, and grass roots participation. The Sports Council has established an advisory service to assist governing bodies and clubs in exploiting sponsorship opportunities more effectively. In many cases sponsorship at a local level does not involve large amounts of money, although some clubs are able to attract significant sums from local companies. Ben Rhydding Hockey Club in West Yorkshire was able to exploit its success on the field of play in 1988/89 by negotiating a £17,000 sponsorship deal over two years with Ametex U.K., the textile company. Advertising in fixture cards, sponsoring matches, and companies providing prizes for raffles and competitions can also make a significant contribution to financial viability.

A further example of income diversification is the commercialisation of the Sports Council itself. In 1987 the Council established itself as a trading company. Marketing activities include the launch of a new clothing range, the marketing of the Council's logo, increased sales from publications and research, advertising revenue, sponsorship, and consultancy.

A former Secretary of State for the Environment, Nicholas Ridley, directly encouraged reduced public-sector support for sport by suggesting that conventional investment programmes by local authorites should be halted; and that in future authorities should use public money to stimulate investment in sport through the commercial sector and should no longer own facilities (Ridley, 1988). However, such a policy reduces opportunities for groups such as the poor, who are least able to take advantage of facilities and opportunities provided by the commercial and voluntary sectors (Fitzjohn, 1988). The Sports Council has, in fact, recognised this problem and foresees two broad markets for sport. The first is affluent, wealthy, well-educated and in work; and the second is generally poor, has poor health, and may be unemployed and living in areas of deprivation. It has been suggested that the commercial sector should be major suppliers to the affluent market, and the public sector should direct more attention to the second category (Benington and White, 1988; Sports Council, 1988a).

The Director's Report (The Henley Centre, 1989a) has demonstrated the increasing number of people in low paid jobs and the widening polarisation of the labour market between a well-rewarded core of professionals and a poorly-rewarded periphery. A 'two nation' state will result in a relatively affluent 70 per cent in full-time employment and an increasingly disadvantaged 30 per cent (The Henley Centre, 1989b).

Regional Councils for Sport and Recreation (RCSR)

The RCSRs were established in England in 1976 in succession to the Regional Sports Councils. The new Councils have a much broader remit and are responsible for producing regional strategies for sport and recreation, preparing subject reports on specific activities, and enhancing the planning process for their respective regions. The Councils are represented by many different bodies including the Water authorities (until 1989), the Countryside Commission, the Nature Conservancy Council, voluntary sports clubs, and the local authorities.

During the ten years between 1980 and 1990 the Regional Councils produced in excess of 120 reports on issues ranging from the problems and needs of motorsport and water recreation, to sport and recreation in rural areas and the provision of artificial turf facilities. A full list of the Councils who produced these, and their dates, is published in *Into the 90s* (Sports Council, 1988a, Appendix 4), and in the strategic plans of the other three Councils. New publications are included in the various Annual Reports. They make useful reference material and are an excellent source of information on policy and planning issues as well as current provision and resources.

The most important function of RCSRs is, however, to grant-aid voluntary, statutory and commercial agencies. Between them, the Regional Councils in England distributed in excess of £7.3m in capital grants and loans in 1988/89 and in excess of £1.5m in regional participation grants. (Sports Council, 1990). Further details on eligible projects and conditions which apply to giving grants and loans are given later.

District and Local Sports Councils

District and local sports councils represent the interests of smaller communities and many of them receive administrative support from local authorities, city councils, and town halls. In Scotland, over fifty local sports councils are under the administrative umbrella of the Scottish Association of Local Sports Councils, and in Northern Ireland local issues are fed through District Sports Committees.

The Central Council of Physical Recreation (CCPR)

The CCPR is the voice of voluntary-sector sports clubs and physical recreation organisations throughout the UK. It represents around 250 governing bodies of sport encompassing around 87,000 clubs. The work of the CCPR is supported in Wales by the Welsh Sports Association and in Northern Ireland by the Northern Ireland Council of Physical Recreation.

The objectives of the CCPR are:

1. To constitute a standing forum where all national governing and representative bodies of sport and physical recreation may be represented and may, collectively or through special groups, where appropriate, formulate and promote measures to improve and develop sport and physical recreation.
2. To support the work of specialist sports bodies and to bring them together with other interested organisations.
3. To act as a consultative body to the Sports Council and other representative or public bodies concerned with sport and physical recreation.

Until 1971, the administration of sport and physical recreation was heavily influenced by the CCPR, and its members worked hand in glove with the Advisory Sports Council. Following the establishment of the Executive Sports Council in 1971, the CCPR was marginalised, its status reduced, and its assets taken over. The control and administration of sport shifted from the voluntary sector firmly towards the public sector. Central government, who were the main financiers of British sport, could now formulate policy and planning, and make the voluntary sector more accountable in its funding. Indeed, the establishment of an executive Sports Council has been seen as a 'major step in the dual process of incorporation and marginalisation of the CCPR' (Coalter, 1986 p. 54).

Despite its reduced power and status, the CCPR is still an important 'watchdog' for voluntary-sector sport and physical recreation. Through its President, the Duke of Edinburgh, the Council voices its opinion on a wide range of sporting matters. The most recent cause has been the loss of playing fields and sports grounds and, through research and media promotions, it has drawn attention to the extensive loss of playing facilities throughout the country due to 'rationalisation' by local authorities. The CCPR has also drawn attention to the effect of the new Business Rate on sports clubs (see pp 219–20).

Further reference to the CCPR and the tension that exists between it and the Sports Council is given in the section on Policy and Planning.

Local Authorities, District and Islands Councils

Local authorities are major providers and operators of sports facilities (Audit Commission, 1989) and District and Islands Councils have important (statutory) responsibilities for sport in Scotland. The range of provision by local authorities is extensive and the spending on sport and recreation in England and Wales accounts for over sixty per cent of total net expenditure on leisure (CIPFA, 1989). Table 7.4 demonstrates the major areas of spending.

Table 7.4   Net expenditure by local authorities on sport and physical recreation (England and Wales, 1988/89 estimates)

Sport and Recreation	*Percentage of Total Expenditure*
Indoor	
Swimming pools	13.3
Sports halls and leisure centres with pools	18.9
Sports halls and leisure centres without pools	7.3
Community centres, public halls	6.1
Outdoor	
Sports facilities	5.0
Golf courses	0.2
Urban parks and open spaces	46.6
Allotments	0.5
Grants and contributions	2.1

Source: Adapted from CIPFA, *Leisure and Recreation Estimates 1988–89.*

The origins of sports and physical recreation provision within local authorities goes back to the nineteenth century and the Baths and Wash-Houses Act (1846). The latter half of the nineteenth century also witnessed the development of new parks, libraries, and museums, as well as the establishment of Baths Departments and Parks Departments within local authorities. It needs to be remembered, however, that provision for sport and physical recreation by local authorities in England, Wales and Northern Ireland has always been discretionary, and this has meant wide variations in the type and extent of provision. As an example, net expenditure per head of population on leisure was £87.83 in Erewash (Derbyshire) in 1985/86, but only £0.93 per head in South Cambridgeshire (CIPFA, 1985). In Scotland, under the 1982 Local Government and Planning (Scotland) Act district and islands councils have a *statutory* duty to ensure provision. The 1982 Act states that district and island councils:

> shall ensure that there is an adequate provision of facilities for the inhabitants of their area for recreational, sporting, cultural and social activities. (Section 14 (1)).

Despite the statutory nature of provision for sport in Scotland, the lack of precision in the Act makes the service highly vulnerable in times of economic constraint. In such circumstances it has proved impossible to identify the appropriate level of block grant that is necessary to ensure 'adequate provision'.

Prior to the reorganisation of local government in 1974 (in Scotland, 1975) all administration of sport and recreation took place in a variety of departments and there was little co-ordination of effort or resources. We saw earlier how local government reorganisation led to the proliferation of facilities by outgoing councils, and comprehensive leisure service departments were created to manage the many new facilities that were being built. Within fifteen years, between 1967 and 1982, some 500 new swimming pools and 500 new indoor sports centres were built throughout the UK. This resulted in current expenditure on sport and recreation within local authorities rising from under £100 million to around £700 million. Up to the late 1980s, expenditure continued to grow at around 8 per cent per annum, despite the Conservative Government's strict spending policies.

Local Education Authorities (LEAs)

LEAs are also significant providers of facilities for sport and physical recreation, particularly through the community use of school, college, and higher education facilities. It has long been recognised that many facilities provided and used by the education sector have not been utilised to maximum efficiency. In many cases the facilities lay idle in the evenings, at weekends, and during holidays. Fortunately, much progress has been made in opening up these facilities for adult and youth use. The 1970s and 1980s witnessed the development of 'dual use' sports facilities designed for school use during the day and community use during evenings, weekends, and school holidays. The Youth Service also provides a wide range of facilities and opportunities for the 11–25 year old age group.

Adult education classes in sport and physical recreation remain popular, and the Sports Council has estimated participation at around 500,000 (Sports Council, 1988a). Most of these activities take place in Further Education Colleges and schools. Many of the classes concentrate on recreational play, and it has been suggested that more emphasis should be placed on training coaches and leaders as well as basic introduction to skills.

The British Olympic Association (BOA)

The BOA represents British interest in the International Olympic movement and raises funds for sports organisations to compete in international events. The BOA also organises a variety of conferences, forums, and seminars on issues such as sports medicine, drug abuse and team training. In 1988, the Sports Council provided £51,000 towards the BOA's new Sports Medical Centre at Northwick Park Hospital, Harrow.

The Association has, however, been involved with a wide range of sports issues over and above those mentioned above. Its membership is open to institutions and individuals, it is concerned with 'mass sport' as well as Olympic sport, and has even had a role in cultivating the fine arts.

For many years, sports participation and progress in the international arena has been hampered by in-fighting and a lack of co-ordination between the various administrative bodies. Now it would appear the wisdom of Don Anthony in his far-sighted book *A Strategy for British Sport*, published in 1980, has at last been heeded. In 1988 the British International Sports Committee (BISC) was established to co-ordinate and develop the work of the BOA, the Sports Councils, and the CCPR.

The Commercial Sector

Sport is big business. Spending on sport is in excess of £3 billion a year and gambling is worth an additional £2.5 billion (The Henley Centre, 1986). Three broad areas stand out as far as commercial interest is concerned; sports goods and equipment; sponsorship; and participation and entertainment. Each area will be considered in turn.

Sports Goods and Equipment

There has been a continuous pattern of strong growth in the sales of sports goods and equipment for over a decade, and the forecast is that growth will continue in the forseeable future. However, high interest rates and mortgage rates affect disposable income and, along with changes in the balance of the population, the high growth of the late 1980s may not be sustained. None the less, The Henley Centre (1986) has estimated that expenditure on sports goods will continue to rise at between 5 and 6 per cent per annum, and that sports clothing and footwear expenditure will grow between 11 and 12 per cent per annum to the mid-1990s.

A particular feature of this sector of the market is the way sports clothing and footwear has become part of everyday leisure wear. It is estimated that over three-quarters of all track suits sold never see an athletics track or sports ground.

Sponsorship

The growth of sport's sponsorship since the early 1970s has been quite staggering and now provides a major source of income for many sports. Growth in direct sponsorship has risen from a modest £2.5 million in 1971 to more than £200 million in 1989. But direct sponsorship is only part of the total, and at least as much again goes into merchandising and hospitality. As an example, Barclays Bank invested £11.5 million over six seasons in the Football League, but part of the deal was ten free tickets to every game in the league each week. The bank uses these tickets (460 a week) to cultivate business contacts and customers. Hospitality 'boxes' and functions at major events such as Wimbledon, Ascot and Lords are sought after by many large companies, and prove excellent environments for making and strengthening business contacts. The Ryder Cup held at The Belfry Golf Club, Warwickshire, in September 1989 attracted two hundred companies, each paying £18,000 for a forty-seat hospitality unit. Individual sportsmen and women also benefit handsomely through advertising, endorsements and appearance money, and the major sponsorship of governing bodies filters down to clubs at the grassroots level. We have also seen how the local sponsorship of clubs and teams is an important source of revenue.

The development of sports sponsorship has not been enthusiastically received in all quarters and there are two major areas of concern. The first is the ethics of tobacco and alcohol sponsorship. When the ban on direct television advertising of tobacco was introduced in 1965, the tobacco companies found sport an ideal vehicle for marketing its products. Sport is popular for the tobacco companies and breweries for a number of reasons. Firstly, sport offers the sort of clean and healthy image that supports brand image. Secondly, identification of a product with sport offers a very strong and long-lasting association. Thirdly, sports sponsorship offers very good value for money compared with direct advertising. The tobacco industry is now limited by government agreement to spend no more than £8 million a year and tobacco sponsorship now accounts for less than 5 per cent of money invested in sport. The Sports Council is also committed to replacing tobacco sponsorship (but not alcohol sponsorship) by other products as and when opportunities arise.

The second area of concern is the financial power exerted by sponsors. Kerry Packer was able to market a new type of floodlit cricket which included new styles of dress, new rules and new equipment. The power to offer players lucrative contracts changed the face of cricket throughout the world. Other examples include the unofficial tours by English cricketers and Welsh rugby footballers in South Africa. Large sponsorship agreements have enabled South African sports administrators to offer tempting contracts to individuals and put in jeopardy other international events and competitions. The power of sponsorship money can also influence the behaviour and attitudes of individuals and teams because of the pressures on winning. Sponsors do not wish to be associated with losers and may withdraw sponsorship money if results are not satisfactory. The power of sponsors is further reflected in the next area to be discussed: the media.

The media comprises television, the press, radio, and photography. Together they exert a strong influence on sponsorship packages. Media coverage is so powerful it can influence when sporting events take place, who takes part, and how sports are conducted. Sports such as American football, basketball, tennis and soccer, have even changed their rules to make the games more attractive to television audiences. Television is the biggest attraction for sponsors, and with the development of cable and satellite television (such as Rupert Murdoch's Sky Television) there are opportunities for even greater sponsorship of sport over the next few years. Until recently only a handful of sports and events were able to gain media attraction (the top ten TV deals in 1988 are given in Table 7.5).

Table 7.5   Top television deals in 1988

Company	Sport	Hours of cover
Cornhill	Cricket	184.40
Embassy	Snooker	96.30
National Westminster Bank	Cricket	37.45
Barclays	Soccer	35.30
Refuge Assurance	Cricket	34.20
Mercantile Credit	Snooker	13.20
Rothmans	Snooker	31.00
Benson & Hedges	Cricket	30.50
MIM Britannia	Cricket	29.40
Fidelity	Snooker	28.45

Source: RSL Sportscan, 1989.

Exercise
Analyse the sports section of various national newspapers, choosing a mixture of 'quality' and tabloid press. What sports receive coverage? How are women's sports represented? Compare the coverage of sports events in each paper and relate it to the socioeconomic group of the readership.

Participation and Entertainment

The financial and administrative interests of the commercial sector in participation and entertainment will be summarised by reference to sport and retail, theme parks, sports villages and activity holidays, health and fitness, and country club hotels.

(i)   Sport and retail

The concept 'leisure and retail mix' has become well-established, and a typical example is the £12 million leisure and retail complex in Basingstoke, Hampshire. Major retail development was allowed, but extensive sports facilities, including a 26 lane ten-pin bowling centre, indoor cricket, an ice-rink and a swimming pool, formed part of the package. It has also been demonstrated that quality sporting and leisure facilities improve the environment and encourage new commerce and industry into an area. By hosting the 1991 World Student Games, the City of Sheffield has attracted over £1000 million of investment, and planning applications for new developments have increased by 50 per cent. This is despite major problems in financing the Games.

Shopping has become a leisure pastime for an increasing number of people and new large-scale sites now cater for multifunctional excursions linking the whole family to a fun-orientated leisure/retail complex. The inclusion of selected sports activities within retail development is seen as advantageous 'both in encouraging and securing a target population of shop users, and also a means of suggesting a 'planning gain' for local populations and authorities' (Spink, 1989). Participation in leisure shopping has been fuelled not only by new facilities, but also by new lifestyle tastes, increasing affluence, developments in new technology such as electronic financial point of sale, and the ease with which credit can be obtained and used.

Sport and retail is, however, not always seen as a profitable financial proposition (the Battersea Power Station venture in London is a case in point). It is also recognised that the more active sports requiring a change of clothing are not appropriate features of the sport/retail mix.

(ii) Theme parks

According to David Reddick (Leisure Management, 1990) 'there are no theme parks in the UK at the moment – they are merely thrill parks'. The first theme park, in the American sense of the term, will be Wonder-World which is planned for a 1000-acre site in Corby. A development of this size will cost in excess of £300 million today, which would require a profit of £1 million a week every week of the year to service the debt. Adopting the English Tourist Board's more general definition of a theme park as 'a general outdoor leisure attraction', most of those in the UK do not depend on a world-wide catchment area, such as Disneyland, but depend largely on day-trippers. Alton Towers, the top park attraction in 1989 with 2.4 million visitors, is able to draw from a 2-hour catchment population of 20 million. Raising the necessary finance for major new developments of this kind is not easy when borrowing is expensive and the return on investment is lengthy and uncertain. The pay-back period for Thorpe Park in Surrey, for example, was in excess of five years (Johnson, 1988).

(iii) Sports villages and activity holidays

Sports villages are based on the concept of Butlin's and Pontin's holiday camps. Lakewoods is a company owned 50 per cent by Granada and 50 per cent by Laing, and between them over £500 million is being invested in a series of five sports villages. As we saw in Example 4 on page 203, IHS, a Swiss company, has established a sports village in Norwich and is in the process of developing a second one in Chigwell, Essex. The concept of the modern sports village is a hotel with a wide range of high quality sports facilities such as squash, tennis, snooker, golf, sports hall and swimming pool plus a sauna. The village is also open to the public on a 'pay-as-you-play' basis.

On a smaller level there are over 3000 organisations offering activity holiday programmes ranging from walking and hiking to traditional team games and coaching.

(iv) Health and fitness

Hotel companies such as Crest (now owned by THF), Thistle, and Embassy have all invested heavily in health and fitness as part of the hotel experience. High quality equipment and service help to attract hotel customers, and at the same time the local community can use the facilities on a pay-and-play basis. Corporate health has also been a growth area, as companies have recognised the importance of maintaining a healthy and fit workforce. It has been estimated that a company of 1000 employees will lose a total of over 5600 days labour each year and will have 4.65 premature deaths per annum at a total annual cost of £200,000 due to heart and other circulatory diseases (Clough, 1989).

(v)   Country club hotels

The golf hotel and country club hotel are concepts that have become increasingly popular for business executives and holidaymakers, although this is not a new concept as hotels such as The Belfry in Warwickshire and Gleneagles in Scotland have combined quality sporting facilities and golf for many years. More recently, Quiet Waters Golf Club and Malden District Council have taken part in a joint £13 million development which includes a 100-bedroom hotel and luxury golf facilities, and Thornbrooks have put over £32.5 million into a golf and hotel development aimed at the American market.

The Voluntary Sector

The administration and financing of voluntary-sector sports clubs varies widely. Some clubs, particularly those linked with trusts and private establishments, are run in a highly efficient and businesslike manner. An increasing number of voluntary clubs now recognise the need for a paid secretary or steward although a vast number of small clubs still rely totally on voluntary help.

The voluntary sector will be considered under three headings: administration; legal responsibilities; and finance.

Administration

The success of most voluntary clubs usually rests on a small core of dedicated, unpaid officials. Some of the major advantages of voluntary clubs consists of the ability of members to pioneer new ideas and projects; to act outside of a bureaucratic structure; for members to retain democratic control over their affairs within an agreed constitution; and to be able to raise funds in whatever manner they please. However, how a club functions depends on dynamic and skilful leadership, as well as the goodwill of elected representatives. Leadership is a significant and often neglected area of research in voluntary clubs, and the health and vitality of many organisations can be seriously affected when leaders are lost.

Legal Responsibilities

It should be noted that voluntary clubs, no matter how they are constituted, have legal responsibilities regarding employees' rights, discrimination, health and safety, the sale of alcohol, contracts of employment, holiday, sickness, and pension rights. There are also responsibilities for premises, including the safety of grounds and buildings, public health, and fire regulations. Ignorance is no excuse in the eyes of the law and members of management committees have to ensure they are aware of their legal responsibiities and, where appropriate, take out suitable insurance. In an unincorporated association, individual members of a management committee can be held personally responsible for the club's obligations and debts.

Finance

Sports Council assistance
The Sports Council operates a scheme of financial assistance to voluntary sports clubs in two ways: firstly by awarding grants and loans for capital cost projects; and secondly by awarding participation grants.

1. Grants and loans
There are a number of conditions imposed, perhaps the most important of which is that the organisation must have 'security of tenure'. This means the club must own its own grounds or have a long lease period. Further details on what constitutes eligible projects and the funding available is now given.

Eligible Projects No assistance is given towards the cost of routine maintenance or repairs or for the replacement of equipment. A range of facilities can be assisted (Sports Council, 1987), including:

(a) Indoor sports facilities such as sport halls, ancillary halls and their associated changing facilities.
(b) Outdoor sports facilities such as pitches, courts, floodlighting, and their associated changing facilities.
(c) Specialist facilities such as gymnastic halls, rifle ranges, and launching slipways.
(d) Purchase of land and sporting rights.
(e) Purchase of sports equipment:
   (i)   Where the equipment is an integral part of the development of a new facility.
   (ii) New major items of equipment with a total capital cost in excess of £1500.
(f) Special facilities for disabled people which meet all the following qualifications:
   (i)   Not sited at a hospital or special school for the disabled (but exceptions may be considered by the Sports Council where adequate community use of the facility is assured).
   (ii) Primarily recreational rather than therapeutic.

(iii) Not capable of being provided by sharing general community provision for similar activities.

(g) Provision of social accommodation to complement an existing sports facility (eligible only for loan).

Amount of grant and loan   The level of assistance for each project is individually assessed on its merits. The total of grants and loans awarded in 1988/89 via the Sports Council was in excess of £7.3 million. Organisations can apply for a minimum grant of £750 or a minimum loan of £1000 (maximum loan £10 000) provided the minimum capital cost of the project is above £1500.

Conditions   There are a range of conditions that have to be met in order to safeguard the use of public funds. Full details are given in the Sports Council publication *Finance for Sports Facilities* available free of charge from any Regional Council or from Head Office.

2. Regional participation grants

These are for innovatory schemes designed to encourage and increase participation in sport. The grants are non-capital expenditure and costs that are allowed include facility hire charge and administration; publicity and promotion; and coaches' fees. In certain cases a grant may be given for capital expenditure on sports equipment and modest building costs as long as such expenditure is part of a scheme to promote participation. In 1988/89 the Sports Council awarded in excess of £1.5 million in regional participation grants.

Finally, it should be remembered when seeking financial assistance that the Sports Council gives preference to schemes which meet with the policy of the Council.

Local government assistance

Historically, local government has played a major part in the funding of voluntary sports clubs by giving grants and loans; allowing rate relief; providing facilities; allocating staff for the upkeep of grounds, and assisting with the administration and management of the organisation. The non-statutory nature of funding for sport and recreation has meant that during periods of financial retrenchment, assistance to voluntary clubs is particularly vulnerable.

As a result of the Local Government Finance Act, 1988 and the introduction of the Uniform Business Rate on 1 April 1990, the CCPR has issued an 'action plan' to assist clubs (CCPR, 1990). The main points can be summarised as follows:

Rate relief for sports clubs   The Local Government Finance Act, 1988 allows up to 100 per cent relief from rates to all sports and recreational clubs that are not established or operated for profit. The government has also issued a 'practice note' to all local authorities entitled *Paying for Local Government – Non-Domestic Rates – Discretionary Rate Relief* which gives guidelines on the criteria authorities should use when considering applications from clubs and societies for relief. The guidelines can be considered under two headings:

1.   Sport and recreational clubs which are registered charities.
2.   Non-profit-making clubs which are not charities.

In the first case (registered charities), organisations are entitled to 80 per cent *mandatory* relief. Local authorities also have *discretion* to increase this relief to 100 per cent. In the second case (non-charities), organisations may be granted up to 100 per cent relief from rates *at the discretion of the local authority*. The decision whether or not to allow relief in this second category, and how much relief to allow, is a matter of local authority policy and the merits of each case. Unfortunately, local authorities vary a great deal in their interpretation of the guidelines.

Rateable value   All non-domestic properties in England and Wales, including sports and recreational clubs, were revalued in the late 1980s to provide information for the Uniform Business Rate introduced in April 1990. In many cases the rateable value of clubs increased sharply and the national average increase was estimated by the government to be eight times higher. The rateable value of any club can be inspected by club officials and an appeal can be made to the Inland Revenue Valuation Officer if the rate is considered excessive.

Action for clubs   The first point that clubs should note is that they do not become ineligible because the accounts show 'a profit' at the end of the financial year. Budgeting for a surplus is, after all, sound financial housekeeping. It might be sensible to refer to the excess of income over expenditure as a 'surplus' in audited accounts rather than a 'profit'. Other actions that clubs may consider undertaking include:

– visiting the Inland Revenue Valuation Office to check on the rateable value of your sports club;
– submitting an application for 100 per cent rate relief to the Director of Finance;
– if a problem exists in obtaining relief, arranging a meeting of treasurers of other sports clubs to agree a course of action;
– keeping local media informed of what action clubs are taking;
– writing to elected Councillors;
– keeping the CCPR informed of the situation;
– seeking the help of officers from your Regional Council for Sport and Recreation; and
– considering the establishment of a charitable youth section which could attract 80 per cent mandatory rate relief.

Other formal avenues of finance include: the Countryside Commission, which will aid projects such as footpath conservation, bridleways, and sites for sport and recreation; the Forestry Commission, which will aid such activities as forest walks, car-rallying, orienteering, fishing, rock-climbing, deer-stalking and potholing; and the Regional Water Author-ities which, until privatisation, assisted in the provision of a wide range of water based sports. This role has now been taken over by the new National Rivers Authority.

Balancing the books

Although the major sources of income for many voluntary sports clubs are bar receipts and receipts from subscriptions and match fees, many clubs utilise a wide variety of methods to increase income, including gate receipts, collections, raffles, and social events. Table 7.6 gives a summary of the major areas of income of voluntary clubs, utilising data from The Henley Centre (column A) with additional material, supplied by the author, based on the 1990 accounts of a Yorkshire golf club (column B).

Table 7.6   Summary of voluntary sector income[a]

	Percentages[*]	
	Column A	*Column B*
Bar receipts[**]	41.4	16.3
Subscriptions & match fees receipts	25.8	53.2
Employers subsidies to clubs (e.g. industrial clubs)	21.1	–
Grants	2.1	0.1
Gaming machines, raffles etc.	5.9	1.4
Hire of facilities to outside groups	1.7	21.6
Interest on deposits, etc.	1.5	6.0
Sponsorship and advertising	0.5	1.4

Source: Figures adapted from The Henley Centre (1986) with additional material supplied by the author.

Notes:
(a)   The table does not include non-monetary sector income such as voluntary work contributed to sports clubs and imputed rent for dual use. Column A is derived from figures based on a small-scale survey (n = 35) of club accounts from seven selected sports (football, rugby, athletics, cricket, tennis, golf, and bowls) conducted by The Henley Centre (1986). The figures in Column B are supplied by the author and are based on the 1990 accounts of a Yorkshire golf club.
   [*]   Percentages rounded to the nearest decimal point
   [**]   Bar receipts are gross and an analysis of various club accounts by the author indicates that net profits range between 20 and 50 per cent. For the golf club studied by the author, the profit was 43 per cent.

The figures in Table 7.6, Column A, include industrial sports clubs, hence for clubs not supported by companies or firms the percentage distribution of income looks very different (Column B). It is clear that unless efficient systems are in operation for servicing the bar and collecting subscriptions and match fees, clubs may suffer badly and it is for this reason that the Club Steward is often the only employee of a voluntary club. There are examples of sports clubs operating with a mark-up (the difference between purchase cost and selling price) of only 15–20 per cent but most are looking for 30 per cent plus and the golf club studied operated at a 43 per cent profit. There is, of course, tension between maximising profits from bar sales and passing on the benefits of cheap drinks to members. The commercial sector has a minimum mark-up of 45 per cent on beer, 60 per cent on spirits and often 100 per cent or more on wine and soft drinks. Wastage and mistakes in serving drinks is no higher than 3 per cent in the commercial sector, but in voluntary sports clubs the figure can be much higher.

Another way to balance the books is to control expenditure, but the ability to hold down expenditure increases is difficult. Wage increases have to keep in line with inflation, and if grounds and playing areas are not well maintained membership will suffer. Table 7.7 shows the main areas of expenditure. The proportionally high cost of ground maintenance for the golf club studied by the author should be compared with The Henley Centre figures, and demonstrate the dangers of making generalisations from aggregate data.

The favourite way for treasurers of voluntary clubs to raise funds is by increasing subscriptions. This is simple to administer and provides money in the bank at the beginning of the playing season, but market forces operate within and between sports clubs and subscription levels have to be kept at a level members can afford. Today, clubs are becoming increasingly proficient at utilising a wide variety of fund-raising methods. Perhaps one of the most significant ways of increasing income since the data for The Henley Centre was collected has been in sponsorship, and many small clubs now utilise local businesses to support and endorse club activities.

In conclusion, many sports clubs will need to review their methods of administration and organisation as well as their financial affairs if they are to have a healthy existence in the future. It was noted earlier that the Sports Council will only grant-aid schemes closely related to participation objectives and the meeting of community needs, and all four Sports Councils wish voluntary clubs to establish closer relationships with other providers.

On a more optimistic note, the voluntary sector has been remarkably resilient in overcoming financial probems. Seemingly bankrupt clubs survive and, through special appeals and events, raise money for a new roof, new pitches, or new showers. We have seen that voluntary effort

Table 7.7   Summary of voluntary sector expenditure[a]

	Percentages*	
	Column A	Column B
Bar purchases, ancillary expenditure	58.2	11.7
Wages	24.9	34.4
Ground Maintenance	10.5	42.4[b]
Ground Hire	2.1	–
Rates	1.9	0.4
Travel	1.5	–
Equipment	0.9	–
Other	–	11.1[c]

Source: Figures adapted from The Henley Centre (1986) with additional material supplied by the author.

Notes:
(a)   The table does not include non-monetary factor expenditure such as voluntary work or imputed rent, or capital expenditure investment. Column A is derived from figures based on a small-scale survey (n = 35) of club accounts from seven selected sports conducted by The Henley Centre (1986). The figures in Column B are supplied by the author and are based on the 1990 accounts of a Yorkshire golf club.
(b)   Ground maintenance for the golf club includes drainage expenditure, clubhouse expenses, and security.
(c)   Additional expenditure for the golf club not detailed in The Henley Centre (1986) analysis includes postage and secretarial (5.3 per cent), and sundries (5.8 per cent).
* Percentages rounded to the nearest decimal point.

has been estimated at £81 million and many clubs have members with the skills and professional knowledge (and contacts) to undertake work on a self-help basis.

Exercise
Evaluate the major items of income and expenditure of a voluntary sports club known to you. It has been suggested that voluntary sports clubs should do more to attract sponsorship and funding from the commercial sector. Assess how a local sports club could do this, and comment on the problems involved.

Policy and Planning

Policy and planning for sport and physical recreation does not take place in a cohesive or co-ordinated manner. Planning has been termed a 'patchwork quilt' – a collection of colourful but distinct initiatives. There is plenty of variety but a distinct lack of centralised policy-making at national and local level. Despite the bewildering number of government departments, agencies, organisations, and 'quangos' involved in sport, at an international level the UK continues to produce individuals and teams which lead the world. In 1989, the British Athletics team won the men's European Cup, beating countries such as the USSR and the then East Germany. The women's team also did well to finish third. In both cases, European countries with a tradition of highly structured and carefully controlled policies finished second best. How is it we can achieve impressive successes in some sports but fail in others? Why, for example, have we consistently failed, in recent years, to produce any tennis players of top international calibre, despite a long tradition in the sport?

In order to gain consistency in performance at international level in a wide variety of sports, something more than *ad hoc* planning is necessary. Those sports that have achieved success in the international arena have the same clear characteristics: a foundation of enthusiasm and commitment; planning; and coaching at the grass-roots level. .

At the heart of international success in athletics is the thriving system of club athletics. Whilst recognising that there are a complex set of economic, social and cultural issues that support individual international success, efficient and enthusiastic coaching and administration by a large bank of volunteers has enabled athletics to cast the net wide. Mass participation, backed by sound coaching and good facilities for the talented, is the secret of finding new stars for the future. Athletics has done this; tennis, in the past, has not. On the contrary, tennis has maintained a class-based system at club level that directly excludes the majority. The Indoor Tennis Initiative, described earlier, is an attempt to improve opportunity, but compared with countries such as France and West Germany we still lag far behind. In 1988, the UK had 250 indoor courts, which was slighty more than Paris! France and West Germany have similar populations to the UK and boast 3000 and 2600 courts respectively. At the same time, a survey of outdoor tennis courts in the UK revealed that 60 per cent of public courts were in a poor state of repair and badly maintained. Between 1980 and 1989 the number of tennis clubs affiliated to the Lawn Tennis Association actually declined, and the UK was alone in Europe in showing a drop in club membership (Sports Council, 1980). However, it is at club level that the crux of the problem lies. Club tennis in the UK has historically been elitist, providing little opportunity for youngsters, and very limited coaching.

A joint survey report, by the Lawn Tennis Association and the Sports Council concluded that 'juniors were not well catered for in terms of the amount of coaching provided'; coaching was 'limited in extent [with] few well qualified coaches and limited opportunities for singles play' (Lawn Tennis Association/Sports Council, 1987).

The examples of tennis and athletics illustrate the distinct approaches to captivating young people into sport. Mass participation and excellence are two sides of the same coin, and success at international level will in turn stimulate greater participation at 'grass roots'.

Let us see, then, what the current policy and planning initiatives of the four Sports Councils are:

Sports Council Policy and Planning

In 1982 the Sports Council published *Sport in the Community: the Next Ten years*, which formed a strategy for sport generally in the UK. In its strategy, the Council sought to increase mass participation in two broad target groups: (i)   the 13–24 age group, and (ii)   the 45–59 age group. The Council recognised that each broad target group could be broken down into a number of subgroups and that certain subgroups would need identifying for particular support. The subgroups were identified as:

(in the 13–24 age group)
–   schoolchildren
–   the unemployed
–   low-income young marrieds with children
–   single parents
and
(in the 45–59 age group)
–   the unemployed
–   low-income people with children still at home.

The Council also recognised that within each subgroup there were those such as ethnic minorities; people with disabilities; and women, who were under-represented in participation figures.

Three strategies were identified in order to meet the objects and targets set:

A.   To channel the skills and expertise of the Council into developing new participation schemes via its headquarters and regional offices.
B.   To operate demonstration projects throughout the country in partnership with local education authorities, local authorities, voluntary and commercial sports clubs, and through its regional offices. Projects would be grant-aided by the Council.
C.   Provide additional grant aid for schemes based on successful demonstration projects.

A major priority for grant-aided projects was to be in the deprived inner cities and among the young. This policy supported the government's concern regarding the young in deprived areas following the inner-city riots of 1980/81.

The Sports Council promised that it would review its ten year strategy mid-term, and in early 1987 circulated a consultation paper *Sport in the Community – Which Ways Forward?* to some 1200 organisations. The paper asked sixty questions about trends and the roles of providers, and the 345 responses were analysed to assist in the formulation of the strategy for sport from 1988–1993 (Sports Council, 1988a). The revised strategy reflects the Council's two broad themes of promoting mass participation and the promotion of performance and excellence. It is also recognised that the facility requirements needed to support these themes are central to its success (Coe, 1988).

Meanwhile, the Sports Council for Wales was formulating its own ten-year strategy for sport for 1986–1996 *Changing Times – Changing Needs* (1986a); and in 1989 the Scottish Sports Council published a strategic plan for the development of sport in Scotland to the end of the century, *Sport 2000* (1986a). The Sports Council for Northern Ireland has not, to date, published a strategy report, but in the Annual Report 1988/89 (1989) a consideration of sport in Northern Ireland up to the year 2000 is made. The plans of each council will be considered in turn.

England

Promoting Mass Participation

In England the Sports Council has identified three main subgroups on which to concentrate efforts until 1993. These are young people, women and 45–59-year-olds (Sports Council, 1988a). In order to help achieve the targets set, new and improved facilities were identified as follows:

- 500 more sports halls
- 150 more pools
- improved pitches
- new artificial pitches
- more safe routes for cyclists and joggers
- improved access to countryside and water.

The Council recognises that one of the most profound influences on the future provision and management of facilities and resources will be the role of local authorities and, in a continuing 'mixed economy' of provision, the Council will have a pivotal role in co-ordinating and co-operating with other sectors, agencies, and organisations. The Council is also concerned to maximise the use of existing resources and seeks to promote further dual-use and links with Local Education Authorities.

Some examples of initiatives that have supported Sports Council policy for promoting mass participation include:

Small Community Recreation Centres   (SCRCs) These have been created to meet the need for small-scale provision and to support deprived rural and village communities. The SCRC project was developed by the Sports Council in 1987 as part of a two-year programme. Rather than providing new facilities, the project concentrated on improving and upgrading existing provision in such places as church halls, school halls, redundant farm buildings, and even open spaces. As an example, the Sports Council (Eastern Region) provided seventy sets of carpet bowls to be used in rural village halls. There are now more than 250 village clubs with over 10,000 participants.

The Countryside and Water Recreation Policy Group   This was set up in January 1988 to advise the Sports Council on ways of safeguarding and improving opportunities for young people to participate in countryside and water activities, and to formulate policies for sport and active recreation which utilise natural resources. Part of the group's role is to co-operate with other agencies and to discuss links between sport and aspects of the environment.

The Indoor Tennis Initiative   (ITI) As mentioned earlier, this was established in 1988 to stimulate investment by local authorities and to provide a national network of indoor tennis facilities. Pilkington Glass has invested £100,000 in Warrington as part of the scheme.

Association Football Schemes   The Sports Council and the Football Trust continue to work together to provide new facilities and to upgrade existing facilities for community use. The Trust is financed by the Football Pools companies (through the Spot-the-Ball competition).

In addition to these initiatives the Sports Council continues to promote Demonstration Projects with community groups and other direct intervention strategies such as Action Sport.

Promoting Performance and Excellence

Promoting performance means fostering a commitment to an activity in its own right and promoting the opportunity and desire for improved competitive results. In other words this means assisting those who want to get better at what they do. Promoting excellence involves assisting those who wish to reach the pinnacle of sporting performance at either national or international level. Accordingly, the Council has selected two broad areas on which to concentrate its efforts and resources:

1.   The development of regional and local performance strategies; and
2.   Promoting the achievement of excellence.

In order to achieve its aims, a number of major new facilities were identified for priorty action (at 1987 prices):

- a national indoor velodrome (for cycle racing) (estimated cost of £7 million)
- a national ice skating training centre (£3–4 million)
- a national centre and arena for movement and dance (£3–4 million)
- a national indoor athletics training centre (£2 million)
- a national outdoor competition centre for bowls (£0.4–0.7 million).

The Council also sought to improve facilities and the management of its own National Centres. Some of the specific initiatives that support Council policy for promoting performance and excellence include:

The National Coaching Foundation (NCF)   This was created in 1983 to improve standards of coaching; share and disseminate research; organise courses and conferences; investigate possible sources of funding for coaching; and provide an advisory service for coaches and performers throughout the UK. In April 1989 the NCF was established as a company limited by guarantee with charitable status, and the Foundation has also established a subsidiary company – Coachwise Ltd. The NCF now has a network of fourteen regional coaching centres throughout the UK and two resource centres. A National Coaching Diploma has also been developed for experienced coaches.

The National Centres Board   This was established in 1987 to manage and develop the five National Sports Centres. The national centres are designed to provide high quality facilities and resources for top-level performers. Some centres are also open to the local community.

Sports Medicine and Science   This will continue to be supported through the offices of the National Coaching Foundation and the governing bodies of sport. Additional developments have included the opening of the British Olympic Medical Centre at Northwick Park Hospital, Harrow, the Football Association's Human Performance Testing Laboratory at Lilleshall in Shropshire, and educational courses for doctors, physiotherapists, and coaches.

The Sports Aid Foundation   This is a limited company formed in 1979, managed by a Board of Governors, who are grant-aided by the Sports Council (£25,000 in 1989/90) and aim to raise funds to assist top amateur performers. Individuals are assisted according to need, and grants go towards items such as transport and travel for training, small items of personal equipment, coaching fees, and costs of special foods.

Wales

A consultative document was circulated to local authorities, governing bodies of sport, national and statutory agencies in October 1985 and responses were taken into account in producing the strategy document *Changing Times – Changing Needs* (Sports Council for Wales, 1986a).

Promoting Mass Participation

The SCW identified the following target groups for the promotion of programmes during the period 1986–1996:

(i)   Children aged 11–16 years, focusing on extra-curricular activities.
(ii) Teenagers and youngsters aged 16–24.
(iii) Mature adults aged 45–59.

It is recognised by the SCW that within these broad groupings there should be particular emphasis on women, the unemployed, the economically disadvantaged, and people with disabilities.

The SCW anticipates attracting an additional 300,000 people in Wales to participate regularly in active recreation by 1996, and a number of priorities for required action have been identified to achieve this target:

- promotional programmes for ten selected sports
- motivation to encourage participation among low participant groups
- more qualified community sports leaders
- the adaptation of 115 existing school sports halls to enable further community use
- the provision of twenty new community sports halls
- upgrading of thirty village/church halls and community centres
- establishing of greater co-operation and partnership between local authorities, schools, sports clubs and the voluntary sector
- the building of thirty low cost sports halls
- the drainage of existing playing surfaces and increased provision of floodlit all-weather areas
- maximising of the use of existing resources.

Promoting Performance and Excellence

The SCW has recognised that many of the governing bodies of sport in Wales are concerned with high-level competition rather than with increasing participation at the grass roots level (Sports Council for Wales, 1986a). A SCW survey of sports centre users has also revealed a high percentage of 'informal' users and that governing bodies are involved with only a small proportion of total participants in sport (Sports Council for Wales, 1986b). Thus the policy of the SCW for promoting performance will concentrate on harnessing the work of other agencies such as local authorities and voluntary agencies who are catering for large numbers of participants. This will allow the governing bodies to concentrate on promoting excellence and the throughput of coaches and trainers. The SCW also recognises that in order to achieve excellence a concentration of resources on selected sports, individual performers, and priorities within sports will be necessary.

Further policy decisions include the development of regional Advanced Training Centres (established initially in 1983) suitable for above-average performers, and the maximisation of use of the National Sports Centre for Wales in Cardiff and Plas Menai, the National Water Centre in the Menai Straits, Gwynedd. In addition to its National Sports Centres, Wales has its own National Coaching Centres, one in Cardiff and one in Bangor.

Scotland

In July 1988 the SSC published *Sport 2000: A Scottish Strategy*, which was a consultative document intended to provoke debate and comment on sport throughout Scotland. This was followed up by over twenty seminars, over a hundred written responses, and a national conference, in order to provide the widest possible forum for formulating a strategy plan. The result was *Sport 2000* (Scottish Sports Council, 1989a) which is the policy document for sport in Scotland until the end of the century.

The SSC policy for developing opportunities for mass participation, performance and excellence is based on the concept of a continuum ranging from an initial interest or foundation at one end, through participation, performance and finally excellence at the other. The foundation level involves non-specific sport and physical recreation promoted mainly through play and physical education. This stage provides a basic 'body literacy' which is essential for purposeful participation. The participation stage is involvement in sport or physical recreation for recreational ends, or for social or health reasons, or for enjoyment, but at this level there are few aspirations to achieve high standards of attainment (Scottish Sports Council, 1989a, 3.6–3.7).

Promoting a Foundation for Sport and Physical Recreation

This is mainly achieved by promoting play and physical education and the SSC aims to:

- encourage co-operation and the co-ordination of agencies involved in children's play
- encourage regional and islands councils to review their current position on physical education
- encourage greater clarity and purpose within the physical education profession in supporting the notion of a solid foundation for the lifetime involvement in sport and physical recreation.

Promoting Participation

This stage involves maintaining the level of interest already secured, maintaining the levels, the frequency, and the quality of performance, and encouraging non-participants. This part of the strategy concentrates on six broad target groups:

- women
- the middle-aged and beyond
- the socially and economically disadvantaged
- unemployed people
- young people
- people with disabilities.

Promoting Performance and Excellence

The SSC recognises that in the past there has been a failure to realise the potential of those who wish to achieve the highest levels of performance (Scottish Sports Council, 1989a: 3.51). In a period of economic constraint the SSC identified three strategies for improving opportunities for promoting performance and excellence:

(i)   improved leadership;
(ii)   improved coaching; and
(iii) greater attention to sports medicine and sports science.

Leadership   One way to encourage improved performance is to develop local leadership. The SSC wishes to develop leadership courses and coaching awards in order to provide trained personnel who can motivate those at the foundation stage. This can be achieved by developing community sports leadership courses within local authorities and through leadership courses in conjunction with the Scottish Vocational Education Council (SCOTVEC).

Coaching   Scotland has its own National Coaching Centres at Jordan-hill College in Glasgow and Moray House College in Edinburgh as well as five regional coaching centres. In 1987 the SSC published a consultative document on coaching and coach education which resulted in a major policy document, the *National Strategy for Coach Education and Coaching Development in Scotland*. The four main strands of the coaching policy are:

1.   *Coach Education Provision* – the revision of existing programmes, the development of new resources and facilities, and the integration of coaching with formal education structures.

2. *Professionalism* – the development of an agreed and systematic body of knowledge, the development of a code of ethics for coaches, and the control of standards, qualifications, and entry into the coaching profession.
3. *Employment and Deployment of Coaches* – to provide examples of good practice for the employment of coaching within local authorities and the private sector and to ensure the equitable deployment of coaches in urban and rural communities.
4. *Support Services* – the development of advisory services and promotion and marketing to support coach education at both local and national level.

Sports Medicine and Sports Science   In 1984 the SSC established a Consultative Group on Sports Medicine and Sports Sciences. This group has assisted in the co-ordination of twenty-three sports medicine centres throughout Scotland, the provision of an education programme for doctors, physiotherapists and coaches, and the co-ordination of the work of sports scientists to ensure practical help for coaches. The SSC also has plans for establishing an Institute of Sports Medicine and Sports Sciences.

The SSC operates three National Sports Training Centres for those aspiring to the highest levels of participation. Glenmore Lodge in the Cairngorms caters for mountain training; the Inverclyde Centre in Largs services a range of indoor and outdoor sports; and the centre at Cumbrae provides top class opportunities for sailing, canoeing, and windsurfing. In addition there has been, since 1987, an initiative called 'TSB Scotland' to meet the costs of fifteen regional and three national Schools of Sport. These schools provide high level coaching for promising young men and women.

Northern Ireland

In 1989 the Sports Council for Northern Ireland (SCNI) produced a strategy statement on extending participation which emphasised the importance of partnership arrangements and co-ordinated initiatives to achieve maximum benefits.

Promoting Mass Participation

The SCNI works closely with the twenty-six district councils in Northern Ireland to promote participation. Target groups include young people, women, and people with disabilities, and the district councils identify areas of special need in their own regions. The SCNI support some twenty-nine Information Points established by the District Councils and co-operate in providing a sports information network through local libraries. Another way participation is promoted is through a Sports Mobile Unit which enables participants to undertake fitness tests and receive advice on exercise schedules.

A further objective in extending participation in Northern Ireland is the development of trained leaders and coaches.

Improving Performance and Excellence

Along with the three other Sports Councils a major way of developing performance and excellence for the SCNI is by grant-aiding and supporting the governing bodies of sport. Other ways of improving performance and excellence have been through the following initiatives:

(i)   *The Ulster Sports and Recreation Trust* – this is an independent charitable Trust which helps those who have ability in their chosen sport. The Trust provides financial awards towards out-of-pocket costs and in 1988/89 made awards amounting to £16,225.

(ii) *Northern Ireland Institute of Coaching* – the Institute provides an extensive programme of coach education courses at various levels and holds an annual conference for members.

(iii) *Regional Schools of Sport* – these schools (three in number) are sponsored by Northern Bank and provide opportunities to improve personal performance and seek to increase the number of qualified coaches. The governing bodies use the schools to bring together talented young performers in regional squads for specialist attention. There are also two schools of sporting excellence sponsored by Dale Farm which provide concentrated high-level coaching for two days each. In addition, there are a number of three-day 'schools of sport' at Craigavon for selected junior squads and individuals.

(iv) *International Sports Academy* – the Academy is an annual event involving twenty-two governing bodies of sport (1988/89) and provides opportunities to develop coaching skills in a wide range of activities.

Other support activities to assist high level performers include a Drug Abuse Panel and a Fitness Testing Project, both supported by the SCNI.

As has previously been noted the strategy and planning documents of the various Sports Councils highlight two distinct markets for sport and physical recreation. One is generally affluent, healthy and well-educated; the other consists of the unemployed and low waged, who are less healthy, and who are concentrated in deprived urban and rural communities. The strategies suggest the former group is best provided for by the commercial and voluntary sectors, whilst the latter group will be best served by the public sector. All four Sports Councils also strongly support much closer links between the various sectors of provision and see improved co-ordination as a central platform to their plans.

Exercise

Find out from your Regional Council for Sport and Recreation or your Local Sports Council what recent policy and planning initiatives have taken place. How are the policy initiatives to be funded? What evidence is there of partnerships between various sectors of provision?

Policy and planning initiatives for sport and physical recreation are not limited to the Sports Councils, or the local authorities and Local Education Authorities. Other important agencies such as the Countryside Commission and the Water authorities (up to 1989) have made policy and planning decisions that directly affect sport and physical recreation. Those policies concerning the countryside have been dealt with in the Countryside Recreation chapter, but it is necessary now to consider the likely influence of the new Water companies and the National Rivers Authority.

Water Privatisation

In November 1989 the ten English and Welsh water authorities were formally floated on the stock market as private companies. Control over rivers, water pollution, fisheries, navigation, harbours, land drainage and flood control is now the responsibility of the new National Rivers Authority (NRA). However, the British Waterways Board continues to have navigational authority for the 2000 miles (3220 km) of canals and rivers in England, Scotland and Wales, around 60 per cent of which is used for cruising, fishing or other leisure activities.

There were in excess of 650,000 acres (263,250 hectares) of land owned by the Water authorities prior to November 1989, and there is fear that the amenity and recreational responsibilities of the old Water authorities, as well as many voluntary agreements for access, will be interpreted differently in the future. The government has pledged that the new NRA and the Water companies will inherit recreational responsibilities, but the question arises as to how seriously these responsibilities will be taken. More than two-thirds of reservoirs in excess of 5 acres (2.02 hectares) are used for fishing, sailing, sail-boarding and canoeing. Despite the fact that these activities generate income, because of the large capital investment that is needed in Britain's water and sewerage business the temptation is to sell off areas of surplus land. Clearly, careful monitoring will be needed if access to these sites for sport and physical recreation is to be safeguarded, and the Sports Council is committed to ensuring a continuity of existing provision and service, and further improvements where possible.

The Commercial Sector

Commercial sector organisations are concerned with one major principle when undertaking new policy and planning initiatives, and that is the principle of 'opportunity cost'. Until the late 1970s it was seldom considered profitable to invest in sport and physical recreation provision that required large capital outlay. There were exceptions, such as ten-pin bowling, but for most commercial organisations there were safer and more handsome returns from developments in housing, office accommodation and shopping.

The growing recognition of the importance of leisure, greater disposable income, attactive interest rates, and partnership incentives from local government, stimulated investment in a wide variety of leisure complexes throughout most of the 1980s. Major areas of investment included theme parks, golf and country club hotels, sports villages, marinas and water-based centres, health and fitness centres, indoor tennis and indoor cricket. The leisure market has also matured. Second-rate facilities are no longer tolerated, and the commercial sector has been able to provide quality and comfort through better furnishings and management. The opening up of public provision for commercial management has also extended an opportunity for commercial sector managers to invest in sport and recreation.

Mixed developments consisting of shopping, office accommodation, housing and leisure opportunities has been another feature of the 1980s, although the high interest rates of the late 1980s and early 1990s has forced many companies to curtail further expansion. Perhaps the most spectacular developments have been the transformation of docklands such as London and Liverpool and the use of the extensive water areas for numerous sports. The emphasis is on industry and commerce, housing and leisure facilities coexisting, and together these features assist the process of urban renewal in areas that previously were derelict and forgotten. Indeed, the opportunity to take part in or observe a wide range of water sports is utilised as a major selling feature to industry and to potential home purchasers. Another example of mixed development is the sports village concept mentioned earlier.

Exercise
What are the commercial advantages of 'mixed development'? Visit a mixed development in your area and note the range of different provision.

Not all developments by the commercial sector have been received enthusiastically and there is a danger that public and minority interests may be jeopardised. Local people have been forced out of areas when developments like London Docklands have taken place. Marine developments such as the new Brighton marina, the Maritime Quarters in Swansea and Liverpool, Glasgow Canal Project, the Dundee Waterfront Development, and the Irvine New Town Development in Scotland, are all examples where, unless specific provision is made, an upgrading of a locality can force up prices beyond the means of local people. There are also examples of large companies such as Mecca and Whitbreads buying up golf courses for the luxury country hotel market. Furthermore, football clubs, cricket clubs and racecourses offer opportunities for development that may not be in the best long term interest of participants, spectators or local inhabitants. Further issues concerning policy and planning for sport and physical recreation will be addressed in the next section.

Future Prospects

There are a number of changes taking place in society that will influence participation in, and consumption of, sport and physical recreation. We have seen earlier how the drop in the number of 16 to 24-year-olds over the next few years could affect sports participation, and the continued move away from physically demanding heavy work to jobs in the service sector may also affect participation rates.

Depending on the government in power, there is also the prospect of further changes in direct taxation and public expenditure. A Conservative Government is likely to support actions to increase the power of consumers and provide greater incentives and opportunities for the commercial sector.

The European Community is also influencing legislation and policy issues in the UK. The Council for Europe in October 1988 highlighted the important role of sport and physical recreation in improving the quality of life in urban areas. As a consequence, an *Urban Charter* has been set up to encourage the involvement of communities in planning and designing localised facilities. The effect of European legislation on sport is going to be significant in areas such as employment, trade, and public safety, and is considered further below.

Increasing numbers of people are concerned about their health and fitness. The trend is for an increased awareness of the benefits of sport and healthy exercise as part of a balanced lifestyle. Spending on sport and fitness is expected to grow thoughout the next decade, yet the time available for leisure will continue to be squeezed for certain sectors of the population. The average number of hours worked each week for many people has actually risen over the last decade, and women are likely to suffer reduced leisure time as they move back into the part-time and full-time labour force. On the other hand, the amount of disposable income for these households is likely to rise.

There is growing pressure to conserve and protect our natural resources, and changes are taking place in the way agricultural land is being used. Although damage to the countryside caused by recreation is small compared with industrial pollution, there will be continued pressure to ensure sound management and planning so that conflicts between recreation and conservation may be minimised.

The changes referred to above will influence the way the public, commercial and voluntary sectors of provision plan for the future. Some of these prospects will now be considered.

The European Community and Sport

The European Community (EC) regards sport as a way of promoting the notion and ethos of the Community as well as encouraging member countries and individuals to identify with it. A small budget of around 1.5m ECUs (1 ECU = £0.74) was granted in 1990 to sponsor events such as the EC Swimming Championships, the EC Cycle Race, and the EC Cross Country Cup. National sports federations are also being encouraged to arrange sports events with the EC in mind, Scotland, for example, received 300,000 ECUs towards the cost of staging the EC Special Olympics in July 1990.

Work in the EC – Freedom of Movement

EC law ensures that professional sportsmen and women, sports coaches, and sports and leisure managers have the right to earn a living anywhere in the EC. The Union of European Football Associations has, for example, proposed the fielding of up to three non-nationals and in addition two players who have accumulated five consecutive years' service in the host member state. This will initially apply for all first division clubs from 1993, but the EC is urging application of this rule to all divisions as soon as practical. A standard contract of employment for football clubs and players is also being considered.

For coaches, sports officers and managers the EC will compel member states to recognise professional qualifications gained in other member states. The competition for vacant or new positions from applicants from other EC states with good command of English will be to the disadvantage of UK workers who are not fluent in foreign languages.

Greater harmonisation for the education and training of leisure professionals is the main objective of the International Association for the Management of Sport (AIMS). This private organisation was established in 1987 and has asked the EC to consider establishing a European Sports Management Institute.

The Committee for the Development of Sport)

This is yet another QUANGO, this time a division of the Council of Europe. The committee has considered present and future initiatives around a number of themes:

- ethical values in sport, including the promotion of fair play
- the concept of sport for all
- safety for participation and safe facilities for spectators
- future issues such as planning, an urban charter, and sports management training.

The issue of management training is again taken up by another organisation called the Standing Committee of Regional and Local Authorities in Europe (CRLAE). This committee is attempting to gain a greater level of equivalence in qualifications, skills and competences across the EC and has already recommended stronger components of generic management and linguistic competences in courses.

Further details of these and other developments are available from the excellent Scottish Sports Council publication *Sport: A European Perspective*, Information Digest PM12, 1990.

The Public and Voluntary Sectors

In the public and voluntary sectors local authorities, local education authorities, parish councils, as well as bodies such as the four Sports Councils, are all in a period of change. Competitive tendering and the drive to make public-sector organisations more cost effective, has produced a major rethink of how sport and recreation should be managed and financed. Future prospects are viewed in two contrasting ways. There are those who see change as an opportunity to reform practices in administration and management, improve the quality of provision, and develop new and productive partnerships. Then there are those who see current patterns of change as a threat. They feel that minority groups and the poor will be priced out, opportunities for high-level performers to practise and train will be reduced, safety standards will fall, and access to opportunities in the countryside will be reduced. A particular area of concern as we saw earlier, has been the loss of sports grounds and recreational spaces over the last few years. The high cost of land has placed many sports grounds and school playing fields under threat. Over the past thirty years, over one hundred industrial sports clubs have been lost in the West Midlands alone and over fifty more are at serious risk (Sports Council, 1988a).

The Community Charge and Capital Control

The Community Charge served to increase pressure to reduce council spending and sharpened demands for improved targeting of subsidies. It is recognised, for example, that the proportion of professional people who regularly take part in sport is about twice as high as that of unskilled manual workers (Audit Commission, 1989). Furthermore, the alteration of the *capital control system* in local authorities in April 1990 means that capital receipts are now taken into account when fixing the borrowing requirements of an individual authority. Hence, capital receipts must now be earmarked to repay debt. In addition, when a local authority enters into a 'planning gain' agreement with a sports developer, the land provided by the authority is treated as a capital receipt and hence brought within the capital control system.

School Physical Education

Another piece of government legislation, the Education Reform Act, 1988, will result in the delegation of budgets to schools and the introduction of local management by governing bodies of schools. The new governing bodies will be able to review the use of their own facilities by the public as well as 'rationalise' the hire of public facilities for their own pupils' use. In addition, there will be pressure on traditional out-of-school activities through tighter financial controls. The role of PE and games as part of the National Curriculum is also giving cause for concern and a preliminary report of a government working party on the place of PE in state schools, was published in April 1991.

Compulsory Competitive Tendering

Finally, the Local Government Act, 1988 (Competition in Sport and Leisure Facilities) Order, 1989, came into force on 28 December, 1989.

Known as Compulsory Competitive Tendering (CCT) the Order requires local authorities to tender the management of sports and leisure facilities. There has been some concern that as a result of CCT, local authorities will become 'residuary bodies' providing minimum services as a safety net to fill the void left by the commercial and voluntary sectors (Benington and White, 1988). The alternative scenario is for the public sector to take on a 'pro-active leadership role' in order to generate 'a strategic vision and framework for the whole sphere of leisure...' (Ibid., p. 246). Benington and White go on to describe three sources of potential power that should provide the platform for future strategies:

1. 'A social role – identifying needs and priorities within the community and developing and distributing services to meet those needs';
2. 'An economic role – using its position as an important employer, purchaser, and economic agent within the local community to influence patterns of investment, job creation and training within the area';
3. 'An ideological and political role – using its authority as the (only) body with an electoral mandate to represent the needs and values not just of one interest group, but of the community as a whole (the employed as well as the unemployed; old as well as young; women as well as men; black people as well as white; management and labour; future generations as well as the present population)'.
    (Ibid., p. 246)

The challenge for local authorities specifically, and the public sector in general, will be in providing a more efficient service, including income maximisation, without damaging social objectives. Local authorities will be held more accountable to both clients and paymasters, and a more rigorous planning strategy and review process, including the use of performance indication, is likely to be imposed (Audit Commission, 1989).

CCT includes the opportunity for 'in-house' bidding by the incumbent leisure services department, or a management buy-out from the local authority sector. An example of success in the second category is that of Circa Leisure which announced a pre-tax profit of £137,000 on a turnover of £1.45 million in their first year of trading. Circa Leisure was formed in January 1988 following the encouragement of Rochford District Council to allow the leisure staff to buy out the management functions. The company is wholly owned by its employees.

The Commercial Sector

The commercial sector will have an increasing impact on sport and physical recreation provision and management. The sports goods market is expected to continue to grow well into the 1990s. A major area of development is expected to be the fun and fitness market, with a move away from traditional team games and formal competitive activities. The commercial sector also makes good use of new technology and improved equipment design. There are likely to be increasing opportunities to take part in a variety of activities utilising high technology equipment, such as golf machines and fitness equipment with 3D graphic displays and simulated experiences. Indoor skiing is now feasible due to a break-through in snow-making equipment, and transportable outdoor synthe-tic ice could change the concept of ice sports. Even more challenging and exciting water flumes and related equipment will continue to boost the leisure pool concept.

The Commercialisation of Sport

Sport is more than active involvement by participants, and includes gambling, spectating, and a wide range of passive sports. Many of these sports are provided and encouraged by the commercial sector and are therefore exposed to commercial pressures. In some cases the conduct, rules and very essence of sports can change; in other cases commercial pressures stretch traditional boundaries of ethics and morality.

The commercialisation of the Olympic movement was obvious in Los Angeles in 1984 and continued in the Seoul Olympics in 1988. The latter event witnessed television revenue of $383 million, sponsorship of $350 million and a final operating profit of $69.5 million. The timing of events each day was seldom for the benefit of the competitors but for the benefit of the television companies. The power of big sponsors is also significant. When asked which city he thought would be successful in the bidding to host the Olympic Games in 1996, Lord Killanin (Chairman of the International Olympic Committee from 1973–80) correctly predicted Atlanta, Georgia, USA, as it was the headquarters of the Coca Cola Company! The Olympic Games have grown to such an extent that, commercial development may be the only way of securing the future of the event.

Many of the changes and additions to sport brought about by commercial interests are not harmful and lead to new and exciting events, increased participation, and more money for clubs and individ-uals. But the commercial sector has to be kept in check, and care will be needed over the next decade to safeguard some of the remaining traditions and values associated with sport.

Further Study

Choose an appropriate geographical area where there is public, voluntary and commercial provision for sport and physical recreation. A 'ward map' would be useful for this exercise and you could add areas of housing density, transport routes and open spaces. Plot different aspects of provision for sport and physical recreation so that you produce a map of facilities.

Visit a selection of the facilities and record information from the following checklist:

- What is the quality of equipment?
- What is the practicality and safety of equipment and playing surfaces?
- Is the lighting and ventilation suitable?
- Are changing areas and showers secure and comfortable?
- What is the quality of first aid provision?
- Who uses the facilities?
- Are there opportunities for beginners, for example instruction and coaching?
- Do the facilities meet the needs of the local community?
- Are the facilities easily accessible by public transport?
- Are the facilities suitable for people with disabilities?
- Is provision made for mothers with young children?

You may like to contrast aspects of provision between different providers. You could also interview members of the public to see what they think of the facilities. Try to discover why particular activities are enjoyed and how often people take part in them. Write down what you think could be done to improve opportunities for participation within the chosen area. Can you cost your suggestions? How feasible are they?

Finally, review media, promotional and advertising materials relating to sport and physical recreation. This could include examining noticeboards, library information points and local papers. Is the material of good quality? Is it representative of all groups (women, the disabled, the elderly, etc.)? Is the material up-to-date and accurate?

Review current and back copies of magazines and journals such as *Leisure Management*; *The Leisure Manager* (the magazine of ILAM); *Sport and Leisure* (the magazine of the Sports Council); and *Leisure Business* (Marcus Leisure Press). Note areas of development, new products, innovations in equipment and playing surfaces, who is investing and how much, issues of concern, features on management and administration. You may be able to identify new trends and fashions. You should also be able to assess the profitable areas of sport and physical recreation that appeal to the commercial sector, as well as minority sporting interests.

Questions
1. Explain why you think it desirable to maintain a healthy mix of provision between the public, voluntary and commercial sectors.
2. Why do you think provision for both mass participation *and* excellence and performance are important?
3. What are the concerns expressed for sport and physical recreation as a result of the introduction of the Education Reform Act 1988?

References

J. Arlott (1975) *The Oxford Companion to Sports and Games*, Open University Press.

D. Anthony (1980) *A Strategy for British Sport*, C. Hunt & Co.

Audit Commission (1989) *Sport for Whom? Clarifying the Local Authority Role in Sport and Recreation*, HMSO .

J. Benington and J. White (1988) *The Future of Leisure Services*, Longman.

J. M. Brohm (1978) *Sport, a prison of measured time*, Ink Links Ltd.

J. M. Buchanan (1965) 'An economic survey of clubs', *Economica*, 32, pp. 1–14, quoted in C. Gratton and P. Taylor (1985).

J. Buswell and C. Escott (1987) *From School to Community*, National Demonstration Project – Interim Report, College of St Paul & St Mary, Cheltenham.

P. Butson (1983) *The Financing of Sport in the UK*, Sports Council Information Service No 8, Sports Council .

B. Carrington and D. Leaman (1982) 'Work for Some and Sport for All', *Youth and Policy*, vol. 1, no. 3.

Central Council for Physical Recreation (CCPR) (1990) *Down with Rates*, CCPR.

CIPFA (1985) *Leisure and Recreation Statistics Estimates*, CIPFA, February 1985.

CIPFA (1989) *Leisure and Recreation Estimates 1988–89*, Chartered Institute of Public Finance and Accountancy.

J. Clough (1989) 'Corporate Health', *Leisure Management*, vol. 9, no. 4, pp. 82–4.

F. Coalter *et al.* (1986) *Rationale for Public Sector Investment in Leisure*, Sports Council/ESRC .

S. Coe (1988), 'The Strategy Launch – Into the 90s', in *Recreational Management 1988* Conference Proceedings, Sports Council, pp. 18–23.

Department of the Environment (1989) *Paying for Local Government – Non-Domestic Rates – Discretionary Rate Relief*, DoE/Welsh Office, HMSO.

Department of the Environment, (1975) *Sport and Recreation*, HMSO, Cmnd 6200.

Department of the Environment, (1977) *Policy for the Inner Cities*, HMSO, Cmnd. 6845.

R. Emes (1988) 'The Implementation of the Strategy: A View from the Voluntary Sector' in *Recreation Management 1988*, pp. 52–8.

P. H. Fentem, E. S. Bassey and N. B. Turnbull (1988) *The New Case for Exercise*, Sports Council & Health Education Authority.

M. Fitzjohn (1988) 'Sport – shifting sands in turning tides', in J. Benington and J. White, pp. 141–54.

C. Gratton and P. Taylor (1985) *Sport and Recreation: An Economic Analysis*, E. & F. N. Spon.

C. Gratton and P. Taylor (1988) *Economics of Leisure Service Management*, Longman.

C. Handy (1989) *The Age of Unreason*, Business Books Ltd.

J. Hargreaves (1984) 'State Intervention in Sport and Hegemony in Britain', L.S.A. International Conference, *Leisure: Politics Planning and People*, Brighton.

L. Haywood *et al.* (1989) *Understanding Leisure*, Hutchinson.

Henley Centre, The (1986) *Leisure Futures*, The Henley Centre.

Henley Centre, The (1989a) *The Director's Report*, May 1989, published monthly by The Henley Centre.

Henley Centre, The (1989b) 'The Second Nation', *Marketing Business*, Feb. 1989, pp. 10–11.

HMSO (1986) *General Household Survey*, HMSO.

S. Johnson (1988) 'British Theme Parks', *Leisure Management*, vol. 8 no. 7, 1988.

Lawn Tennis Association/Sports Council (1987) *LTA Affiliated Clubs – National Study for Tennis*, LTA/Sports Council.

Leisure Consultants (1988) *Leisure Forecast*, Leisure Consultants, Autumn 1988.

Leisure Management (1990) 'A Theme for the Future', Leisure Management, vol. 10, no. 10, 1990.

N. Ridley (1988) *Enabling not Providing*, Department of the Environment.

RSL Sportscan (1989) *Marketing/Sportscan Quarterly Survey*, May 1989, RSL Sportscan.

T. Sandler and J. T. Tschirhart (1980) 'The economic theory of clubs: an evaluative survey', in C. Gratton and P. Taylor (1985), p. 128.

Scottish Sports Council (1988) *Sport 2000: a Scottish strategy: A consultative document*, Scottish Sports Council.

Scottish Sports Council (1988) *National strategy for coach education and coaching development in Scotland*, Scottish Sports Council.

Scottish Sports Council (1989a) *Sport 2000: A Strategic Approach to the Development of Sport in Scotland*, Scottish Sports Council.

Scottish Sports Council (1989b) *Annual Report 1988/89*, Scottish Sports Council.

R. J. Shephard (1986) 'Economic benefits of enhanced fitness', Campaign III: *Human Kinetics*, M8 222, US.

J. Spink (1989) 'Leisure and Retailing', in F. Kew (ed.) *Leisure : Into the 1990s*, Bradford & Ilkley Community College.

Sports Council (1980) *Report of the Minister's Lawn Tennis Inquiry Committee*, Sports Council.

Sports Council (1982) *Sport in the Community: The Next Ten Years*, Sports Council.

Sports Council (1985) *Actual Life Styles*, Coventry City Council, Interim Report on the Results of the Pupils' Leisure Survey, Sports Council.
Sports Council (1987) *Finance for Sports Facilities*, Sports Council.
Sports Council (1988a) *Sport in the Community: Into the 90s*, Sports Council.
Sports Council (1988b) 'A Sporting Future', *Recreation Management 1988*, Conference Proceedings, Sports Council.
Sports Council (1990) *Annual Report 1988–89*, Sports Council.
Sports Council for Northern Ireland (1989) *Annual Report 1988–89*, Sports Council for Northern Ireland.
Sports Council for Wales (1986a) *Changing Times – Changing Needs*, 10-year Strategy for Sport in Wales 1986–1996, Sports Council for Wales.
Sports Council for Wales (1986b) *National Survey of Sports Centre Users in Wales*, Sports Council for Wales.
Sports Council for Wales (1989) *Annual Report 1988/89*, Sports Council for Wales.
R. Terry (1989) '*Norwich Sports Village*', Leisure Management, vol. 9, no. 1, pp. 48–50.
G. Torkildsen (1986) *Leisure and Recreation Management*, 2nd edition, E. & F. N. Spon.
M. Whitehead (1987) *The health divide: inequalities in health in the 1980s*, Health Education Authority.

Further Reading

J. Bale (1989) *Sports Geography*, E & F. N. Spon.
Central Council of Physical Recreation (1983) *Committee of Enquiry Into Sports Sponsorship* (The Howell Report), CCPR.
E. Cashmore (1982) *Black Sportsmen*, Routledge and Kegan Paul.
J. J. Coakley (1982) *Sport in Society: Issues and Controversies*, C. V. Mosby Co.
Department of the Environment (1989) *Developing Sport and Leisure, Good Practice in Urban Regeneration*, HMSO.
T. Donohue and N. Johnson (1986) *Foul Play : Drug Abuse in Sport*, Blackwell.
T. Duffy and P. Wade (1983) *Winning Women: Changing Image of Women in Sport*, Queen Anne Press.
C. Gatton and P. Taylor (1985) 'The Economics of Sport Sponsorship', *National Westminster Bank Quarterly Review*, August 1985.
H. Griffiths (1985) *Fund Raising for Sport – A Guide for Sports Clubs*, The Sports Council.
C. W. N. Miles and W. Seabrooke (1977) *Recreational Land Management*, E. & F. N. Spon.
T. Moule (1986) *Fit for Sport*, PSL Thorsen.
G. Pearson (1983) *Hooliganism, A History of Respectable Fears*, Macmillan Press.
Scottish Sports Council (1983) *Disabled People and Sport*, Scottish Sports Council.
M. Shoebridge (1987) *Women in Sport – A Select Bibliography*, Mansell Publishing Ltd.

The Sports Council (1985) *Doping Control in Sport*, Sports Council.
G. Whannel (1983) *Blowing the Whistle: the Politics of Sport*, Pluto Press.

Note also the wide range of publications available from the Sports Council and the Countryside Commission.

Cabin cruisers on the Norfolk Broads

8 Tourism

John Walsh-Heron

Today almost everyone aspires to a holiday, to travel, to see the world, to experience new cultures, and to participate in an exciting activity. Tourism is a word used to describe all these actions and desires. But to define tourism is not easy as it covers such a multitude of activities. The tourist is often referred to as: an excusionist, a day-tripper, a visitor, a holidaymaker, or a traveller. A broad definition that covers most uses of the term has been given by Professor David Jeffries in *The Development of Tourism*, (1985):

> Essentially tourists and excusionists are people...staying overnight or on a day trip in places other than their normal place of residence for any of a wide range of purposes – *leisure*, ie recreation, holiday, health, study, religion, or sports; *business*, and for other purposes.

An interesting aspect of this definition is the reference to *leisure* and *business*.

Leisure tourism, in its simplest form, is all about humans indulging in an experience which should be pleasurable, satisfying, and happy. Achieving these objectives for each individual on holiday requires a complex mix of services to combine together, at a specific point in time, to provide the customer with what he/she requires. *Business tourism* can involve an overnight stay, but is often a day trip away from the usual place of work and residence. Many businesses arrange conferences, exhibitions, meetings, and staff development and training activities, as well as promotional functions, which often mix business with pleasure. A planning workshop for business executives at the Gleneagles Hotel in Scotland combining work, high-quality hotel service, and golf, is a good example.

The tourism industry is a 'people business'. The service side of tourism is about fulfilling peoples' dreams, providing a memorable experience, and extending a high level of 'customer care'. Tourism is an industry that provides not only enjoyment, but direct benefits to the national economy. During 1988, Britain attracted approximately 15.8 million overseas tourists, whose total expenditure amounted to £6085 million. To this must be added the earnings from domestic tourism, which amounted to £7850 million in 1988. This expenditure creates some 1.5 million jobs in the UK, which represent about 6 per cent of total UK employment.

Tourism as part of the world economy also continues to grow, with some 390 million tourist arrivals in 1988, up by nearly 9 per cent on the previous year. Spending by these visitors was estimated to be US$195 billion, an increase of 23 per cent on 1987. However, the drive for tourism growth has already provided many long-term problems for the industry. Cheap flights and the marketing of 'mass tourism' in Spain and other European destinations has led to a price war. Many customers have become dissatisfied with poor-quality provision and service, and have lost confidence with the promises of travel agents. But, overseas visitors to the UK are expected to increase by 5 per cent per annum and this would mean an additional 32 million visitors by the mid-1990s. Domestic tourism is also on the increase, especially short weekend breaks and business tourism. So by the mid-1990s an additional 250,000 new jobs could be created.

Exercise

Find out by consulting your library and/or your National Tourist Board, statistics for current overseas and domestic tourism. How have the numbers of visitors changed in recent years? What are the predictions for the future? You could also attempt to discover figures and trends for your area by contacting your Regional Tourist Board.

A major problem to tourism growth in the UK is the upgrading and extending of basic infrastructure – our roads, airports, and hotels. Furthermore, planners need to appreciate the delicate dividing line between continued tourism growth in harmony with nature, and tourism which leads to the despoilment and destruction of the very environment the tourist seeks.

Throughout this chapter the elements that make up tourism will be investigated and explained. The problems that tourism faces if it is to continue to grow will be examined, and some of the misconceptions and fallacies that relate to tourism will be challenged. Tourism is a vast national and international business, hence discussion will be limited to domestic tourism and the importance of services for incoming tourism within the UK. The first section will examine the various facilities and types of provision utilised by tourists.

Provision and Facilities

The tourist industry is subject to a range of pressures outside its immediate control. Fluctuating currency exchange rates affect all incoming tourism, and the United States' market is particularly prone to terrorism scares. The strength of domestic tourism is influenced by the level of interest rates (high levels reduce disposable income) and the cheapness and value for money of holidays abroad. All these factors make long-term planning hazardous.

The provision of accommodation for tourists in the UK has been criticised as being antiquated and of poor-quality. Some resorts have made efforts to improve the quantity, quality and variety of accommodation, but there has been little forward planning across the country as a whole. This section will initially examine hotels and serviced accommodation, and then review provision for camping, caravanning, and self-catering tourists. The section will conclude by explaining a range of facilities and visitor attractions.

Hotels and Serviced Accommodation

The hotel industry has its roots in the development of the Victorian resort and the railway terminus hotel. Comparatively little development took place from the beginning of this century until the 1960s. So, although the Trust Houses Group was founded in 1902 (which became Trust House Forte (THF) in the early 1970s), massive expansion of the company into a major hotel group in the world can be traced to the 1960s. The main impetus for this expansion emanated from Sections 7, 8 and 9 of the Development of Tourism Act, 1969. This gave the newly-formed statutory tourist boards for England, Scotland and Wales the power to give grants and loans for the development of new hotels and the extension or upgrading of existing hotels. This system of grant aid was known as the Hotel Development Incentive Scheme (HDIS).

When the Labour Government introduced the Development of Tourism Bill into Parliament in 1968, they predicted that the HDIS scheme would cost the Exchequer £8 million. At the end of the scheme in 1973, it had actually cost the government £60 million in grants and loans, had created 40,000 new hotel beds in four years, and generated £200 million investment in the industry.

Whilst the incentive scheme was a necessary boost for the hotel business it had some fundamental flaws. To appreciate these problems the system of grant aid needs to be understood. This scheme was based on three sections of the Development of Tourism Act:

Section 7
This was for the building or conversion of an existing building into a hotel of ten bedrooms or more.

Section 8

Provided for the provision of an extension to an existing hotel of at least five bedrooms which would provide, at its completion, a hotel of 10 bedrooms or more.

Section 9

Allowed for grants for the provision of certain items of fixed equipment, such as central heating, lifts, kitchen equipment, bathroom and toilet equipment.

Grants were provided under Sections 7 and 8 at the level of £1000 per bedroom (£1250 in development areas) or 20 per cent (25 per cent in development areas) of the eligible capital cost. Under Section 9, 20 per cent (or 25 per cent) of the total eligible costs were payable.

These grants were provided of right, subject to certain conditions:

(i)   building had not commenced prior to 1st April, 1968;
(ii)   building had commenced prior to 1st April, 1971; and
(iii) building was completed prior to 31st March, 1973.

Subject to the above, a grant was deemed payable to a hotel development, but there were major imperfections. Nowhere within the Development of Tourism Act, as it relates to the HDIS scheme, were any specific standards laid down. Therefore, bedrooms could be of any size so long as a bed could be fitted into them. There was no requirement for en-suite bathrooms, and no standard relating to construction, such as sound-proofing, heating or lighting levels.

The legacy of the HDIS scheme can still be seen today and can be held responsible for most of the modern city-centre hotels. In London many of the major hotels owe their development to this scheme. However, the advent of a vast chain of hotels did not materialise. The creation of the Trust House Forte Post House chain did emerge, with a typical 150-bedroom Post House receiving £150,000 in grant aid, approximately 15 to 20 per cent of the capital cost. But the true budget-style hotel/motel did not appear, primarily due to the inherent conservatism in development and building techniques of hotel companies. Also, the lack of competition (this did not apply to London) did not provide an incentive to the innovative. Nevertheless, the period between the mid-1970s and today has seen a considerable change in direction by hotel/leisure companies. A number of factors have been responsible for this:

• Increasing consumer sophistication.
• Development of the motorway system.
• Vast increase in the leisure/second holiday market.
• Improved construction techniques.

These factors, alongside a decrease in the costs of development of budget hotels, have now brought the serviced accommodation sector well within the price band of the majority of the population.

The hotel sector now covers a wide range of serviced accommodation, grouped as:

- Hotels – generally 10 bedrooms or more.
- Guest houses – usually between 4 and 9 bedrooms.
- Bed and breakfast – usually small private houses.
- Farm guesthouses – located on a working farm.
- Inns/pubs – licensed premises that also provide accommodation.

Table 8.1 gives the proportions of British residents (as tourists) in various types of accommodation in England. It can be seen that apart from staying with friends or relatives, hotels and serviced accommodation predominate. Approximately 90 per cent of all serviced accommodation within the UK is in small individual units, average size 20 bedrooms, owned by families or small companies. There are about 50,000 such units within the UK with only about 1500 establishments owned by large groups such as Trust House Forte, Bass, or Ladbrokes (Hilton). It is estimated that there will be a shortfall of 19,000 hotel rooms in London alone by the year 2000, this represents the equivalent of ninety-eight new hotels.

Table 8.1   Accommodation of British tourists in England

1988	Trips	Nights	Spending
millions	110 (100%)	410 (100%)	£6,275 (100%)
Accommodation used:	%	%	%
Licensed hotel	17	14	36
Unlicensed hotel of guesthouse	5	5	8
Holiday camp	3	5	5
Camping	3	4	3
Towed caravan	2	3	3
Fixed caravan	7	9	7
Rented flat or flatlet	1	2	3
Rented chalet	2	3	3
Other rented	3	5	5
Paying guest	2	2	2
With friend or relative	51	45	24
Second home	1	2	1
Boat	1	1	2
Other or in transit	2	1	1

Source: BTA, National Facts of Tourism (1989a).

Brewery-linked chains of hotels are becoming stronger but, with the exception of Bass, have been slow in developing out of beer into other sectors. The Monopolies and Mergers Commission Report (HMSO, 1989) did, however, nudge companies towards diversification. As we saw in the previous chapter, there is a growing emphasis on the development of sports and leisure experiences within the hotel scene. To attract weekend visitors as well as business travellers, many hotels have incorporated health and fitness suites, golf courses, swimming pools and extensive sports facilities into their developments. THF, who own Crest Hotels, control the Crest Sensation Leisure Clubs with the emphasis on health and fitness. There are currently fifteen of these clubs in a total of forty-five Crest Hotels. In the chapter on Sport and Physical Recreation it was noted how a number of hotel chains are moving into the golf market and in some cases incorporating championship courses into luxury hotel developments. Crest Hotels have reportedly earmarked £40 million to 'leisurise' their hotels over the next few years and current thinking is that leisure clubs in hotels are essential to increase profit margins. Another development is the revamping of the holiday village concept – established many years ago by Butlin's and Pontin's. A recent partnership between Granada and Laing has resulted in £500 million-worth of investment for a series of five holiday villages around the country.

Exercise
Find out what hotel developments have been taking place in your region. Write for a brochure and note any health, fitness, or sports facilities that may be offered. What are the charges? Can the public, as well as the hotel guests, utilise them?

Although the UK hotel industry has, for generations, lagged behind its counterparts in both the USA and Europe, the signs are that we are learning from overseas developments and gradually improving the quality and quantity of provision. Two clear examples are based on the success of the American motel, and the French Novotel concept. Both come under the broad heading of budget Hotels.

Budget Hotels

These fill the gap in the market between luxury hotels and bed-and-breakfast establishments. A number of chains have identified this gap and are building 'two-star' and 'three-star' accommodation. The philosophy for this type of development is exemplified by the French company Novotel. Its aims are:

- to provide guests with all primary facilities and amenities without their having to pay for secondary services they rarely require;
- to achieve the optimum in hotel design which will enable the company to provide all these primary facilities and better value for money than is available from competitors; and
- to provide a price structure which is as good as a three star hotel but 25–30 per cent cheaper.

The French are leading the way in budget hotel development in Europe, and companies such as Ibis and Companile have established a strong branding and image alongside a standardised layout. This enables the visitor to be secure and confident when booking accommodation at the lower end of the market. Budget does *not* mean cheap quality. The aim is to produce a friendly and economical hotel with an emphasis on value for money. A further development in this sector of accommodation is the budget motel. The French company Accor are leaders in Europe with their Novotel brand aimed at business travellers with a car. Accor have also developed a brand of hotel called Formula 1. This was conceived in 1984 and now operates in many localities throughout France. These 'hotels' are built in factories and then erected on site. Credit card check-in provides guests with coded entry into the hotel and their room. The rooms are basic and standard, and each shares a bathroom and toilet facilities with four other rooms. Development costs of approximately £1000 per room (1988 prices) allow the unit to be developed on locations previously considered unviable. Whether this concept will succeed outside France is as yet unknown.

In Japan they have created capsule hotels which provide cylindrical tubes of 82.74 inches (210cm) long, 47.28 inches (120cm) high and 43.34 inches (110cm) wide. All modern conveniences provided (except a private bathroom), including TV, radio and alarm clock. An Oriental solution which might not catch on in Europe! Within the UK, Trust House Forte is adding bedrooms to its Little Chef restaurants; Rocco Forte is adding further 'two-star' accommodation to its chain, and the Ibis hotel group is moving strongly into the low-cost, standard-design hotel market. The latter group plan thirty-nine new hotels by 1995.

Country House Hotels

These look set to expand in the 1990s as they combine comfort and character with good value for money, although the economic recession is causing severe problems for the less well established. Thistle have planned a new division of country-house-style hotel and they aim to have twenty new developments completed within the next few years.

The distinct lines that previously existed between different styles of accommodation are blurring. Hotels now offer self-catering, and self-catering operators provide services. The hotel industry is not the only sector of accommodation in the UK that has undergone change. The self-catering sector, particularly the caravan and camping sector, is also in the throes of modernisation.

Caravan, Camping and Self-Catering

This sector of tourist accommodation arouses the greatest conflict of opinion. The environmentalist and planner considers most caravan parks a blot on the landscape. On the other hand, caravan and camping holidays represent nearly 25 per cent of all holiday trips taken in the UK; in 1988 this meant over £774 million to the economy (see Table 8.1 on page 253).

What also must be taken into account are the parks and other locations operated by organisations such as the Caravan Club and the Camping and Caravan Club of Great Britain, which are exempt from planning controls.

Recent History of Development

The caravan and camping industry can be traced back to 1905 when the Camping and Caravan Club of Great Britain was founded. But it was in the early 1930s that the growth of the trailer caravan and the improvement in roads produced the first big boom in modern motorised caravanning. In 1936, the Public Health Act formally laid down standards for camping/touring parks and in 1939 The National Caravan Council was established to represent all the facets of the caravan industry. At the end of World War II, poor roadways and a comparatively empty coastline combined to provide the second major development in this sector, the static holiday caravan park. It may be simplistic to consider that these were the only elements that led to the massive growth of caravan parks after the war, but they did provide the impetus.

The need to provide cheap holiday accommodation in locations near the beach, within easy rail travel distance of main conurbations, also put the embryo caravan manufacturing industry on its feet. The assortment of huts, sheds, and ex-railway carriages which at first provided this type of accommodation, were slowly replaced by the shape of caravans as known today. By the mid-1950s the majority of the caravan parks, particularly in coastal locations, had established themselves. They provided much of the population with the only affordable opportunity for a holiday that was practical in the post-war population explosion. The uncontrolled growth of caravan parks along the coast caused considerable concern amongst planners, who demanded that planning controls be introduced. The result of their action was the Caravan Sites

and Control of Development Act, 1960, which still provides the framework of control for the development of the caravan park sector.

Each park (other than those organisations granted exemptions under
the 1960 Act) required planning permission and a site licence to operate.
The Act outlines the basic operating framework within which most parks
have to operate today, and has the following features:

- length of operating season;
- number of caravans allowed on the park;
- what types of caravan (static, touring, motor caravan);
- ratio of toilets and wash basins to be provided; and
- fire precautions.

The above elements, plus many others, are all detailed within the site
licence. At present no other sector of tourist accommodation has such
restrictive statutory controls placed on its operators.

This sector went through a period of growth and prosperity from 1960
until the mid-1970s. With the domestic holiday market expanding, park
operators felt there was little need to invest. There emerged in 1974 a
number of issues which demanded attention from the industry if it was
not to enter terminal decline. As a result of local government reorganisation, all county councils were obliged to formalise planning policy into a
Structure Plan. Most included planning policies which would severely
restrict or prohibit the future growth of the static holiday caravan park.
These policies, allied to the dramatic growth of overseas holidays taken
by UK residents, as well as an upswell in demand for improving
standards, painted a gloomy picture for the future. A series of excellent
summers masked these problems until the turn of the decade, when
disaster seemed to face the sector.

The reality of a change in the demands of the market, together with
the down-market image of the caravan and caravan parks, stirred the
industry into action. The two main caravan trade organisations put
together public relations, promotional and advertising campaigns to
dispel the poor image. These are ongoing schemes comprising long-term
image-building goals, as well as short-term objectives for bookings and
the sales of holiday caravans. The main organisation for the caravan
park operators, the British Home and Holiday Park Association
(BH&HPA) took a number of steps to achieve the objectives, primarily
through the commissioning of a consultative report on the health of the
industry. This report has been the basis from which the image-building
campaigns have evolved.

The other main trade organisation is the National Caravan Council
(NCC), which primarily represents the caravan manufacturers, traders
and suppliers. The NCC has put massive financial support into improving the marketing effort of the industry (£3 million between 1988 and

1990). The combined efforts of these two bodies (BH&HPA and NCC) have been underpinned by two other major initiatives: the introduction of a caravan park grading scheme, and the establishment of a Caravan Industry Training Organisation.

The Caravan Park Grading System

This was introduced in 1986 and is a partnership between the two trade organisations and the National Tourist Boards of England, Scotland, and Wales. The system is based on an annual inspection of each caravan park, carried out by an officer of the respective National Tourist Board. All criteria are set and agreed by a co-ordinating committee of the trade organisations and tourist boards. This initiative, which originated from the trade, is vital to the industry if the consumer is to be assured of standards. The system is soon to become mandatory for all caravan parks in membership of either a trade body or tourist board.

The Caravan Industry Training Organisation

Another step necessary in establishing the caravan industry as a credible sector, was the introduction of a recognised training system. In 1988, a government-recognised industry training organisation was established to enhance the growth of professionalism within the sector. Investment in the industry is now considerable, with many large companies such as Rank and Bourne Leisure, as well as individual operators, showing their confidence in new training methods.

Caravan Park Development

The changing patterns of the market place, aspirations for 'value added' goods, and the continued expansion of activity/special interest holidays and shortbreaks, will ensure that those caravan park operators who are flexible and responsive will survive and prosper well into the next century.

A new style of layout for parks has been initiated in East Anglia. Entitled 'Caravanscape' it has concentrated on three ways of improving the visual impact of parks:

- upgrading of park features, including improved landscaping and layout;
- village grouping, to achieve significant improvement to the layout; and
- 'themeing', to include painting of existing caravans, the remodelling of central facilities, and fun themes to enhance the holiday atmosphere.

The theory of the village approach is simple. By grouping caravans more closely together rather than further apart, a more interesting environment can be created and more amenity space provided on the park. The principles of themeing may also be applied by taking a particular architectural style – historical or futuristic. Themeing can be extended to the caravans themselves, and some examples considered in the Caravanscape project are: space stations, *Jaws* or a Wild West town. Whatever the visual appearance of the caravan park of the future, certain features are already emerging as priorities for integration into a park:

Parks
  – hall mains services underground
  – service 'hook-ups' to all pitches for touring/camping
  – all pitches cabled for satellite TV
  – individually landscaped pitches

Larger Parks
  – themed indoor leisure centres with multiple pool/leisure areas
  – fast-food outlets
  – activity instruction
  – ski-slopes/ice rinks/bowling greens

Caravans
  – insulated for year-round occupation
  – central heating
  – air conditioning
  – video/teletext/satellite
  – telephones
  – daily cleaning and maid service.

Many of the features are being integrated into existing park development. The Haulfryn Group, which owns a number of parks in North Wales and Scotland, have been developing the caravan of the future. These units has been manufactured to the highest specification and finished to the highest quality. The caravans sell for as much as ten times the price of a standard caravan (at around £100,000, 1990 price).

Exercise
Visit a caravan park and make notes of the following: the caravans themselves, including their design and the quality of comfort; the layout of the park; services within the park such as mains services, shops, and sports provision; the cost of utilising the park; your own assessment of the quality and range of amenities and any improvements you consider desirable.

At present, overseas visitors using caravan and camping accommodation account for only 2 per cent of all holiday occupation. In the past, caravan park operators were content to tap a buoyant domestic market, and did not put any effort into attracting overseas visitors. There is also a lack of any centralised booking system, and this makes the reservation process cumbersome and frustrating. This is compounded by a lack of 'packaging' of caravan and camping accommodation within the business. The industry must address these problems if it is to increase its share of the overseas visitor market.

Visitor Attractions

In many ways, the development of visitor attractions has been one of the most obvious changes in tourism within the last decade, and Center Parcs in Nottinghamshire, Alton Towers in Staffordshire, and the Jorvik Viking Museum at York are now well known. The popularity of the top twenty visitor attractions for 1987 and 1988 is given in Table 8.2.

Table 8.2   Visits to tourist attractions, 1988 (thousands)

		1987	*1988*
Top 20 attractions where there is an admission charge:			
1	Madame Tussaud's, London	NC	2705
2	Alton Towers, Staffordshire	2300	2510
3	Tower of London	2289	2182
4	Blackpool Tower	1523	1478
5	Natural History Museum, London	1291	1367
6	London Zoo	1304	1326
7	Kew Gardens, London	1336	1181
8	Chessington World of Adventures	841	1151
9	Magnum Leisure Centre, Irvine	1078	1081
10	Thorpe Park, Surrey	1060	1028
11	Flamingo Land, North Yorkshire	882	987
12	Royal Academy, London	769	987
13	Drayton Manor Park, Staffordshire	972	985
14	Edinburgh Castle	967	958
15	Roman Baths and Pump Room, Bath	873	954
16	Windsor Safari Park	813	951
17	Chester Zoo	862	897
18	Jorvik Viking Centre, York	887	886
19	Swansea Leisure Centre	741	808
20	Louis Tussaud's Waxworks, Blackpool	600[*]	705[*]

Source: BTA, Britain's Tourism (September 1989c).
[*]Estimate   NC Not Comparable

Visitor attractions cater for a wide range of tastes and interests and include historic buildings and gardens, museums and art galleries, zoos, and an increasing number of theme parks and leisure parks. In excess of 50 per cent of the thousands of visitor attractions throughout the UK have opened since 1970, which indicates the high level of interest and investment in tourism over the last two decades.

By definition, attractions attempt to provide a unique experience and that is part of the magic they have to offer. A succinct definition of an attraction does not exist. Attractions do, however, have a number of similar features – they all:

- set out to attract visitors;
- are managed and developed as an attraction; and
- perceive and recognise themselves to be a tourist attraction.

All visitor attractions are not necessarily artificially constructed and they can be classified in several different ways. There are essentially three methods of classification:

1. As determined by the *resource basis* of the attraction (for example, artificial heritage feature, natural heritage feature).
2. As determined by the *nature* of the appeal to the visitor (for example, exhibition and displays, events and demonstrations).
3. As determined by the *purpose* of the attractions (for example educational, recreation).

While artificial attractions can in principle be located wherever suitable land is available, other types of attractions are clearly more site-specific. For example, Walt Disney World chose from any number of potential sites thoughout Europe for Euro Disney, but, there is only one Windsor Castle, one Niagara Falls, and one Taj Mahal. However, this neat classification can be overturned by modern developers. Epcot, part of Disney World, has built a World Showcase in one location. Chessington World of Adventures has brought the Mystic East to Surrey. Lake Havesin City has purchased, transported, and rebuilt London Bridge in Arizona. Thus anything is possible and the neat classification of types of attraction is becoming increasingly confused.

The importance of visitor attractions as the focus of tourism development becomes more important as the planning of attractions becomes more sophisticated. The emergence of National Garden Festivals is a recent development designed to improve and revitalise the image and local economy of a designated 'depressed' area.

Unlike the hotel and self-catering sectors, little national regulation or concerted development assistance has been directed to visitor attractions. The Tourist Boards (Section 4 of the Development of Tourism Act) have, however, targeted certain strategic developments.

Some UK developments have run into trouble by trying to copy large-scale schemes from overseas. Land prices in the UK, the availability of large areas of land for development, and the difficulties of raising finance, threaten the viability of many attractive ideas. For example, we saw in the last chapter the futuristic theme park planned for the old Battersea Power Station in the heart of London, which has repeatedly suffered from a lack of proper financing.

Despite difficulties with some large-scale ventures, innovation and continual development is necessary in order to attract a public who have high expectations and an increasingly sophisticated outlook.

Exercise
Visit your local Tourist Board and find out the range of visitor attractions in your area. Contact one or two of them and try to find out a little more about their operations. What do they charge? How many visitors do they have? How do they market themselves?

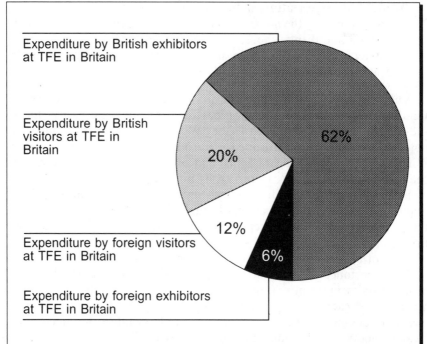

Expenditure by British exhibitors at TFE in Britain

Expenditure by British visitors at TFE in Britain

Expenditure by foreign visitors at TFE in Britain

Expenditure by foreign exhibitors at TFE in Britain

62%

20%

12%

6%

Figure 8.1 Estimated pattern of expenditure, trade fair exhibition and related industries, 1983

Source: BTA, *British Travel Brief* (1987).

Business tourism

A major growth area is the trade fair and exhibition market, and it is estimated that revenue from British and foreign exhibitors exceeds £1 billion. As well as the leading trade fair centres such as Earls Court, Olympia, and Harrogate, there are many small and medium-sized venues and organisers operating on a regional basis and in highly specialised areas. The wide range of trade shows and events they present serves as a shop window for British industry.

The proportion of spending by overseas visitors stood at around 18 per cent in 1983 (see Figure 8.1) but the British Tourist Authority believes that this composition is changing due to the improvement of air links, more co-ordinated promotions, the opening up of the European Community from 1992, and the completion of the Channel Tunnel.

Administration and Finance

Until 1969, tourism was administered by voluntary bodies mainly financed by commercial organisations, local government and some central government funding. In the 1967 Development of Tourism Bill (see page 251) the following objectives were set out:

(i)   the establishment of the British Tourist Authority to promote the UK as a whole overseas;
(ii)   the establishment of The Wales Tourist Board and The Scottish Tourist Board to promote and develop tourism for their respective countries, but not overseas;
(iii)   the creation of the Hotel Development Incentive Scheme (Sections 7, 8 and 9 of the Act);
(iv)   the establishment of statutory registration, classification and grading, of tourist accommodation; and
(v)   the ability to fund special tourism projects (Section 4 of the Act).

These, together with other sections, formed the Bill. Following parliamentary debate on the Bill, the Development of Tourism Act, 1969 was approved, and laid the foundation of a formal structure of tourism within the UK. This created the statutory tourist boards (see Figure 8.2). Since the establishment of the statutory tourist boards, various governments have had an ambivalent attitude towards tourism, with numerous investigations into their cost-effectiveness. None the less, the statutory tourist boards have contributed considerably to the management of tourism, the evolution of the other necessary administrative levels of tourism, and the development of a range of initiatives.

British Tourist Authority (BTA), and the three National Tourist Boards for England (ETB), Scotland (STB), and Wales (WTB). Each is equal within the terms of the Act.

Development of Tourism Act, 1969

BTA British Tourist Authority	ETB English Tourist Board	WTB Wales Tourist Board	STB Scottish Tourist Board
Promotes Britain overseas	12 regional tourist boards	3 regional tourist councils	32 area tourist boards

The four organisations are all Quasi-Autonomous Non-Governmental Organisations, popularly known as QUANGOs. Each has a Chairman appointed by the appropriate Secretary of State, who also appoints a Board of nine members for the BTA and six members for each of the National Boards.

Figure 8.2   The statutory Tourist Boards

As previously outlined, each National Tourist Board has developed a regional structure. Each of these structures is different – but this is necessary in order to provide the most appropriate platform for the tourism industry within each area.

England

England is split into twelve tourist regions, each with its own Director and support staff. The Regional Tourist Boards are autonomous organisations funded by the ETB, the local authorities and the regional tourism industry. The proportion of funding varies from region to region. Each is attempting to increase the proportion of its funding from commercial sources. A review by central government of the organisation of tourism in England in 1989 demanded that more functions be devolved to the Regional Tourist Boards, thus making them more powerful.

Scotland

After the 1982 Local Government Act for Scotland the Scottish Tourist Board, with the Highlands and Islands Development Board (HIDB), set up thirty-two autonomous Area Tourist Boards. The structure of tourism in Scotland is somewhat more complex, as the HIDB has a statutory responsibility for tourism in the Highlands and Islands area. The Scottish Development Agency also has an important role in the development of tourism in Scotland and is considered below in the section on local government administration.

Wales

There are three regional offices, based in North, Mid- and South Wales. The Managers and most of the support staff are Wales Tourist Board (WTB) staff. Each has a Regional Tourism Council (RTC) for which WTB provide the majority of tourist information centre staff. At present the majority of the permanent staff of the regional councils are employed and paid for by the Wales Tourist Board. However this will change in 1991 as the WTB are restructuring and these staff will be seconded to regional companies which will replace the regional councils. In North Wales the regional office also supports the North Wales Marketing Bureau. In 1990, the Wales Tourist Board announced that certain functions would become 'privatised'. These would include inspection and advisory services which are now established within Tourism Quality Services, a company limited by guarantee. Other regional functions will also become 'privatised'.

Each of the National Tourist Boards, and the BTA, are funded by central government plus revenue raised from commercial activity. In Wales and Scotland the tourist boards also administer the Tourist Projects Grant Scheme. This scheme was discontinued in England in 1989.

Northern Ireland

The Northern Ireland Tourist Board (NITB) was established as a Statutory Tourist Board in the mid-1950s. At the same time, schemes of financial assistance for projects, together with a statutory system of registration, classification and grading were introduced.

All liquor licensing certificates within Ulster need the approval of NITB. In 1989, the Northern Ireland Office reviewed the functions of the NITB and a massive reconstruction of the Statutory Tourist Board was undertaken, including the abandonment of the statutory systems of registration, classification and grading.

The Isle of Man

The Isle of Man has statutory tourism functions allied to its own governmental system. This has included, since the mid-1970s, a statutory system of registration for tourist accommodation. There is considerable co-operation between the Isle of Man Tourist Board and those of the English Regional Tourist Boards.

The British Tourist Authority has the power to market all the UK areas overseas, but both the English and Wales Tourist Boards do not have any statutory power to spend their budgets in marketing their respective countries abroad. Based on an amendment to the Development of Tourism, Act, the Scottish Tourist Board was, from 1984, granted the power to market Scotland overseas. The government has consistently refused to grant Wales similar powers as it has been considered unnecessary, despite numerous representations that have been made to the government.

Local Government Administration

Most resorts such as Blackpool, Brighton and Llandudno, have been involved in tourism for many years. The administration of local government, and therefore tourism at that level, changed in 1974 with the reorganisation of local government in England and Wales (and Scotland in 1975). The broad split of local government left strategic planning, education, highways and other services with county, metropolitan or, in Scotland, regional councils. The provision of services such as refuse collection, parks and leisure, and housing were left within the district councils.

The actual responsibility for tourism within an area remains unclear, as certain functions of the county and the district overlap, but as time has gone on the district councils have, in general, become the prime movers in this sector. The Association of District Councils (ADC) has a tourism committee which has proved to be an effective lobby for tourism at the local level. Funding for these tourism activities is generated from the rates (since April 1990, the Uniform Business Rate), with many large resorts generating considerable income from the operation of tourism and leisure facilities. However, the administration and funding of tourism does not just remain with these bodies; it also lies with a number of others within the public and charitable sectors. The National Trust controls vast tracts of land utilised as a recreational resource, as well as many historical properties. The new Water companies have the ownership of vast areas of water space, again a valuable tourism resource. These, together with other bodies such as the National Rivers Authority, the Countryside Commission, English Heritage, and Cadw, all have considerable influence on how the tourism product is managed and operated.

Exercise
Find out how tourism is administered within your local authority. What are the policies? How is tourism development encouraged and resourced by the local authority? Are there partnerships with other public bodies, commercial and voluntary organisations or groups?

The Tourist Boards at national and regional levels all have to work together in conjunction with the local authorities and other interested bodies. Partnership between these organisations has grown as central government funds have contracted. However, true co-ordination of effort is sometimes difficult with varying priorities leading to conflicts in certain situations.

In Scotland, the Scottish Development Agency (SDA) has a strategic role in the development of tourism. The SDA sees Scotland as one unit – indeed, Scotland has been described as one large theme park! The SDA operates under an Act of Parliament that enables it to raise finances and give grants. The agency will explore the risks of new projects; will take initiatives in sponsoring new ventures; and will also assist in the raising of finance. The SDA also has a unique statutory responsibility for derelict land clearance, and will arrange for infilling derelict dock areas, improving buildings; and the enhancement of the environment. Tourism in Scotland, as in other parts of the UK, is seen as having a direct influence on economic regeneration and improving the general fabric of society.

It is appropriate in the context of the administration of tourism to look at two examples of the way that tourism is organised.

Overseas Marketing

As previously outlined, the Development of Tourism Act, 1969 gave powers to the British Tourist Authority to market the whole of the UK overseas. The National Boards were not allowed to market directly overseas. If the English Tourist Board wished to market overseas it required BTA approval before the promotion could be licensed. (The 1989 review of the ETB means that most of the marketing functions have now devolved to the Regional Boards, which are allowed to market overseas). The promotion would be handled by BTA staff overseas. The system is fraught with difficulties as national priorities for England, Scotland, and Wales do not always coincide with BTA's plans.

We have seen how Scotland obtained an amendment to the Development of Tourism Act, 1969, which allowed them to market themselves directly overseas, whereas the Wales Tourist Board has been unsuccessful.

Classification and Grading

Another example of administration which creates difficulties for the tourist industry is the classification and grading of accommodation. The BTA have refused to include in their publications examples of different

National Tourist Board classifications and grading systems. It is argued that this would further confuse the foreign visitor. There is an element of logic in this, but the diversity of product within the UK demands that separate systems are evolved to properly inform the consumer of what is available. The BTA developed a system, Commended Hotels, principally targeted at overseas markets, although promoted within the UK. This system has no formalised system of grading and classification and does not generally involve the National Tourist Boards, who operate their own inspectorate. The BTA Commended Scheme commenced in 1973 and still continues, even though the National Tourist Boards have established a British serviced accommodation scheme – the Crown Scheme, and in 1989 launched a grading system to work in conjunction with this. Under the review carried out in 1989 by the Secretary of State it was decided to discontinue the BTA Commendation Scheme.

During the two decades of Statutory Tourist Boards there have been three or four (depending on which country is concerned) government or parliamentary investigations into the effectiveness of Tourist Boards. Each has tinkered with the operation of Tourist Boards, or concluded that they were actually doing a creditable and important job.

Policy and Planning

Tourism has been described as a 'benefit and a blight'. Indeed, many public organisations have mixed feelings about tourism as a worthwhile contribution to the economy. Figures available from the Tourist Boards underline the growing volume of tourism and revenue-earning capacity. The Department of Employment estimate 1.2 million people in the UK directly rely on tourism to provide employment.

The 1980s and early 1990s witnessed tourism being used as a catalyst for major urban and rural regeneration and tourism is at last becoming an integral part of local, regional, and national planning. There has been an increasing realisation that many of our heritage sites have immense tourist value. It has also been recognised that to capitalise on our natural heritage, far higher quality facilities and services are needed. The reality is that, to date, there is no central government policy for the planning of tourism.

Leisure consultants Howarth and Howarth believe that:

> successive British Governments' intervention in tourism...has been largely a reaction to changes rather than a definite policy to bring change; reactive rather than pro-active. We feel that there is a real need for a central government policy on tourism with a nationalisation

of public sector involvement into a combined strategy which can be implemented at a national level. (*Leisure Management*, 1986)

The National Tourist Board has, for many years, suffered from a lack of direction from the government. This has led to a piecemeal approach to planning. Planning for tourism came about through the Development of Tourism Act, 1969 and comparatively little thought was put into the Act. Of course, there were few individuals in the late 1960s who had any experience in planning for tourism, so inevitably much was by trial and error. The first evidence of planning for tourism was contained in the county councils' strategic plans, which began to emerge after the local government reorganisation of 1974. In many ways these were naïve attempts to regulate for a business few had knowledge of. Experience has ensured that these strategies have become more realistic and yet sensitive to community needs. Tourism can be intrusive and have a negative impact on a culture, a heritage, or a natural resource, if not managed and developed properly. Examples of growth for short-term economic gain, rather than long-term benefit to the community, can be seen throughout the Mediterranean, and may well be beginning to emerge in the South Pacific. However relevant the debate to control tourism development, the reality is that tourism will happen, and it must be managed and shaped to the direct benefit of the community.

Exercise
Choose a popular tourist facility in your region and make a site visit during a peak season period. Note access routes to the facility; provision for car and coach parking; public transport access; the level of use; the quality of provision; congestion; litter; noise; and many other features of significance. Is the facility being managed sensitively? Is there evidence of undue stress on the environment? What could be done to improve the situation?

Two publications of the late 1980s, one by the English Tourist Board and another by the Wales Tourist Board, provide a feasible framework for planning.

The ETB's five year *A Vision for England* plan provides an outlined strategy. The emphasis is on private/public partnership agreements, and the programme sets an ambitious investment target of £3–4 billion from 1987 to 1992. The Wales Tourist Board's *Developing the Potential* report, combined with its *Golden Opportunity* development proposal, has provided a realistic scenario for tourism in Wales well into the 1990s.

In the absence of central planning, the benefits of which may be dubious, only National Tourist Boards can apply a realistic approach to the future planning for tourism. Planning tourism also requires a certain co-ordinated approach from the government in its legislative and fiscal programmes. Lord Young produced a document on behalf of the government in 1985, entitled *Lifting the Burden* (Department of the Environment, 1985). This was a recipe for eliminating unnecessary bureaucracy which had been imposed on the private sector, to allow growth. This was followed in July 1985 by *Pleasure, Leisure and Jobs*, which provided a framework for the government to more properly co-ordinate schemes for the benefit of tourism.

As an industry, tourism already has seventy-eight Acts of Parliament, plus many statutory instruments which applied prior to 1985. An imaginative vision for tourism should have promised less regulation and a co-ordinated effort from central government. However, a number of proposals, now law, have appeared, which demonstrate a lack of co-ordination from the government towards the industry. Examples are the new business rating and community charge system introduced in 1990. The caravan sector was faced with the impossible situation of each holiday caravan being subject to the community charge. The legislation did not initially seem able to cope with those establishments which were guesthouses in the summer and private houses in the winter, or to differentiate between a second home and a self-catering unit. Through considerable pressure and ultimate acceptance of advice, the more ill-considered applications of the legislation have now been changed. Other difficulties were also apparent in legislation relating to the privatisation of electricity; television licence reform; VAT regulations; and certain aspects of the liquor licensing reform legislation.

Future Prospects

This chapter has already drawn attention to many new initiatives in the tourist product. It is clear that tourism is an industry of change. Predicting the future for an industry which is subject to the vagaries of international exchange rates, the horrors of terrorism, and civil and industrial strife, combined with the increasing market sophistication and awareness of the consumer, may appear impossible. However, as the 1990s lead to the new century, certain external factors can be predicted which will shape the tourism sector.

Population Change

The demographic predictions for the early 1990s to 1995 show some dramatic shifts in the UK population, particularly the 16 to 19-year age group. These demographic features are applicable across Europe (with the exception of the Irish Republic) and to a lesser extent in North America. These shifts have two main implications for tourism.

The first implication concerns employment for the industry. As school-leavers decrease, competition for young workers will be immense. The tourism industry will have to turn to less traditional sectors of the labour market, such as the five million non-working married women in the UK. However, other industries will also be targeting this sector, and tourism as an industry, not renowned for its high wages or pleasant working conditions, is going to have to improve its image as an employer considerably. An inevitable consequence of increased competition in the labour market is that the higher cost of labour within this sector will have to feed through in the form of cost increases.

The second implication of demographic change is that those businesses targeted at younger members of the population will have to consider their product's future. Examples include fast food, sport, and sections of teenage entertainment.

A Combined Europe

From 1992, a number of changes may take place which will have a considerable impact for domestic tourism:

1. The deregulation of air routes

The free competition policy supported by the EEC may well mean the opening up of the European skies. Cheaper flights to and from different destinations, may have a similar impact on the travel and tourism industry as the deregulation process had in the USA in 1978/79. There is no doubt that in the USA the boom in hotel/motel building was attributed primarily to deregulations of air fares and routes. However, Europe is smaller than the USA and existing air traffic control problems will have to be solved before this could become a realistic option.

2. Frontier controls

These will disappear for EEC nationals and will obviously help to speed up the movement of traffic through major gateways, but existing Customs and Immigration controls will still apply for travel outside the EEC and visitors from non-EEC destinations.

3. *Fiscal harmony*

A similar rate of VAT throughout Europe is a goal. This could be a benefit or a handicap for operators in the UK. In France, higher rates of VAT (or consumption tax) apply to the luxury end of the hotel market, and duty-free shopping may disappear on routes between European destinations. The prospect of a European currency is another factor that will influence tourism.

4. *Time*

There have been demands from the EEC that the UK cease British Summer Time at the end of September each year. This has not been welcomed by the tourist operators, particularly the visitor attraction and hotel sectors. A recent Policy Studies Institute document proposes a typical British compromise to this problem. In future, Britain should add two hours in the summer, and continue in the winter with an extra hour on Greenwich Mean Time. These proposals have been submitted for government backing. The suggestions have been supported by the Royal Society for the Prevention of Accidents (ROSPA), who have reported that such a proposal would improve road safety.

Channel Tunnel

It is questionable whether the completion of the Channel Tunnel will benefit UK tourism. At present there are still a number of logistical and financial decisions to make on the routing of the rail tracks and where through trains will run to in the UK. However, two factors need to be considered.

Firstly, the tunnel is only a rail-link, therefore all those wishing to travel will still have to book tickets, travel to the point of access, and be the subject of possible industrial action: the same situation as now. Secondly, Euro Disney opens in 1992, 17.4 miles (28 kilometres) outside Paris, with a projected 11 million visitors for the first year. There are also seventeen theme parks planned in the Pas de Calais area of France.

Further Study

A reading list is detailed at the end of the chapter but to understand some of the issues raised more fully, the following assignments are suggested.

Assignment 1

Develop a tourism marketing plan for a chosen area, based on existing data. This will require reference to the county or regional council Structure Plan, together with any local plans issued by your district/ borough council. Reference to National/Regional Tourist Board development and marketing objectives should also be made.

The plan should identify strengths and weaknesses of the existing tourism product. Outline proposals for implementing the plan relating to target markets. Detailed costings are not required, but an indication of the overall cost should be included. The methods to be used in implementing the strategic plan should also be outlined.

Assignment 2

Examine the AA and RAC hotel inspection schemes and compare them with the National Tourist Board's Crown Scheme. Identify the prime differences, particularly the subjective elements within these systems.

Establish the difference between classification and grading systems and devise an integrated system that all organisations could use within the UK.

Assignment 3

The division between serviced and self-catering accommodation is already blurring. Project what will occur in development terms to both these sectors in the next decade. Outline how the design of new built establishments will change and specify what impact these changes will have on operational management. References to external factors of change must be taken into account.

Questions
1. Outline the main objectives of the Hotel Development Incentive Scheme. List the basic criteria together with the total amount of grant paid in England, Scotland and Wales respectively.
2. List six of the English Regional Tourist Boards and outline the main operational activities carried out by them.
3. The Channel Tunnel is scheduled for completion in 1993. Outline the impact that the opening of the tunnel will have upon the existing cross-channel ferry operators.

References

British Tourist Authority (1987) *British Travel Brief*, BTA.
British Tourist Authority (1989a) *National Facts of Tourism*, BTA.
British Tourist Authority (1989b) *Tourism Statistics*, BTA.
British Tourist Authority (1989c) *Britain's Tourism*, BTA.
Department of the Environment (DoE) (1985a) *Lifting the Burden*, HMSO.
Department of the Environment (DoE) (1985b) *Pleasure, Leisure and Jobs – The Business of Tourism*, HMSO.
English Tourist Board (1987) *A Vision of England: A Strategy For Tourism Development*: England, ETB.
HMSO (1986) *The Supply of Beer,* Cm. 651.
Howarth and Howarth (1986) *Leisure Management*, vol. 6 no. 12, December.
D. Jeffries (1985) *The Development of Tourism*, Inaugural Lecture, Union of Strathclyde, May 1985.
Wales Tourist Board (1988) *Tourism in Wales – Developing the Potential*, (A Wales Tourist Board Strategy) June 1988.
Wales Tourist Board (1988) *The Golden Opportunity. Where in the World but Wales*, Wales Tourist Board, June 1988.

Further Reading

A. J. Burkart and S. Medlik (1981) *Tourism – Past, Present and Future*, 2nd ed, Heinemann.
D. Foster (1985) *Travel and Tourism Management*, Macmillan.
J. C. Holloway (1983) *The Business of Tourism*, MacDonald & Evans.
J. C. Holloway and R. V. Plant (1988) *Marketing for Tourism*, Pitman.
V. T. C. Middleton (1988) *Marketing in Travel & Tourism*, Heinemann.
L. Lickorish and A. Jefferson (1989) *Marketing Tourism, A Practical Guide*, Longman.
J. Walsh-Heron and T. Stevens (1990) *The Management of Visitor Attractions and Events*, Prentice-Hall.

Useful Addresses

Publications which provide further sources of information can be found at the end of the Useful Addresses section. Many of the organisations whoses addresses are given here have a wealth of publications, facts, advisory leaflets, and research findings at their disposal.

Entertainment and the Arts

Arts Council of Great Britain, 14 Great Peter Street, London SW1P 3NQ.
Association of County Councils, 66a Eaton Square, London SW1E 6LE.
Association of Business Sponsorship of the Arts, 2 Cluster Street, London SW1X 7BB.
Association of District Councils, 9 Buckingham Gate, London SW1E 6LE.
Association of Independent Radio Contractors, Radio House, 46 Westbourne Grove, London W2 5SH.
British Broadcasting Corporation, Portland Place, London W1A 1AA.
British Council, 10 Spring Gardens, London SW1A 2BN.
British Film Institute, 127 Charing Cross Road, London WC2H 0EA.
British Phonographic Industry Ltd, Roxburghe House, 273/278 Regent Street, London W1R 8BN.
British Theatre Association, 9 Fitzroy Square, London W1P 6AE.
British Videogram Association, 22 Roland Street, London W1V 3DD.
Cable Television Association, 50 Frith Street, London W1V 5TE.
Convention of Scottish Local Authorities, 16 Moray Place, Edinburgh EH3 6BL.
Council of Regional Arts Associations, 13a Clifton Road, Winchester, Hants SO22 5BP.
Crafts Council, 12 Waterloo Place, London SW1A 4AU.
Independent Broadcasting Authority, 70 Brompton Road, London SW3 1EY.
Independent Television Association, Kingston House, 56 Mortimer Street, London W1N 8AN.
National Music Council of Great Britain, 10 Stratford Place, London W1N 9AE.
National Organisation for Dance and Mime, 9 Rossdale Road, London SW15 1AD.
Office of Arts and Libraries, Horse Guards Road, London SW1P 3AL.
Publishers Association, 19 Bedford Square, London WC1B 3HJ.
Scottish Arts Council, 19 Charlotte Square, Edinburgh, EH2 4DF.
Scottish Film Council, 74 Victoria Crescent Road, Glasgow G12 9JN.
Sky Channel, 6 Centaurs Business Park, Grant Way, off Syon Lane, Isleworth, Middlesex TW7 5QD.
Variety Club of Great Britain, 32 Welbeck Street, London W1M 7PG.
Welsh Arts Council, Holst House, Museum Place, Cardiff CF1 3NX.

Libraries

Booksellers' Association of Great Britain and Ireland, 154 Buckingham Palace Road, London SW1N 9TZ.

British Association of Picture Libraries and Agencies, 13 Woodberry Crescent, London N10 1PJ.

British Library – Research and Development Department, 2 Sheraton Street, London W1V 4BH.

Library Association, The, 7 Ridgmont Street, London WC1E 7AE.

Library and Information Services Council, Offices of Arts and Libraries, Horse Guards Road, Great George Street, London SW1P 3AL.

Library and Information Services Council (Wales), Welsh Office (ED23), Cathays Park, Cardiff CF1 3NQ.

National Library of Scotland, George IV Bridge, Edinburgh EH1 1EW.

National Library of Wales, Aberystwyth SY23 3BU.

Museums

Association of Independent Museums, Weald and Downland Museum, Singleton, W. Sussex.

British Museum, The, Great Russell Street, London WC1B 3DG.

Cadw – Welsh Historic Monuments, 9th Floor, Brunel House, 2 Fitzalan Road, Cardiff CF2 1UY.

Civic Trust, 17 Carlton House Terrace, London SW1Y 5AW.

Civic Trust for Wales, Room 4, Llandaff Court, Fairwater Road, Llandaff, Cardiff CF5 2LN.

Department of the Environment, Room C11/10, 2 Marsham Street, London SW1A 3EB.

Historic Buildings and Monuments Commission for English Heritage, Block D, Brooklands Avenue, Cambridge CB2 2BU.

Imperial War Museum, Lambeth Road, London SE1 6HZ.

Museums Association, The, 34 Bloomsbury Way, London WC1A 2SF.

Museums and Galleries Commission, 16 Queen Anne's Gate, London SW1H 8AA.

National Dairy Museum, Wellington Country Park, Riseley, Reading RG7 1SP.

National Horseracing Museum, 99 High Street, Newmarket CB8 8JL.

National Maritime Museum, Greenwich SE10 9NF.

National Mining Museum, Lound Hall, Haughton, Retford DN22 8DF.

National Motor Museum, Beaulieu SO42 7SN.

National Motorcycle Museum, The, Coventry Road, Bickenhill, Solihull B92 0EJ.

National Museum of Photography, Film, and Television, Prince's View, Bradford BD5 0TR.

National Museum of Wales, Cathays Park, Cardiff CF1 3NP.

National Railway Museum, Leeman Road, York YO2 4XJ.

Royal Museum of Scotland, Chambers Street, Edinburgh EH1 1JF.

Science Museum, Exhibition Road, South Kensington, London SW7 2DD.

Scottish Agricultural Museum, Ingliston, Newbridge Edinburgh.

Scottish Civic Trust, 24 George Street, Glasgow G2 1EF.
Welsh Folk Museum, St Fagans, Wales CF5 6XB.
Welsh Industrial and Maritime Museum, Bute Street, Cardiff CF1 6AN.

Countryside Recreation

Association of Countryside Rangers, The Bunting, Kingsley, Stoke-on-Trent ST10 2AZ.
British Trust for Conservation Volunteers, London Ecology Centre, 80 York Way, London N1 9AG.
Broads Authority, The, Thomas Harvey House, 18 Colegate, Norwich NR3 1BP.
Conservation Foundation, The, Fairholt House, 2 Pont Street, London SW1X 9EL.
Council for the Protection of Rural England, Warwick House, 25/27 Buckingham Palace Road, London SW1W 0PP.
Council for the Protection of Rural Wales, Ty Gwyn, 31 High Street, Welshpool SY21 7JP.
Countryside Commission, John Dower House, Crescent Place, Cheltenham GL50 3RA. Publications Despatch Department, 19-23 Albert Road, Manchester M19 2EQ.
Countryside Commission for Scotland, Battleby, Redgorton, Perth PH1 3EW.
Countryside Council for Wales, Plas Penrhos, Fford Penrhos LLS7 2LQ.
Countryside Recreation Research Advisory Group, School for Advanced Urban Studies, Rodney Lodge, Grange Road, Bristol BS8 4EA.
Field Studies Council, Central Services, Preston Montford, Montford Bridge, Shrewsbury SY4 1HW.
Game Conservancy, Burgate Manor, Fordingbridge, Hampshire SP6 1EF.
Nature Conservancy Council, Northminster House, Peterborough PE17 4NG.
Nature Conservancy Council (Scotland), 12 Hope Terrace, Edinburgh EH9 2AS.
Open Spaces Society, The, 25A Bell Street, Henley-on-Thames RG9 2BA.
Ramblers Association, The, 1/5 Wandsworth Road, London SW8 2XX.
Royal Society for Nature Conservation, The, The Green, Nettleham, Lincoln LN2 2NR.
Wildfowl Trust (HQ), Slimbridge, Gloucestershire GL2 7BT.

Parks and Amenities

Agricultural Development and Advisory Service, M.A.F.F., Nobel House, 17 Smith Square, London SW1P 3HX.
Arboricultural Advisory and Information Service, Forestry Commission, Forest Research Station, Alice Holt Lodge, Wrecclesham, Farnham GU10 4LH.
Arboricultural Association. Ampfield House, Romsey SO51 9SA.
Association of County Councils, Eaton House, 66a Eaton Square, London SW1W 9BH.
Association of District Councils, 9 Buckingham Gate, London SW1E 6LE.
Association of Playing Fields Officers and Landscape Managers, 1 Cowley Road, Tuffley, Gloucester GL4 0HT.
Brecon Beacons National Park, 7 Glamorgan Street, Brecon LD3 7DP.

British Association of Golf Course Constructors, Telfords Farm, Willingale, Ongar, Essex CM5 00F.

British Association of Landscape Industries, Landscape House, 9 Henry Street, Keighley BD21 3DR.

British Effluent and Water Association, 5 Castle Street, High Wycombe HP13 4RZ.

British & International Golfcourse Greenkeepers Association, Aldwark Manor, Aldwark, Alne, York YO6 2NF.

Camping and Outdoor Leisure Association, 1 West Ruislip Station, Ruislip HA4 7DW.

Centre for Alternative Technology, Llwyngwern Quarry, Machynlleth SY20 9AZ.

Centre for the Conservation of Historic Parks and Gardens, The Institute of Advanced Architectural Studies, University of York, The King's Manor, York YO1 2EP.

Centre on Environment for the Handicapped, 35 Great Smith Street, London SW1P 3BJ.

Civic Trust, 17 Carlton House Terrace, London SW1Y 5AW.

Committee for Plant Supply and Establishment, C/O Horticultural Trades Association (see below).

Community Land Use, 192–6 Hanbury Street, London E1 5HU.

Conservation Foundation, The, Fairholt House, 2 Pont Street, London SW1X 9EL.

Council for National Parks, 45 Shelton Street, London WC 2H 9HJ.

Dartmoor National Park, National Park Officer, Haytor Road, Bovey Tracey TQ13 9JQ.

Department of the Environment, 2 Marsham Street, London SW1P 3EB.

English Heritage, Fortress House, 23 Savile Row, London W1X 2HE.

Exmoor National Park, Exmoor House, Dulverton TA22 9HL.

Forestry Commission, 231 Corstorphine Road, Edinburgh EH12 7AT.

Garden History Society, 5 The Knoll, Hereford HR1 1RU.

Groundwork Foundation, The (HQ), Bennetts Court, 6 Bennetts Hill, Birmingham B2 5ST.

Historic Buildings and Monuments Commission, English Heritage, as above.

Horticultural Trades Association, 19 High Street, Theale, Reading RG7 5AH.

Inland Waterways Association, 114 Regents Park Road, London NW1 8UG.

Institute of Groundsmanship, 19–23 Church Street, The Agora, Wolverton, Milton Keynes MK12 5LG.

Lake District National Park, Busher Walk, Kendal, Cumbria LA9 4RH.

Landscape Institute, 7 Barnard Mews, London SW11 1QU.

Landscape Research Group, Leuric, North Road, South Kilworth, Near Lutterworth LE17 6DU.

Ministry of Agriculture, Fisheries and Food, Victory House, 30–34 Kingsway, London WC2B 6TU.

National Council for the Conservation of Plants and Gardens, The Pines, The Royal Horticultural Gardens, Wisley, Woking GU23 6QB.

National Society for Allotment and Leisure Gardeners Ltd, 22 High Street, Flitwick, Bedford MK45 1DT.

National Trust, 36 Queen Anne's Gate, London SW1H 9AS.

National Trust for Northern Ireland, Rowallane House, Saintfield, Ballynahinch, Co. Down BT24 7LH.

National Trust for Scotland, 5 Charlotte Square, Edinburgh EH2 4DU.

National Turfgrass Council, 3 Ferrands Park Way, Harden, Bingley BD16 1HZ.
North Yorks Moors National Park, The Old Vicarage, Bondgate, Helmsley YO6 5BP.
Northumberland National Park, Eastburn, South Park, Hexham NE46 1BS.
Peak District National Park, Aldern House, Baslow Road, Bakewell S30 2WB.
Pedestrians Association, 1 Wandsworth Road, London SW8 2XX.
Pembrokeshire Coast National Park, County Offices, Haverfordwest SA61 1QZ.
Royal Botanic Gardens, Kew, Richmond TW9 3AB.
Royal Forestry Society of England, Wales and Northern Ireland, 102 High Street, Tring HP23 6AH.
Royal Scottish Forestry Society, 11 Atholl Crescent, Edinburgh, EH3 8HE.
Scottish Rights of Way Society Ltd, 1 Lutton Place, Edinburgh EH8 9PD.
Snowdonia National Park, Penrhyndendraeth LL48 6LS.
Sports Turf Research Institute, Bingley BD16 1AU.
Timber Research and Development Association, Stocking Lane, Hughenden Valley, High Wycombe HP14 4ND.
Woodland Trust, Autumn Park, Grantham NG31 6LL.
Yorkshire Dales National Park, Yorebridge House, Bainbridge, Leyburn DL8 3BP.

Play and Playwork

Association for Fair Play for Children in Scotland, Unit 9 Six Harmony Row, Govan G51 3BA.
Child Accident Prevention Trust, 75 Portland Place, London W1N 3AL.
Fair Play for Children, 8a The Precinct, West Meads, Bognor Regis POZ1 5SB.
Federation of Resource Centres, 'Playworks', 25 Bullivant Street, St Anne's, Nottingham NG3 4AT.
Handicapped Adventure Playground Association, The Head Office, Fulham Palace, Bishops Avenue, London SW6 6EA.
Joint National Committee on Training in Playwork, 'Playtrain', 99 Clifton Road, Birmingham B12 8SR.
Kids' Clubs Network, 297–281 Whitechapel Road, London E1 1BY.
Leeds Polytechnic, Playwork Team, Room 1002, Calverley Street, Leeds LS1 3HE.
Local Government Training Board, Arndale House, The Arndale Centre, Luton LU1 2TS.
National Association for the Welfare of Children in Hospital, Argyle House, 29–31 Euston Road, London NW1 2SD.
National Association of Hospital Play Staff, 40 Brunswick Square, London WC1N 1AZ.
National Centre for Play in Scotland, Moray House College of Education, Holyrood Road, Edinburgh EH8 8AQ.
National Children's Bureau, 8 Wakley Street, Islington, London EC1V 7QE.
National Children's Play and Recreation Unit, The, 359–361 Euston Road, London NW1 3AL.
National Institute of Playwork, Mike Hardwick, Community Recreation Manager, The Well Springs Civic Centre, Bolton BL1 1US.

National Playbus Association, Unit G, Arnos Castle Trading Estate, Junction Road, Brislington, Bristol BS4 5AJ.

National Playing Fields Association, (NPFA) 25 Ovington Square, London SW3 1LQ.

National Playing Fields Association (Scotland), 20 Queen Street, Edinburgh EH2 1JX.

National Voluntary Council for Children's Play, C/O National Children's Bureau, as above.

Play Wales, Custom House, Custom House Street, Cardiff CF1 5AP.

Playboard Northern Ireland, 123–137 York Street, Belfast BN15 1AB.

Playmatters, National Toy Library Association, 68 Church Way, London NW1 1LT.

Pre-School Playgroup Association, 61–63 Kings Cross Road, London W1X 9LL.

Royal Society for the Prevention of Accidents, Cannon House, The Priory, Queensway, Birmingham B4 6BS

Woodcraft Folk, The, 13 Ritherdon Road, London SW17 8QE.

Sport and Physical Recreation

British Amputee Sports Association, Harvey Road, Aylesbury HP21 9PP.

British Colleges Sports Association, 28 Woburn Square, London WC1H 0AD.

British Deaf Sports Council, 54 Boroughgate, Otley LS21 1AE.

British Olympic Association, 1 Wandsworth Place, London SW18 1EH.

British Paraplegic Sports Society, Ludwig Guttman Sports Centre for the Disabled, Stoke Mandeville, Harvey Road, Aylesbury HP21 8PP.

British Polytechnics Sports Association, B223 Birmingham Polytechnic, Perry Bar, Birmingham B42 2SU.

British Sports Association for the Disabled, Hayward House, Corton, Warminster BA12 0SZ.

British Students' Sports Federation, 28 Woburn Square, London WC1H 0AD.

British Universities Sports Federation, 28 Woburn Square, London WC1H 0AD.

Calvert Trust Adventure Centre for Disabled People, The, Little Crosthwaite, Underskiddaw, Keswick CA12 4QD.

Central Council of Physical Recreation, Francis House, Francis Street, London SW1P 1DE.

Institute of Baths and Recreation Management, Gifford House, 36/38 Sherrard Street, Melton Mowbray LE13 1XJ.

National Association of Swimming Clubs for the Handicapped, 219 Preston Drive, Brighton BN1 6FL.

National Coaching Foundation, 4 College Close, Beckett Park, Leeds LS6 3QH.

National Federation of Gateway Clubs, Mencap National Centre, 117 Golden Lane, London EC1Y 0RT.

Physical Education Association of Great Britain and Northern Ireland, Ling House, 162 Kings Cross Road, London WC1X 9DH.

Scottish Sports Association for the Disabled, Mr W. Fenwick, 14 Gordon Court, Dalclaverhouse, Dundee DD4 9DE.

Scottish Sports Council, 1 St Colme Street, Edinburgh EH3 6AA.

Sport and Recreation Information Group, C/O National Coaching Foundation, 4 College Close, Beckett Park, Leeds LS6 3QH.

Sports Council, The, 16 Upper Woburn Place, London WC1H 0QP.

Sports Council for Northern Ireland, House of Sport, Upper Malone Road, Belfast BT9 5LA.

Sports Council for Wales, National Sports Centre for Wales, Sophia Gardens, Cardiff CF1 9SW.

Welsh Paraplegic and Tetraplegic Association, Rookwood Hospital, Llandaff, Cardiff CF5 2YN.

Women's Sports Foundation, London Women's Centre, Wesley House, 4 Wild Court, London WC2B 5AU.

Tourism

Association of British Travel Agents, National Training Board, 7–11 Chertsey Road, Woking GU21 5AL.

Backpacking Club, 20 St Michaels Road, Tilehurst, Reading RG3 4RP.

Brewers' Society, 42 Portman Square, London W1H 0BB.

British Association of Tourism Officers, c/o Plymouth Marketing Bureau, St Andrews Street, Plymouth PL1 2AH.

British Holiday and Home Parks Association, Chichester House, 31 Park Road, Gloucester GL1 1LH.

British Tourist Authority, Thames Tower, Blacks Road, London W6 9EL.

Camping and Caravanning Club, The, 11 Lower Grosvenor Place, London SW1W 0EY.

English Tourist Board, Thames Tower, Blacks Road, London W6 9EL.

Guild of Guide Lecturers, Grandma Lees Restaurant, 2 Bridge Street, London SW1A 2JR.

Institute of Travel and Tourism, 113 Victoria Street, St Albans AL1 3TJ.

National Caravan Council, Catherine House, 88 Victoria Road, Aldershot GU11 1SS.

Scottish Tourist Board, 23 Ravelston Terrace, Edinburgh EH4 3EU.

Tourism Society, The, 26 Grosvenor Gardens, London SW1W 0DU.

Wales Tourist Board, Brunel House, 2 Fitzallen Road, Cardiff CF2 1UY.

Other Professional Bodies and Institutes

Hotel and Catering Training Company, International House, High Street, Ealing, London W5 5DB.

Institute of Leisure and Amenity Management, Lower Basildon, Reading RG8 9NE.

Leisure Studies Association, Membership Secretary, John Capenerhurst, Bradford and Ilkley Community College, Ilkley Campus, Wells House, Ilkley LS29 9RD.

Recreation Managers Association, 710a High Road, Finchley, London N12 9QD.

Sources for Further Information

Excellent sources for further addresses and a great deal of other useful information can be found in the following texts:

A Practical Approach to the Administration of Leisure and Recreation Services, 2nd Edition, Croner Publications, 1989.

English Tourist Board, *The Handbook of Tourism and Leisure*, Hobson Publishing, Annual.

Leisureforce Index, Leisureforce, Friary Press, Annual.

Leisure Services Year Book, Longman Group, Annual.

Index